Problem-solving
and
Thinking Skills Resources
for Able and
Talented Children

Barry Teare

Published by Network Continuum Education
The Tower Building, 11 York Road, London SE1 7NX

An imprint of The Continuum International Publishing Group

www.networkcontinuum.co.uk
www.continuumbooks.com

First published 2006
© Barry Teare 2006

ISBN-13: 978 1 85539 071 3
ISBN-10:   1 85539 071 X

Acknowledgements

Page 52 *Oxford Guide to Word Games*, reprinted with the permission of Oxford University Press,
www.oup.com
Page 79 *Teaching Children to Think*, Robert Fisher, 0 7487 2235 1, reproduced with the permission of
Nelson Thornes Ltd, first published in 1995.

Every effort has been made to contact copyright holdersof materials reproduced in this book.
The Publishers apologize for any omissions and will be pleased to rectify them at the earliest opportunity.

Edited by Dawn Booth
Design & layout by Neil Hawkins, Network Continuum Education
Cover illustrations by Kerry Ingham
Illustrations by Kerry Ingham

Printed in Great Britain by
Ashford Colour Press, Gosport, Hants

Contents

Introduction

In recent years there has been a central paradox in what is asked of our schools in teaching children. There has been a growing support for emphasis upon thinking skills and problem-solving skills. Each area of the National Curriculum 1999 includes details of how they would be achieved in the particular subject.

In 1999 the Department for Education and Employment (DfEE) published, and publicized widely, *From Thinking Skills to Thinking Classrooms: A review and evaluation of approaches for developing pupils' thinking* by Dr Carol McGuinness of Queen's University, Belfast. Her remit was clear:

  The purpose of the review was (1) to analyse what is currently understood by the term 'thinking skills' and their role in the learning process; (2) to identify current approaches to developing children's thinking and to evaluate their effectiveness; (3) to consider how teachers might be able to integrate thinking skills into their teaching both within subject areas and across the curriculum; (4) to identify the role of ICT in promoting a positive approach to thinking skills; and (5) to evaluate the general direction of current and future research and how it might be translated into classroom practice (page 1).

To its great credit, the government has also devoted considerable attention to improving provision for what it calls gifted and talented children. There has been encouragement for teachers to increase the challenge for able pupils by paying more attention to the higher-order thinking skills of analysis, evaluation and synthesis.

In 2002, the Qualifications and Curriculum Authority (QCA) launched its project 'Creativity: find it, promote it'. One of the areas of stated interest is how teachers promote pupils' creativity by specifically teaching creative thinking skills.

Excellence and Enjoyment: A Strategy for Primary Schools was published in 2003 for the Department for Education and Skills (DfES). One of the principles of education and teaching is to enrich the learning experience by building learning skills across the curriculum. Group problem solving is also suggested as one of the features of making learning vivid and real.

The other pressure, however, and therefore the paradox, has been the emphasis placed upon content. There have been detailed programmes of study that have led to some teachers complaining about an overfull curriculum. This, in turn, has led a number of professionals to be concerned about where the space was coming from for thinking skills and creativity. This worry has been exacerbated by the demands of test situations that, it has been claimed, do not always lead to, nor reward, higher thinking.

Terry Pratchett in his novel *Pyramids* (Victor Gollanz, 1989), typically and mischievously, has one of his Discworld characters, Artela, saying:

People never learn anything in this place. They only remember things.

Clearly content is important and, for certain careers, it is essential. The trick is to incorporate content with exciting teaching and learning. Too much content, or content delivered in a dull way, can be damaging. Able students are often in a position where they are a long way ahead of others in terms of content and understanding. They certainly should not be repeating what they already know, nor be forced to go through steps that they do not need, nor doing more examples at the same level of difficulty than is absolutely necessary. The greatest gift that you can present to able children is exciting and challenging learning that has, at its core, transferable thinking skills and problem solving. That is what *Problem-solving and Thinking Skills Resources for Able and Talented Children* is about and it takes its place in a series of books for Network Continuum Education. Many of the materials have strong curriculum links. Others prepare able children in more general ways to tackle situations across the curriculum. After all, why is a historian, such as the author, of use to various companies and organizations? It is not that he or she can tell you what Catherine the Great did at a particular time but, rather, that he or she possesses a strong grounding in the higher-order thinking skills of analysis, evaluation and synthesis that can be applied not only to other periods of history but also to situations outside the subject content.

Even more relevant is the experience gained while working with able children on courses all over the country. In many cases the author could soon see the learning regime that the children were used to. Those who had a very straight-down-the-middle background took time to adjust to material presented in different ways, even though they were very able. On the other hand, those who had experienced a varied approach in the classroom, including some unusual materials, were not fazed by anything. Rather, they applied the skills that they had gained to the new situations to find solutions. It is this confidence, promoted by a wide armoury of skills, that we should be encouraging in able children.

Using this Book

Problem-solving skills and thinking skills do not operate in isolation from each other. The allocation of pieces to particular sections, therefore, has to be far from exact. Resources have been placed in the section where the most important skill in that piece is to be found but there is considerable overlap. Emphasis has been put on problem-solving skills and thinking skills rather than subject content but, even so, there is much that fits particular curriculum areas. To assist the reader, tables of each section follow, detailing other skills in use and obvious subject links. There is one more, extremely important, consideration. Many pieces that do not have direct subject content are still invaluable in a number of curriculum areas, for the transferable skills that are involved. Subject teachers will, therefore, find the 'general' pieces of great relevance for the development of pupils' skills that are essential to success in that curriculum area.

Contexts

The resources within this book can be used in a variety of ways. Since the government's emphasis upon better provision for able pupils, teachers have recognized a need to find suitable materials for a variety of situations. Details for each piece can be found in the teaching notes that accompany it but the full, composite list for their use is as follows:

- as extension material to particular subject content
- as resources to be included in thinking skills' courses
- as an enrichment activity for those who have completed other tasks quickly and well
- as the subject of a class debate

- as differentiated homework or homeworks, depending upon the length of the piece
- as an activity during an enrichment session, day, weekend or summer school
- as an open-access competition where, normally, the extension task can be used as a discriminator, if needed
- as an activity for an extra-curricular club or society
- as part of the identification process of able pupils; reaction to particular pieces can help to build up a profile of the strengths and needs of individual children.

Solutions and the Concept of 'Some Answers'

Solutions are given in the teaching notes. Sometimes there is a single, correct answer, as in the case, for example, of a matrix problem involving logical thought. Codes are interesting in that there is an answer in the form of a message that makes sense but other ideas, even if they do not produce the solution, are of interest and are worthy of credit. The author has encouraged children on enrichment courses to record unsuccessful routes and then discuss them to see whether they were appropriate to try or not.

Open-ended material, especially where personal judgement is involved, does not produce neat answers. Even so, success criteria can be teased out, so that an evaluation of the responses can be made.

A number of teaching notes contain the phrase 'some answers'. To help teachers using the resources, suggestions are made as to some of the possible responses. This cannot be, however, the complete story. Readers familiar with Gödel's Theory of Incompleteness will be aware that even in mathematics, exactness is elusive. Many years ago the author became aware of a debate that had taken place within a meeting of physics examiners. In one question candidates were expected to quote a learned example of a particular theory. One candidate had forgotten that example but had worked out another successfully from first principles. The argument raged as to whether he should have been given credit for the response. One of the principles behind this book, and the others in the Network Continuum Education 'Able and Talented Children' series, is that assessment must be flexible and sensible, giving credit for unexpected but valid answers. This is in sharp contrast to the organizer of a quiz who says to the teams 'there is only one answer that will be given a point – the one on my answer sheet, whether it is right or wrong!'. One can appreciate that the quiz organizer has a problem for there can't be a huge debate over every answer or the event would go well beyond the allocated time. It is very frustrating, nevertheless, to have an alternative answer that is as good, or even better, than the one on the sheet and get no marks for it. 'Some answers' stresses the point that able students should receive credit for a different reply, so long as it is valid and fits the data.

Section 1   PROBLEM SOLVING

Title	Page	Other skills involved	Direct subject links
'It's Your Problem'	18	Research, strategic thinking, analysis, evaluation, synthesis, decision making, prioritization, working with other people	Many, especially design and technology, personal and social education, citizenship
'On Your Best Behaviour'	20	Analysis, evaluation, synthesis, research, interpersonal skills	Personal and social education
'The Problem Is'	22	Deduction, inference, creativity and imagination, interpretation of data, alternative answers	Many, including science, physical education, personal and social education
'Perplexing Posers'	24	Analysis, deduction, inference, close engagement with data, logical thinking, lateral thinking	History, geography, science, design and technology
'A Piece of Cake'	28	Decision making, empathy, cause and effect, engagement with data, analysis, evaluation, research	History (Henry VII in particular)
'Getting the Balance Right'	31	Analysis, synthesis, evaluation, decision making, deduction, inference, careful use of data	Personal and social education, mathematics
'Timetable'	38	Analysis, synthesis, evaluation, logical thinking, close engagement with information, lateral thinking, decision making	Mathematics

Section 2   WORDPLAY

Title	Page	Other skills involved	Direct subject links
'Merlin'	54	Word humour, use of a dictionary	English, science
'Grateful for the Ghost'	56	Close engagement with text, dictionary work	English
'The Avid Diva'	58	Word humour, use of a dictionary, application	English
'The Last Shall Be First'	60	Subject-specific vocabulary, dictionary work, handling cryptic data	English, science, history, geography
'Gremlin'	63	Deduction, inference, hypothesizing, imagination, creative writing, research, use of different forms of dictionaries	English, history
'Dictionary Delia'	66	Research, succinct writing, creativity and imagination, analysis, sense of humour	English, music, sport, history, science, politics, mathematics
'Turning the Corner: A Mathstory'	68	Deduction, inference, engagement with text, mathematical terms	Mathematics, English
'Hide and Seek Solve a Problem'	73	Homographs, homophones, deduction, inference, creative writing, use of an atlas, geographical knowledge of Britain	Geography, English
'The Name of the Game'	76	Homographs, homophones, logical thinking, lateral thinking, alphabetical order, following instructions, engaging with cryptic information	English

Problem-solving and Thinking Skills Resources for Able and Talented Children

Section 3   LOGICAL THINKING

Title	Page	Other skills involved	Direct subject links
'Key to the Room'	81	Synthesis, alternative methods of working	Mathematics
'Fit the Bill'	83	Synthesis, alternative methods of working	Physical education
'Larry Literacy's Love of English'	85	Synthesis, careful analysis of data, figures of speech, parts of speech, vocabulary extension	English
'Willowmere'	87	Synthesis, information processing, span of concentration, wordplay	Science
'Suit Yourself'	98	Synthesis, strategy, following instructions, span of concentration, analysis of data, information processing	Mathematics

Section 4   LATERAL THINKING

Title	Page	Other skills involved	Direct subject links
'Life's Little Mysteries'	122	Deduction, inference, fluency, handling data accurately	Personal and social education
'England Expects'	126	Connections and associations, creativity and imagination, wordplay, succinct creative writing, abstract thinking, deduction, inference	English, history, art, music, science, geography, politics, citizenship
'In My Mind's Eye'	128	Interpretation of visual information, analysis, wordplay, classification, process of elimination, imagination and creativity	English, mathematics, art, science, history, geography, religious education
'The Crustacean of Fashion'	134	Wordplay, word humour, visual interpretation, imagination and creativity, drawing	Art
'No Words Needed'	136	Visual interpretation, symbolic thinking, creativity and imagination, design, succinct visual presentation	Media studies, art, English

Section 5   PREDICTION

Title	Page	Other skills involved	Direct subject links
'Crystal Ball'	141	Synthesis, analysis, use of existing data, research, creativity and imagination	History, technology, politics, science, sport
'Let Us Suppose ...'	143	Synthesis, logical thinking, lateral thinking, research, analysis of existing information	Science, politics, art, citizenship, mathematics, environmental studies
'Final Curtain'	145	Deduction, inference, analysis, evaluation, seeing connections, logical thinking, lateral thinking, prioritization, synthesis, close engagement with text and data, putting together a reasoned report	History, geography, science, English

Section 6   EVALUATION

Title	Page	Other skills involved	Direct subject links
'Myself'	164	Analysis, synthesis, intrapersonal intelligence	Personal and social education
'Those In Favour? ... Those Against?'	167	Research, appreciation of both sides of an argument	Citizenship, politics, religious education, personal and social education, law, environmental studies
'The Going Rate'	169	Analysis, synthesis, personal values, interpersonal intelligence	Citizenship, politics, personal and social education
'Decisions by the Decade'	172	Empathy, analysis, synthesis, research, prioritization, selecting key elements from a huge amount of data	History
'Looking for Clues'	174	Close engagement with text, deduction, inference, analysis, synthesis, using success criteria, writing a synopsis	English, media studies
'Devon Loch'	176	Analysis, synthesis, research, working as a team, presentational skills, organizational skills, careful interpretation of data	History, English, media studies

Problem-solving and Thinking Skills Resources for Able and Talented Children

Section 7   CLASSIFICATION

Title	Page	Other skills involved	Direct subject links
'In a Class of their Own'	185	Research, strategy, organizational skills, mental agility, use of a dictionary, deduction, inference	English, geography, science, sport, mathematics, music, religious education, geology
'Spoof Proof Reader'	189	Spelling, grammar, plurals, punctuation, use of capital letters, use of a dictionary, close engagement with text, deduction, inference	English
'Pawn in the Game'	192	Derivation of words, use of a dictionary, wordplay, application, appreciation that language changes	English, religious education, French, mythology, history, ancient languages, computer studies, popular music, science
'The Following Parties'	197	Wordplay, sense of humour	English, history, science

Section 8   SEQUENCING

Title	Page	Other skills involved	Direct subject links
'Next in Line'	201	Research, mental agility, explaining 'rules', application	Mathematics, science, history, geography
'Tries So'	205	Analysis, engagement with text, deduction, inference, a very particular form of writing	English
'Letters Rearrange'	209	Wordplay, mental agility, strategic thinking	History, science, English, mathematics, art
'In Good Order'	212	Analysis, evaluation, logical thinking, problem solving	Citizenship, technology

Section 9   CODES

Title	Page	Other skills involved	Direct subject links
'The School for Surreptitious Spies'	218	Analysis, synthesis, deduction, inference, close engagement with text, good working methods, following instructions, logical thinking, abstract thinking	Mathematics, history
'New Meanings for Mnemonics'	226	Synthesis, logical thinking, wordplay, mnemonics, close interpretation of data, abstract thinking	Mathematics
'The Case of the Confused Chemist'	229	Synthesis, following instructions, logical thinking, deduction, inference, engagement with text, abstract thinking, application	Science
'Spellbinding'	233	Synthesis, analysis, deduction, inference, careful use of data, spelling, homophones, following instructions, abstract thinking	English

Section 10   THINKING LIKE CRAZY

Title	Page	Other skills involved	Direct subject links
'Hiss, Moo, Quack, Baa'	236	Imagination and creativity, analysis, wordplay, application, word humour, abstract thinking, creative writing of a particular kind	English, politics, citizenship
'The Pentire Point'	239	Wordplay, word humour, imagination and creativity, idioms, similes, proverbs, research	English, geography
'Humanimals'	241	Seeing connections, creativity and imagination, lateral thinking, identifying key characteristics, drawing, painting or modelling	Science, art
'You don't need to be Christopher Columbus'	243	Seeing connections, wordplay, word humour, creativity and imagination, succinct creative writing of a very particular kind	English, media studies, politics, sport, music, science, history, art

Links with Other Books in the Network Continuum Education Series on Able and Talented Children

- Those responsible for good provision for able children need a wealth of resources to draw upon.

- The resources should play to higher-order thinking skills, as the books detailed below clearly demonstrate. Many also deal with prescribed areas of subject content. Others are not so directly curriculum linked but develop ways of thinking and working that enable able children to come to new problems with a range of appropriate tools.

 **SEE ALSO**

- There is a wealth of challenging and exciting materials in this, the seventh book, in the series by Barry Teare for Network Continuum Education that have been created and used very successfully by the author with able children throughout the country, and that have thinking skills and problem solving at their centre. As with all the resources books, activities are accompanied by comprehensive solutions and notes for teachers. Each theme is preceded by a commentary outlining key principles and links with curriculum guidelines, giving general guidance for teachers. Books in the series include the following:

Effective Provision for Able and Talented Children
This is a book aimed mainly at teachers on how to provide successfully for able children in the wide sense and includes:

★ school policy ★ identification ★ strategies to combat underachievement ★ pastoral issues ★ personnel matters ★ classroom management ★ monitoring and evaluation ★ a small section of materials for use with pupils ★ recommendations on resources.

Effective Resources for Able and Talented Children
The book starts with a section on the curriculum principles behind good provision for able children. The huge majority of the book consists of challenging and exciting materials that are divided into 11 themes but have overlap between them:

★ literacy ★ language across the curriculum ★ reading ★ writing ★ numeracy, mathematics ★ science ★ logical thought ★ codes ★ humanities ★ detective work ★ alternative answers, imagination, creativity.

More Effective Resources for Able and Talented Children
A total of 65 new materials appear in this book. Many of the sections are similar to the previous books but with some new areas:

★ English, literacy ★ mathematics, numeracy ★ science ★ humanities, problem solving, decision making, information processing ★ modern foreign languages ★ young children ★ logical thought ★ detective work, codes ★ lateral thinking ★ competitions.

Challenging Resources for Able and Talented Children
All 62 activities in this book are brand new – most are based around entirely new topics, while some take a fresh approach to revisited topics from previous books:

★ English, literacy ★ mathematics, numeracy ★ science ★ humanities ★ young children ★ logical thought ★ detective work and codes ★ lateral thinking ★ competitions

Enrichment Activities for Able and Talented Children
Based upon a very large number of courses run by the author for able children in various parts of the country, this book starts with the theory behind successful enrichment activities:

★ aims and objectives ★ selection of participants ★ creating an encouraging atmosphere ★ the role of the teacher ★ pastoral issues ★ the key curriculum elements ★ how to judge the success of the event.

The huge majority of the book is a treasure trove of brand-new resources covering:

★ English ★ reading ★ mathematics ★ humanities ★ lateral thinking ★ logical thinking ★ detective work ★ tournaments ★ presentations ★ events ★ treasure hunts.

Also included are full details of commercial materials that have been used to great effect by the author with able and talented children. There is also a detailed explanation of teaching methods and techniques.

Parents' and Carers' Guide for Able and Talented Children
The book's prime target is that of parents and carers. However, teachers and schools have also been enthusiastic about the contents, which are divided into three main sections:

- The discussion of issues and practices that give parents and carers information, and to assist understanding of their able and talented child. This also allows schools to give appropriate advice and strengthen home–school partnerships, as stressed by government initiatives.

- Advice for all curriculum areas about places to go, resources to use, activities to do, websites to visit and how to provide beneficial support, especially by parents and carers but also by teachers.

- The question 'What makes a novel suitable reading for able and talented children?' is examined. There is a detailed and lengthy list of recommended authors and titles, with comments and explanations as to their inclusion. This section is equally valuable for parents, teachers and librarians.

Section 1

Problem Solving

The *Chambers Dictionary* defines a 'problem' as 'a matter difficult to settle or solve; a source of perplexity; a question or puzzle propounded for solution'. Problem solving is fundamental to success in life, within personal relationships, at home, at work and at school. It is present in all areas of human experience. There is a clear link between theoretical problem solving and the situations that are faced on a day-to-day basis. This is made clear in the introduction to Edward de Bono's *Children Solve Problems* (Penguin, 1972):

> Problem-solving may seem to be a rather specialized part of thinking. But if we change the name to 'dealing with a situation', 'overcoming an obstacle', 'bringing about a desired effect', 'making something happen', then it can be seen that the thinking involved is very much the thinking that is involved in everyday life even though the actual problems may appear exotic (page 11).

The skills involved were regarded as so important by the authors of the National Curriculum 1999 that every subject area had to show where problem solving fitted into the programme. A selection of quotes follows:

> … through recognizing geographical problems and issues as part of the geographical enquiry process, identifying and undertaking sequences on investigation, interpreting and explaining results, and making decisions about geographical issues.
> *(geography)*

> The subject calls for pupils to become autonomous and creative problem solvers, as individuals and members of a team.
> *(design and technology)*

> … through becoming involved in political and community issues.
> *(citizenship)*

> … through achieving intentions when comparing and presenting performances to different audiences and in different venues.
> *(music)*

> … through recognizing the nature of the task or challenge, thinking of different ways to approach the task and changing their approach as the need arises … .
> *(physical education)*

> … through finding ways to answer scientific questions with creative solutions.
> *(science)*

> … through selecting and using methods and techniques, developing strategic thinking and reflecting on whether the approach taken to a problem was appropriate.
> *(mathematics)*

> … through modelling real situations and developing solutions to problems when working with ICT.
> *(information and communication technology)*

… through finding out about the past by investigating a specific question or issue, deciding what information they need to know, identifying relevant sources of information and discussing their conclusions.
(*history*)

Problem solving is not a single skill, but rather an overlapping of a number of thinking skills. Likely to be involved in it are logical thinking, lateral thinking, synthesis, analysis, evaluation, sequencing, decision making, research and prediction.

There have been many models on the steps to be taken when solving problems. An early and important step is to understand the nature of the problem. It was G.K. Chesterton who wrote in *Scandal of Father Brown* (1935):

 It isn't that they can't see the solution. It is that they can't see the problem.

The Art of Solving Problems by Keith Jackson was published in 1975 by St Martin's Press as part of the Bulmershe–Comino Problem-Solving Project. He defined the stages of problem solving as:

1 formulating the problem, which involves its detection, identification and definition
2 interpreting the problem
3 constructing courses of action
4 decision-making
5 implementation.
(*page 14*)

In *Teaching Children to Think* (Stanley Thornes, 1995), Robert Fisher identifies four main strategies:

1 understanding the problem
2 planning the action
3 tackling the task
4 reviewing the situation.

Following collaborative work with Harvey Adams, Belle Wallace created a TASC (thinking actively in a social context) problem-solving wheel. This was the central piece in a series of books edited by Belle Wallace and published by NACE/David Fulton: *Teaching Thinking Skills Across the Primary Curriculum* (2001), *Teaching Thinking Skills Across the Early Years* (2002) and *Teaching Thinking Skills Across the Middle Years* (2002, co-edited with Richard Bentley). The stages identified are:

1	Gather/organize	What do I know about this?
2	Identify	What is the task?
3	Generate	How many ideas can I think of?
4	Decide	Which is the best idea?
5	Implement	Let's do it!
6	Evaluate	How well did I do?
7	Communicate	Let's tell someone!
8	Learn from experience	What have I learned?

(*Teaching Thinking Skills Across the Primary Curriculum*, pages 14–15)

● 'It's Your Problem' gets pupils to use a problem-solving model and its stages to deal with a problem at school, home or anywhere else that they know well. This makes the exercise a very personal experience.

● 'On Your Best Behaviour' looks at a situation that is causing growing concern: behaviour among school pupils. The pupils are put into the role of members of the School Council. They are then asked to investigate the problem and make suggestions as to how the situation can be improved. Evaluation is important here, as is the area that Howard Gardner refers to as interpersonal intelligence. The results may well be of practical value to schools.

● A well-known and highly successful piece of work of the author's is 'The Question Is', where a normal process is reversed. Children are given answers and asked to suggest suitable questions. The same thinking has been applied here to problems and solutions in '**The Problem Is**'. Twenty solutions are given and the students are asked to be creative and imaginative in constructing unusual problems to which the given solutions may provide an answer. Differentiation by outcome clearly takes place, as could differentiation by task if the teacher asks pupils to choose only a certain number of solutions.

● '**Perplexing Posers**' works on the premise that some situations are not world shattering in their importance but they do pose interesting conundrums that exercise the mind. Five novel and contrasting short problems from real life have to be solved. A puzzle format is used. A number of key skills are required – analysis, deduction, inference, close engagement with data, logical thinking and lateral thinking.

● The reign of Henry VII is the setting for '**A Piece of Cake**'. Pupils are asked to put on their crowns as, on this occasion, they will be their thinking hats. The problem solving concerns plots and rebellions faced by Henry VII at the beginning of his reign. The piece is best tackled before the students know the real outcomes. In this way, the children are placed at their own 'frontier of knowledge' and have to work things out for themselves.

● '**Getting the Balance Right**' is, in content terms, very close to students in secondary schools. As part of a work-shadowing project, the children are placed as helpers to Mr Zavi, the Head of Year 7. He has had the task of placing students from four primary schools into forms on the basis of a number of principles. The task is to work out what those principles are by studying the form lists for the new Year 7. There is a considerable quantity of data to synthesize. Pupils are also asked to evaluate the system and make a judgement upon it.

● The final piece is also from school life. Timetablers in secondary schools have a great deal of problem solving to do. '**Timetable**' poses a series of problems in the preparation of timetables, their construction and an evaluation of their strengths and weaknesses. As with many other problem-solving situations, a number of skills come into play – analysis, synthesis, evaluation, logical thinking and close engagement with information.

It's your problem

Problems come in all shapes, sizes and types. Some can be seen as puzzles. There is one school of thought which says that the only problems that really matter are real-life problems. Here is your chance to enter that particular area.

Your Tasks

1 Identify a problem at school, home or anywhere else that you know well. This could be, for instance, that car parking at school is not very well organized. It could be that the atmosphere in your class is damaged by bullying. Another possibility is that storage of personal possessions in your bedroom has become a problem.

2 Use the list of stages given below.

3 Try to find a solution or solutions to the problem.

The Stages

1 **Identification of the problem**
This may well involve research, a questionnaire and extensive conversations with other people.

2 **Defining the objective**
Work out what it is that you hope to achieve. What would be a successful conclusion?

3 **Analyse the obstacles to success**
Understand what factors there are in the way of a successful solution to the problem. Which obstacles are the most serious? How could you remove these obstacles?

4 **Constructing courses of action**
Collect ideas and information from various sources. Talk to other people to see if they have any suggestions. Think carefully about the problem yourself. Research similar problems to see if their solutions can help thinking on the present problem.

5 **Evaluate the possible courses of action**
What would be the consequences of each proposal? How much would each cost? How realistic are they? Do they contain insurmountable obstacles?

6 **Decision making**
Compare the various alternatives that are available. Decide which one seems the best solution when all factors are considered.

7 **Implementation**
Make a plan as to how the decision can be put into practice. The planning should involve a timetable for action and a detailed list of the order in which actions should be carried out. It would be helpful if some flexibility could be built into the planning.

8 **Review**
Once the actions have been completed you need to review what has taken place.

? Has the problem been solved?
? Was the objective brought to a successful conclusion?
? Do some difficulties still remain?

? What has been learned from the problem solving?
? Did everything go according to plan?
? Could some things have been done better?

Problem-solving and Thinking Skills Resources for Able and Talented Children
© Barry Teare (Network Continuum Education, 2006)

It's your problem

Teaching Notes

The title has been chosen to stress that, in this piece of work, the pupils will be tackling a problem of their own choice and, indeed, a real-life problem that affects them personally. This contrasts with other resources in this book where problems are presented to the pupils for them to solve.

Note:
All the stages have been detailed but, for practical reasons, implementation may be outside the pupils' control. In which case, the teacher would need to explain the circumstances. Even so, appreciation of the full process is valuable. Where possible, full pupil participation in real-life problem solving is well worth pursuing.

Key Elements

- ❖ problem solving
- ❖ research
- ❖ strategic thinking
- ❖ analysis
- ❖ evaluation
- ❖ synthesis
- ❖ decision making
- ❖ prioritization
- ❖ working with other people
- ❖ the art of compromise in the 'real world'.

Contexts

'It's Your Problem' can be used in the following ways:

- ❖ as part of a thinking skills and problem-solving course
- ❖ as work within an appropriate curriculum area; for instance design and technology, personal and social education, citizenship
- ❖ as part of the work of the School Council
- ❖ as a differentiated homework project (certainly up to the decision-making stage)
- ❖ as an activity for the Problem-solvers' Club
- ❖ as an open-access competition (up to, and including, the decision-making stage).

ON YOUR BEST BEHAVIOUR

Congratulations!

You have been elected to the School Council. Obviously your schoolmates feel that you have good powers of evaluation and problem solving.

The first main subject for discussion after you join the School Council is that of pupil behaviour. There is a nationally growing concern that behaviour among school pupils is getting worse. The staff believes that such might be the case at your own school.

Now you can use your judgement, your problem-solving skills and your interpersonal skills.

Your Tasks

1 Carry out research in your school to identify the main problems. Talk to other pupils to learn about their concerns.

2 Try to analyse the causes of these problems. Without understanding the causes, it clearly will be very difficult to improve the situation.

3 After consultation with others, make suggestions as to how problem areas can be tackled so that the general level of behaviour improves.

4 Make a written report for consideration by staff and pupils. In that written report, refer to the problems, their root causes and possible solutions.

ON YOUR BEST BEHAVIOUR

Teaching Notes

Many able children have good interpersonal skills. They also have ability in terms of the higher-order thinking skills of analysis, synthesis and evaluation. There are well-documented cases of pupils being used as negotiators, mediators and 'buddies' in attempts to improve behaviour within schools. Listening to the views of able children is often a productive route to follow.

The Office for Standards in Education (OfSTED) and others have expressed concern at the worsening level of behaviour, especially in secondary schools, so we have here a very real problem to solve. The data could be put to very practical use in the school.

Key Elements

- ❖ analysis
- ❖ evaluation
- ❖ synthesis
- ❖ problem solving
- ❖ research
- ❖ interpersonal skills
- ❖ real-life situation.

Contexts

'On Your Best Behaviour' can be used in a variety of ways:

- ❖ as part of personal and social education
- ❖ as an activity within a problem-solving course
- ❖ as differentiated homework(s)
- ❖ as an activity during an enrichment day, weekend or summer school
- ❖ as an open-access competition
- ❖ as part of the work of the School Council.

The Problem Is

You are normally faced with a problem and asked to try to find a solution. On some occasions there can be more than one possible solution. So, what about reversing the process? In this piece of work you are going to be given the solutions.

Your Tasks

1 For each of the solutions given below, provide a suitable problem that would be answered by the suggested solution.
2 If you can do so, write down more than one problem that would be solved by the given solution.
3 Some may fit into a very logical line of thinking in your mind. However, also try to be creative and imaginative in order to construct unusual problems to which the given solutions could provide an answer.

The Solutions

1 Use breaks with gaps in the fences and hedges.
2 Put adverts into the local newspapers.
3 Replace red with blue.
4 Gradually increase the periods of real exertion.
5 See if you can meet her, with nobody else present.
6 Go and talk to the bank manager.
7 Think of ☐☐☐☐ rather than ▭
8 Move it into a different part of the garden.
9 Have at least two drinks a day, made mainly with milk.
10 Rub the surface with ice cubes in a pack.
11 Ask about the possibility of a civil ceremony.
12 Make sure that the percentage of cotton is as high as possible.
13 Switch it on a few minutes before you really need it.
14 Do a greater share of the housework without making too much of a fuss.
15 Read an interesting book for a few minutes.
16 Check with the local police station.
17 Arrange some lessons with the club professional.
18 Try moving to an alphabetical system.
19 Set limited, short-term targets.
20 Accept that the teddy bear is there to stay and ignore it.

Extension Task

Create some more solutions of your own. Try to include a variety of topics. Make some of them open-ended so that more than one problem would fit. Then ask somebody else to suggest problems to lead to the solutions.

Problem-solving and Thinking Skills Resources for Able and Talented Children

The Problem Is

Teaching Notes

One of the author's most successful and productive pieces of work has been 'The Question Is', in which the pupils are given answers and asked to create the questions that would lead to those answers. Now, that same technique has been applied to problems and solutions.

Key Elements

- ❖ problem solving
- ❖ deduction
- ❖ inference
- ❖ creativity and imagination
- ❖ open-endedness
- ❖ interpretation of data
- ❖ alternative answers
- ❖ differentiation by outcome
- ❖ differentiation by task.

Note: As the items can be tackled in many different ways, differentiation by outcome takes place. The teacher may ask pupils to choose only a certain number of items; then differentiation by task also occurs.

Contexts

'The Problem Is' can be used in the following ways:

- ❖ as a piece of general classroom work
- ❖ as part of a problem-solving/thinking skills course
- ❖ in sections, as 'starters' or 'icebreakers' in the classroom
- ❖ as normal homework
- ❖ as differentiated homework
- ❖ as an activity during an enrichment day, weekend or summer school
- ❖ as an activity for the Problem-solvers' Club
- ❖ as an open-access competition.

Some Suggestions

The nature of the solution will guide thinking into certain areas. Even so, responses can be extremely varied. Credit should be given for any appropriate problems that are put forward.

Examples

1 This could concern the problem caused by heavy winds on the other side of solid walls, created by windbreaks.

9 A health problem is likely, especially calcium deficiency, which can lead to brittle bones and poor condition of teeth.

10 The ice cubes could be the solution to bruising of the skin or to help remove depression marks in carpets revealed when items of furniture are moved.

Perplexing Posers

Some problems are not world-shattering in their importance but they do pose interesting conundrums that exercise the mind.

See what you make of these five 'Perplexing Posers'.

Poser one 'CANDLE POWER'

If you visit Blists Hill Open Air Museum, near Coalbrookdale, you will see a number of old shops operating under conditions that would have existed many years ago. One of the shops produces candles by an old-fashioned method, using a number of coatings until the candles are the correct weight. The natural colour of such candles was originally determined by the type of animal fat used and this was normally a shade of yellow. The operator explains to visitors that the largest regular order was for the nearby mines but the owner requested that colouring be added so that the candles for the mining industry were green.

What was the reasoning behind this request?

Poser two 'THE LYNTON–LYNMOUTH RAILWAY'

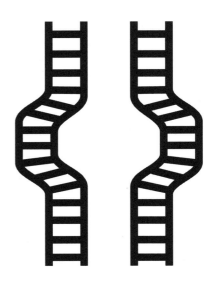

Harriet Holiday visited the world-famous cliff railway that runs between Lynton, at the top of the cliff, and Lynmouth, down below, in North Devon. She stood at the bottom of the cliff, looking up towards the higher station at Lynton. She was somewhat alarmed to see that the tracks had a kink in them, as shown in the diagram.

How could you persuade Harriet Holiday that it was safe to use the cliff railway? What would your reasoning be concerning the 'kink'?

Having been persuaded to take a journey on the cliff railway, Harriet Holiday got into conversation with the operator, who said that an Act of Parliament had been passed to give perpetual right to water from the West Lynn River to the railway company.

What did Harriet learn, to explain why this right was vital to the operation of the cliff railway?

Poser three 'SEA OF GRASS'

A visitor to Grange-over-Sands in Cumbria was very surprised to see sheep grazing on the beach at low tide.

Why should sheep be in such an unusual environment for them?

Problem-solving and Thinking Skills Resources for Able and Talented Children
© Barry Teare (Network Continuum Education, 2006)

Perplexing Posers

Poser four 'THE CHURCH CLOCK'
(with acknowledgement to Colin Dexter and Inspector Morse)

The church at Telltime has a clock on the south face of the tower. This clock is run by electric power. Each October Mr Warden has the task of putting the clock back one hour as British Summer Time comes to an end.

Mr Warden has some difficulty in carrying out this annual task. The hands of the clock are moved by lever equipment behind the clock-face, which is reached by a narrow spiral staircase. This equipment allows movement both clockwise and anti-clockwise. From that position, Mr Warden cannot see where he has moved the hands to. He is out of sight from anybody on the ground outside the church.

Mrs Preacher offered to help by standing below, outside the church, looking up at the clock on the tower.

1 What was Mrs Preacher hoping to do until she realized that the walls of the church were far too thick for her to succeed in helping Mr Warden?

2 Forced back on his own devices, Mr Warden adopted a long-winded and very energetic way of putting the clock back one hour. What was that method?

3 A new parishioner, Miss Service, eventually found a better way of solving the problem and saving Mr Warden time and energy. What was it?

4 At a neighbouring church, looked after by Mr Parson, there was a similar problem, but there the lever equipment only moved the hands in an anti-clockwise direction. Why was the method used by Mr Warden, before Miss Service's arrival, even more difficult for Mr Parson to use at his church? Why was Miss Service's suggestion less useful each spring?

Poser five 'MUSEUM PIECE'

A visitor to a museum in Norwich was interested by a particular exhibit. Part of the equipment was a dial, like the one in the illustration.

The visitor also heard a rhythmic noise of two speeds – 17 'beats' in 20 seconds, followed by five 'beats' in three seconds, and then the pattern repeated. There were other visual components that told the visitor exactly the purpose of the exhibit.

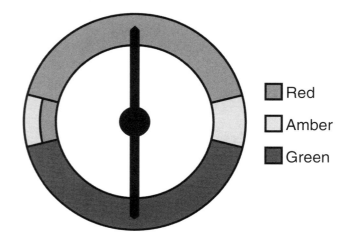

■ Red
□ Amber
■ Green

Can you suggest what it might have been from the information given?

Perplexing Posers

Teaching Notes

This piece presents five novel and contrasting short problems to solve. In this case something approaching a puzzle format is used.

Key Elements

- ❖ analysis
- ❖ deduction
- ❖ inference
- ❖ close engagement with data
- ❖ problem solving
- ❖ logical thinking
- ❖ lateral thinking.

Contexts

'Perplexing Posers' can be used in the following ways:

- ❖ as material within a thinking skills course
- ❖ as an enrichment activity for those who have completed other tasks
- ❖ as differentiated homework
- ❖ as an activity during an enrichment day, weekend or summer school
- ❖ as an activity for the Problem-solvers' Club.

Solutions

'CANDLE POWER'

The miners had access to the candles for work purposes only. If they were caught with company candles in their homes they were liable to punishment, possibly dismissal. The only candles that were green belonged to the company, therefore their identification was simple.

'THE LYNTON–LYNMOUTH RAILWAY'

The railway is completely safe. The 'kink' is the passing place for the two cars as one goes up and the other goes down. What is not clear is why the cars were constructed too wide for them to be able to pass (unless this was necessary for the amount of traffic) and why the tracks were not laid far enough apart to allow the cars to pass.

What tends to mislead the reader is that it is not stated in the problem that these are the tracks for both cars, rather than the two tracks for one car.

The water is used as ballast in the base of the car going down. When the passengers are on board in both cars, a tank is filled in the car at the top of the railway. When sufficient water has been added, the top car moves down towards Lynmouth and pulls the other car up the other side. At the bottom the water is emptied out and again the top car is weighted with water. It normally takes 700 gallons (2,728 litres) of water ballast to operate the counter-balance system.

This is the 'real answer' but sensible suggestions on steam power, for instance, are worth investigating.

Perplexing Posers

'SEA OF GRASS'

A foreign, invasive form of grass was threatening other native species of grass. It was not checked in its growth by salt. Tractors could not be used as they would cause damage. Chemicals were no use because of their effect on the marine environment. Sheep were introduced and the grass is now kept in check. The sheep have the good sense to retreat when the tide comes in. The girl who tends the sheep has the local nickname of 'Bo-Peep'. Holker Hall, the local estate, sells salt-marsh lamb.

'THE CHURCH CLOCK'

1   Mrs Preacher was hoping to shout instructions up to Mr Warden, but the church walls were too thick for him to be able to hear without coming down the staircase and outside the church.

2   He guessed an adjustment and then went down the staircase and out of the church to see where the hands were pointing. He repeated this several times until the clock was exactly one hour back.

3   As the clock was run by electricity, Miss Service suggested removing the fuse for exactly one hour.

4   Mr Parson could manoeuvre the hands back in time but, if he went too far, he could not adjust in a clockwise direction. Miss Service's suggestion was as useful to Mr Parson as to Mr Warden in October but it was much more problematic in spring when clocks go forward one hour and a fuse would have to be removed for 11 hours.

'MUSEUM PIECE'

This is a model of the system used to operate traffic lights at a two-way junction. One light is red while the other is green, and one is red and yellow prior to red while the other is yellow prior to green.

The slower beat accompanies the movement of the marker over the long periods of red and green, whereas the quicker beat takes the marker through the short yellow and red, and yellow sections.

A Piece of Cake

Do you sometimes wish you were somebody else? Perhaps even royalty? Now is your chance. In this piece of work you are going to be Henry VII, first of the Tudor monarchs, back in the year 1487.

Put on your crown for, on this occasion, it is your thinking hat! Then the work will be 'A Piece of Cake'.

Your Tasks

Read the two passages below on background information and Lambert Simnel, and then answer the questions that follow.

Background Information

In 1485, Henry Tudor fought and defeated Richard III at the Battle of Bosworth Field. Richard died during the fighting. The victor took over the throne under the title Henry VII. This followed a period of war and fighting for possession of the crown between the House of York and the House of Lancaster, known as the Wars of the Roses.

Henry VII did not have a strong claim to the throne. The Beaufort side of his family had been barred from the line of succession by Henry IV. There was a number of stronger claimants – the two sons of Edward IV (the 'Princes in the Tower' who had disappeared); the three sons of John de la Pole (Duke of Suffolk); and the grown-up daughter of Edward IV, Elizabeth of York. There were many people who wanted to get rid of Henry VII and plots against him were inevitable.

Lambert Simnel

In 1487, Richard Symonds used a boy called Lambert Simnel in a plot against the king. At first it was planned that Simnel would impersonate Richard of York, the younger of the two Yorkist princes who had disappeared. The scheme was then changed, with Simnel impersonating the young Earl of Warwick. Warwick was imprisoned in the Tower of London by the king but (false) rumours of his murder encouraged the plotters to use his name. Simnel was 'crowned' in Dublin and a rebel army landed in England. Henry VII defeated the rebels at the Battle of Stoke in June 1487.

1 No king likes plots and rebellions, but why do you feel particularly worried and vulnerable?

2 When you learn that Warwick's name is being used, what obvious course of action can you take to try to weaken the conspiracy? Your actions fail to convince enough people – why? (Remember that this is 1487!)

3 After the Battle of Stoke, the young Simnel is your prisoner. How are you going to deal with him? Write down the various possibilities. What would be the advantages and disadvantages of each option? What is your decision and why have you made it?

4 Do some research to find out what really happened. Do you think Henry VII's decision was a wise one? Incidentally, do you now know why this piece of work was given the title 'A Piece of Cake'?

Problem-solving and Thinking Skills Resources for Able and Talented Children
© Barry Teare (Network Continuum Education, 2006)

A Piece of Cake

Teaching Notes

'A Piece of Cake' is a problem-solving and decision-making exercise. It is best tackled before the pupils have studied the events in question, so that they have to think the problems through for themselves. They can be said to be at their own 'frontier of knowledge'.

Key Elements

- ❖ problem solving
- ❖ decision making
- ❖ empathy
- ❖ cause and effect
- ❖ engagement with data
- ❖ analysis
- ❖ evaluation
- ❖ consideration of alternative routes
- ❖ research (for question four)
- ❖ Henry VII in particular; threats to the crown in general.

Contexts

'A Piece of Cake' can be used in a number of ways:

- ❖ as a preliminary to work on the Tudors
- ❖ as part of a problem-solving/thinking skills course
- ❖ as an enrichment activity for those who have completed other work
- ❖ as differentiated homework
- ❖ as an activity during an enrichment day, weekend or summer school
- ❖ as an open-access competition
- ❖ as an activity for the History Society or the Problem-solvers' Club.

Success Criteria

Responses are likely to be judged in relation to a number of factors including:

- ❖ the quality of judgement displayed
- ❖ an understanding of what was appropriate for 1487
- ❖ the number of alternatives considered before making decisions
- ❖ the degree to which empathy is shown
- ❖ the appreciation of cause and effect – particular decisions have particular consequences.

Some Answers

Task 1 Henry knew that he was not in the strongest of positions. His claim was weak and he had many enemies. Other claimants gave a focal point for opposition. There had been a long period of unrest and his reign was only two years old.

Task 2 Henry had the opportunity to show the real Warwick. In fact he paraded Warwick through the streets of London. However, communications were poor and news spread slowly. As a result, Henry's action had little effect outside London.

A Piece of Cake

Task 3 Pupils need to examine the consequences of a strong punitive line or, alternatively, a lenient view towards Simnel. They need to assess the likely effects upon Henry's position in the country. Would strong action deter other plots or would it cause more resentment? Would a kind approach defuse opposition and win support, or would it be taken as a sign of weakness?

Task 4 Henry VII put Simnel to work in the royal kitchens. He was later 'promoted' to the position of falconer. There was another plot in 1495 in which Perkin Warbeck impersonated Richard of York. He was captured and imprisoned in the Tower of London. In 1499 both Warbeck and Warwick were executed on dubious charges of escape and plotting, after which there were no further attempts to dethrone Henry. Is this evidence that Simnel should have been treated more harshly, or was Henry more firmly established on the throne by that time?

The title 'A Piece of Cake' refers to Simnel cake, which is linked with Lambert Simnel's position in the royal kitchen. The cake contains currants, sultanas and candied peel, and it is topped with jam and almond paste.

A Piece of Cake

Getting the Balance Right

You attend Furness Ridge High School. In the future you hope to become a teacher yourself. When, therefore, it was work experience week, you were delighted to work-shadow Mr Zavi, the Head of Year 7. During the week, Mr Zavi set you a task based upon the work that he had carried out the previous summer.

He had visited the four linked primary schools – Green Bank, Dent Hill, Renton Valley and Hopton Lake – to gather information about the pupils who would be starting at Furness Ridge High School in the September. Details of musical ability, sporting ability and other talents and interests had been handed over to appropriate members of staff. Mr Zavi himself had used the data to place the children into four Year 7 forms. He had carried out his work following key principles of school policy about the establishment of forms.

Your Tasks

1 Study the four form lists on the separate sheets.
   NOTES
   (a) The range of ability is described in sequence as – needs extra help, weak, below average, average, above average, very good, excellent. Obviously this has to be a general comment and does not reflect special abilities.
   (b) Initials by the side of the pupils' names state whether the child is male (M) or female (F). This is to avoid any embarrassment where the first name could refer to a boy or a girl, such as Pat or Evelyn.
   (c) The second set of initials refers to the primary school that each pupil previously attended – Green Bank (GB), Dent Hill (DH), Renton Valley (RV) and Hopton Lake (HL).

2 Work out the principles of school policy that Mr Zavi had to follow to place the children into their new forms. You are looking for five principles. Give exact details to support your views.

3 Comment as to whether you believe that this is a sensible set of principles to follow. If so, what are the advantages of such a system? If not, what don't you like and what would you prefer?

4 At Furness Ridge High School, the four Year 7 forms are named Austen, Dickens, Hardy and Shakespeare. If it was your choice, what names would you give to the forms?

Extension Task

Imagine that you are Mr Zavi and it was you who placed the pupils into the four forms. This is looking at the problem from the other end. You would have had all the information from the four primary schools. How would you have set about creating the forms? In what order would you have worked?

Getting the Balance Right

FORM 7 AUSTEN

NAME			LEVEL OF ABILITY	SPECIAL FRIENDS AT PRIMARY SCHOOL
JEREMY BACON	M	HL	Weak	Michael Douglas
DAWN BOONE	F	GB	Needs extra help	None
BRENT CARLING	M	DH	Excellent	Hadji Kahn
SHIRLEY CARLTON	F	GB	Weak	None
CHRISTINE COWGILL	F	GB	Average	None
MARGARET CULLEN	F	HL	Average	None
IRENE DANIELS	F	HL	Average	Carol Finney/ Jan Kennedy/John Bates
MICHAEL DOUGLAS	M	HL	Average	Jeremy Bacon
ROSEMARY GEORGE	F	RV	Very good	Fatima Griffiths
ELIZABETH GREENOCK	F	HL	Below average	Vicki Pointou/Ali Patel
FATIMA GRIFFITHS	F	RV	Excellent	Rosemary George
BERNARD HART	M	GB	Above average	None
RUTH HOLLAND	F	GB	Average	Patsy Peters
DEAN HORTON	M	GB	Needs extra help	None
PETER HOWARTH	M	HL	Average	None
HADJI KAHN	M	DH	Very good	Brent Carling
ANNA KARSKI	F	GB	Excellent	None
JUNE MCALLISTER	F	RV	Above average	None
ALI PATEL	M	HL	Above average	Vicki Pointou/ Elizabeth Greenock
PATSY PETERS	F	GB	Average	Ruth Holland
VICKI POINTOU	F	HL	Very good	Elizabeth Greenock/Ali Patel
SALLY RENFREW	F	GB	Average	Brenda Makin
CHRISTINE SCOTT	F	RV	Needs extra help	None
COLIN SEFTON	M	RV	Below average	Duncan Earle
SUSAN SKIPTON	F	GB	Average	None
BARRY WALTON	M	DH	Average	None

Special notes from the primary schools:

1 Sally Renfrew and Brenda Makin tend to chatter rather than get on with their work.

2 When Colin Sefton and Duncan Earle get together they tend to be aggressive to other pupils.

3 Irene Daniels, Carol Finney, Jan Kennedy and John Bates have a very bad influence on each other.

FORM 7 DICKENS

NAME			LEVEL OF ABILITY	SPECIAL FRIENDS AT PRIMARY SCHOOL
KAREN ADAMS	F	GB	Average	Helen Smith/Roger Parks
GAIL BENTON	F	GB	Below average	Joyce Lander
JOAN CAMPBELL	F	HL	Below average	Angela O'Brien
ALED DAVIES	M	HL	Excellent	Norman Pinner
DUNCAN EARLE	M	RV	Above average	Colin Sefton
CAROL FINNEY	F	HL	Average	Irene Daniels/ Jan Kennedy/John Bates
IMRAN GAVASKAR	M	RV	Weak	Gordon Oliver
KATIE HAILES	F	HL	Average	Fiona Maxwell
SHEILA HUSH	F	HL	Above average	None
PAUL HUTTON	M	GB	Average	None
RITA JONES	F	DH	Average	Mary Stevens
ROY LAMPETER	M	RV	Needs extra help	Nicholas Swain
JOYCE LANDER	F	GB	Very good	Gail Benton
BRENDA MAKIN	F	GB	Needs extra help	Sally Renfrew
FIONA MAXWELL	F	HL	Excellent	Katie Hailes
ANGELA O'BRIEN	F	HL	Average	Joan Campbell
GORDON OLIVER	M	RV	Average	Imran Gavaskar
ROGER PARKS	M	GB	Average	Karen Adams/Paul Winston
NORMAN PINNER	M	HL	Below average	Aled Davies
SOLOMON RICHARDS	M	GB	Very good	Bruce Sharples
ANNE RIDGE	F	DH	Average	None
HELGA SEELER	F	DH	Very good	None
BRUCE SHARPLES	M	GB	Average	Solomon Richards
HELEN SMITH	F	GB	Very good	Karen Adams
MARY STEVENS	F	DH	Average	Rita Jones
NICHOLAS SWAIN	M	RV	Average	Roy Lampeter
PAUL WINSTON	M	GB	Weak	Roger Parks

Special notes from the primary schools:

1 Brenda Makin and Sally Renfrew talk instead of work.

2 Duncan Earle and Colin Sefton are not a good combination to have together.

3 Carol Finney, Irene Daniels, Jan Kennedy and John Bates behave badly together.

Getting the Balance Right

FORM 7 HARDY

NAME			LEVEL OF ABILITY	SPECIAL FRIENDS AT PRIMARY SCHOOL
LUCY BURNS	F	GB	Average	Maria Walenska/Tessa Lloyd
DIANE CAINE	F	HL	Needs extra help	Heather McCann/Tony Forbes
HOWARD CARPENTER	M	DH	Needs extra help	Vernon Golding
MOIRA CARTER	F	HL	Average	Neville Reid
FRANK CLIFFORD	M	GB	Below average	Harry Young
PAMELA DALY	F	HL	Above average	None
RICHARD DEXTER	M	RV	Average	None
TONY FORBES	M	HL	Average	Heather McCann/Diane Caine
VERNON GOLDING	M	DH	Average	Howard Carpenter
SUSAN GREALISH	F	RV	Very good	None
CLYDE HALL	M	GB	Very good	Greg Plant
JAN KENNEDY	F	HL	Average	Irene Daniels/ Carol Finney/John Bates
ROBERT LISTER	M	GB	Needs extra help	Greg Plant
TESSA LLOYD	F	GB	Above average	Lucy Burns
HEATHER McCANN	F	HL	Excellent	Tony Forbes/Diane Caine
GREG PLANT	M	GB	Average	Robert Lister/Clyde Hall
GRETA POULTON	F	DH	Very good	Polly Ince
CHERYL RICHMOND	F	HL	Average	None
ASIF SALIH	M	RV	Excellent	None
BRIAN SHARP	M	GB	Below average	Graham Barnes
ETHEL SIMPSON	F	RV	Average	Jenny Williams
MOIRA UNDERHILL	F	GB	Very good	Vanessa Walker
MARIA WALENSKA	F	GB	Weak	Lucy Burns
VANESSA WALKER	F	GB	Weak	Moira Underhill
JENNY WILLIAMS	F	RV	Average	Ethel Simpson
HARRY YOUNG	M	GB	Average	Frank Clifford

Special notes from the primary schools:

1 Brian Sharp and Graham Barnes behave badly when together.

2 Greta Poulton and Polly Ince tend to be rather silly together.

3 It is not a good idea to have Moira Carter and Neville Reid together.

4 Jan Kennedy, Irene Daniels, Carol Finney and John Bates should be kept well away from each other.

Problem-solving and Thinking Skills Resources for Able and Talented Children
© Barry Teare (Network Continuum Education, 2006)

FORM 7 SHAKESPEARE

NAME			LEVEL OF ABILITY	SPECIAL FRIENDS AT PRIMARY SCHOOL
DAVID ASTON	M	GB	Above average	None
GRAHAM BARNES	M	GB	Very good	Brian Sharp
JOHN BATES	M	HL	Weak	Irene Daniels/ Carol Finney/Jan Kennedy
WENDY BILLINGS	F	RV	Average	None
GILLIAN BOYDE	F	HL	Average	None
LANA BRIGGS	F	DH	Needs extra help	Regina Soudja
CONRAD BURTON	M	GB	Average	Ashley Furnell
JENNIFER DIGBY	F	GB	Excellent	None
HILARY EMERSON	F	GB	Average	None
ASHLEY FURNELL	M	GB	Excellent	Conrad Burton
LUTHER GARNER	M	HL	Very good	Ian Quigley
HANNAH GARSTON	F	GB	Excellent	None
MANDY GREGG	F	RV	Average	Wendy Billings
ERROL HUNTE	M	HL	Very good	Nigel Jones
POLLY INCE	F	DH	Average	Greta Poulton
NIGEL JONES	M	HL	Needs extra help	Errol Hunte
JOSEPHINE LINKS	F	HL	Average	None
JANET PRENDERGAST	F	GB	Below average	None
ANNE PRICE	F	RV	Average	None
IAN QUIGLEY	M	HL	Needs extra help	Luther Garner
ALAN RAFFAN	M	RV	Average	Dale Underwood
NEVILLE REID	M	HL	Very good	Moira Carter
MARGARET SHORT	F	GB	Average	None
PAULA SMITH	F	GB	Average	None
REGINA SOUDJA	F	DH	Weak	Lana Briggs
TRACEY TURNER	F	GB	Average	None
DALE UNDERWOOD	M	RV	Weak	Alan Raffan

Special notes from the primary schools:

1. Graham Barnes and Brian Sharp tend to 'act the fool' together.
2. Polly Ince and Greta Poulton do not have a good working relationship.
3. John Bates, Irene Daniels, Carol Finney and Jan Kennedy have a very bad influence on each other.
4. Neville Reid and Moira Carter waste time when together.

Getting the Balance Right

Teaching Notes

'Getting the Balance Right' gives pupils the chance to carry out a piece on problem solving that is close to their own lives. The situation is fictional but it is based closely on real life.

Key Elements

- ❖ problem solving
- ❖ analysis
- ❖ synthesis
- ❖ evaluation
- ❖ decision making
- ❖ deduction
- ❖ inference
- ❖ careful use of data.

Contexts

'Getting the Balance Right' can be used in a number of ways:

- ❖ as part of a problem-solving/thinking skills course
- ❖ as part of personal and social education
- ❖ as an enrichment activity for those who have completed other tasks
- ❖ as an activity during an enrichment day, weekend or summer school
- ❖ as differentiated homework
- ❖ as an activity for the Problem-solvers' Club.

Some Answers
The Principles of School Policy

1 **The forms should be of the same size if possible.** The 106 primary school children cannot be placed into four exactly equal forms. The closest solution is to have two forms of 27 and two forms of 26.

2 **There should be an equal proportion of boys and girls in each form.** The preponderance of girls means that the boys will be outnumbered but this imbalance should be weighted equally among the four forms.

3 **The forms should be mixed ability**, in other words each form should contain a good mixture of pupils right through the ability range, from those who need extra help because they have major learning problems to those who have a high level of ability.

4 **No one primary school should dominate any of the Year 7 forms.** The number from each primary school varies considerably, so each form will have more children from Green Bank than from Dent Hill but a similar proportion applies.

5 **Every effort should be made to keep children with their particular friends unless the friendships led to trouble, in which case the children should be put into separate forms deliberately. In any case, they should know some children in their new forms.**

NOTE: With potentially conflicting claims, the principles cannot be followed absolutely exactly. However, the following observations show that great attention has been paid to school policy.

Getting the Balance Right

Policy	7 AUSTEN	7 DICKENS	7 HARDY	7 SHAKESPEARE
1	26	27	26	27
2	16 girls, 10 boys	15 girls, 12 boys	15 girls, 11 boys	15 girls, 12 boys
3	Extra help 3 Weak 2 Below average 2 Average 10 Above average 3 Very good 3 Excellent 3	Extra help 2 Weak 2 Below average 3 Average 12 Above average 2 Very good 4 Excellent 2	Extra help 3 Weak 2 Below average 2 Average 11 Above average 2 Very good 4 Excellent 2	Extra help 3 Weak 3 Below average 1 Average 12 Above average 1 Very good 4 Excellent 3
4	GB 10, DH 3, RV 5, HL 8	GB 10, DH 4, RV 5, HL 8	GB 11, DH 3, RV 5, HL 7	GB 11, DH 3, RV 5, HL 8
5	Sally Renfrew is not with Brenda Makin; Colin Sefton and Duncan Earle have been kept apart.		Brian Sharp and Graham Barnes are not in the same form; Greta Poulton and Polly Ince have been kept apart; Moira Carter and Neville Reid have been kept separate.	
	Irene Daniels, Carol Finney, Jan Kennedy and John Bates have been placed one in each of the four forms.			

Other answers depend very much upon the personality and philosophy of individual pupils. Their responses do help to build up a personal profile for pastoral purposes. If alternative principles are suggested that fit with the data, credit should be given.

Extension Task

Credit should be given for any valid answer. A suggested order is:

1. Analyse the original data to record the total number of pupils, the number of boys and girls, how many children come from each primary school and the frequency of pupils in each of the seven ability groups.

2. Work out the ideal pattern for each form – the total, the balance of boys and girls, the balance of primary school origin and the desired frequency of ability groups.

3. Place the children who need to be separated.

4. Place the children who should be kept together.

5. Keep a rolling total of where the various balances now are.

6. Place children with no special friends, keeping a close eye on the desired outcome.

7. Change a small number of children, if necessary, to complete the placements while getting the desired outcome as close as possible.

Special Note

The pupils and schools are purely fictional. Any links with real children or schools is completely coincidental.

Timetable

In secondary schools, each year one of the teachers has the difficult and complicated task of drawing up the school timetable for the following year. When completed, this timetable shows what every pupil and teacher is doing for each lesson. It has to be accurate or chaotic situations can result, such as one teacher being down to look after two classes at the same time!

Careful thought and planning are necessary. A good quality timetable improves the day-to-day conditions in which everybody works. The amount of data to be dealt with is enormous. There are many processes along the way. Much has to be done before actual timetabling begins. The timetabler has to be a really good problem solver.

Could you do such a job?
There are five challenges to pit your wits against.

Lesson One	'Teachers' Time'
Lesson Two	'Combing Out the Knots'
Lesson Three	'Years 10 and 11 in Conflict'
Lesson Four	'Steering Wheel'
Lesson Five	'Quality Control'

Are you ready to pick up the gauntlet? Come and take a journey through the intriguing world of 'Timetable'.

LESSON ONE: 'TEACHERS' TIME'

Before you can start timetabling, it is essential to have the correct number of teachers available for each subject. Solving this sort of problem needs to take place earlier in the school year. Teachers always say they have never got enough time. The challenge here is to decide whether 'Teachers' Time' is sufficient.

Your Tasks

1 Study the data on the opposite page concerning the teaching of history at the William Pitt High School.

2 Work out how many history lessons have to be taught in total.

3 Work out how many lessons are available from those who teach history at the school.

4 Decide upon the course of action required. Is the staffing just right? Is more teacher time required? If so, is there a need to appoint another history teacher, or is the deficit small enough to be dealt with in a different way?

Problem-solving and Thinking Skills Resources for Able and Talented Children
© Barry Teare (Network Continuum Education, 2006)

Timetable 2/10

History lessons at the William Pitt High School

- The school is eight-form entry, in other words there are eight classes in each year, apart from Years 12 and 13 (the 'sixth form').
- William Pitt High School has 25 one-hour periods a week.
- Each class in Years 7, 8 and 9 has one lesson of history a week.
- Not every pupil takes history in Years 10 and 11.
- In both Years 10 and 11 there are four groups taking history.
- The allocation of time in Years 10 and 11 for history is three periods per group.
- In Year 12 there is one advanced-level history group.
- An advanced-level group has a time allocation of six periods.
- The position in Year 13 is the same as for Year 12.

History teachers at the William Pitt High School

- Mrs Disraeli is in charge of history. She is also the Head of the Humanities Faculty.
- Mr Gladstone has just been appointed to the school to start next September. This is his first job following qualification.
- Miss Palmerston is a classroom teacher with no extra responsibilities. Her main subject is history but she is committed each year to teach six periods of politics.
- The teaching loads for various members of staff vary. Heads of Faculty teach 19 periods a week. Newly qualified teachers teach 20 periods a week. Classroom teachers, with no additional responsibilities, have just three non-teaching periods a week.

LESSON TWO: 'COMBING OUT THE KNOTS'

A knot in your hair is a tangle and sometimes you have to comb out such a knot. In timetable terms, there is a different meaning. A combing chart is used to make sure that teacher teams fit into the number of lessons available. This is an exercise carried out before timetabling proper begins.

An example

Let us look at a very simple exercise. In a particular school there are 40 lessons in a week, eight for each of the five days. The English department plans to use teachers 1 and 2 for 15 periods together, teachers 2 and 3 for 15 periods together, and teachers 1 and 3 for 15 periods together. Also teachers 4 and 5 will work together for 10 periods, as will teachers 6 and 7. This seems reasonable, but is it?

With a combing chart, teacher teams that can operate at the same time are placed underneath each other as there are no clashes. However, if one or more teachers overlap teams, those lessons cannot take place at the same time. This is shown by drawing lines not below each other.

Timetable

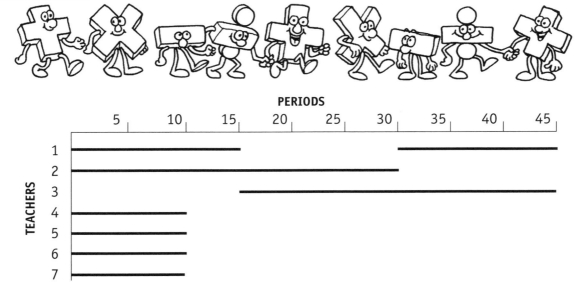

Teachers 4, 5, 6 and 7 pose no problem. However teams 1 and 2, 2 and 3, and 1 and 3 must operate at separate times as there is overlap of teachers. The English department's plans use 45 periods but there are only 40 periods in the week. Teams have to be changed before the timetabler can get to work. This example shows that even when there are sufficient teacher lessons available in total, the plan might not work.

Your Tasks

1 Study the information below on the mathematics department's plans at Cartesian Community College, an 11–16 school.

2 Draw a combing chart using the information.

3 State whether the arrangements work or not and what changes, if any, are required; thus 'Combing Out the Knots'.

The suggested timetable arrangements for the mathematics department at Cartesian Community College:

NOTES

1 There are 25 periods per week, five for each of five days.

2 As Cartesian Community College is an 11–16 school, there are no Years 12 and 13 to plan for.

3 There are seven teachers involved in the teaching of mathematics. All do a little teaching in other subjects. Teacher 7 is a senior member of staff.

4 The availability of each teacher for mathematics lessons is as follows:

Teacher 1	20 periods
Teacher 2	20 periods
Teacher 3	16 periods
Teacher 4	20 periods
Teacher 5	20 periods
Teacher 6	16 periods
Teacher 7	8 periods

- In Year 7 the teachers teach in two teams for four lessons a week. One team consists of Teachers 1, 2 and 3. The other team is made up of Teachers 1, 4 and 5.
- In Year 8 the classes are taught in pairs for four lessons a week. Similarly the teachers are organized in pairs. The pairings are Teachers 1 and 2, 1 and 6, and 1 and 5.
- There are similar arrangements in Year 9 as for Year 8. The teacher pairs are 2 and 4, 3 and 4, and 5 and 6.
- In Year 10 all the pupils are taught at the same time for four lessons a week. The teacher team is 2, 3, 4, 5, 6 and 7.
- In Year 11 the arrangements are exactly the same as for Year 10.

LESSON THREE: 'YEARS 10 AND 11 IN CONFLICT'

Pupils in Years 10 and 11 take subjects chosen from option pools, as well as compulsory subjects such as English and mathematics. All the subjects in an option pool are timetabled at the same time. This involves a team of teachers from different curriculum areas and might consist of history, geography, religious education, French and German. Each pupil would then have to choose one of these five subjects. The same process applies to all the option pools. Some subjects appear in more than one option pool to allow greater choice for the pupils.

To make the timetable work, option pools in Year 10 have to be taught at the same time as other option groups in Year 11. However, that can only happen if the same teacher is not expected to teach a group in both options.

Years 10 and 11 may or may not be in conflict socially in school, but the phrase has a different meaning for the timetabler who constructs a conflict matrix to show which options can be scheduled at the same time (in other words, where no teachers are placed in both options under consideration). An easy example is shown in the diagram below:

Diagram 1

		YEAR 11		
		OPTION 1	OPTION 2	OPTION 3
YEAR 10	OPTION 1			
	OPTION 2	X	X	X
	OPTION 3		X	

In diagram 1 only three options for each year are used to simplify the example. Year 10 Option 1 can be placed against any of the three Year 11 options, as there are no teachers clashing. The biggest problem is Year 10 Option 2 where there are clashes with all three Year 11 options. These clashes are indicated by crosses. Without some changes the timetabler would be put in a very difficult position. To make decisions about changes to the planning, the timetabler needs to know who the problem teachers are. This additional information is shown below:

Diagram 2

		YEAR 11		
		OPTION 1	OPTION 2	OPTION 3
YEAR 10	OPTION 1			
	OPTION 2	3, 6	1, 5	7
	OPTION 3		4	

Timetable

Diagram 2 displays the same data as diagram 1, but now there is important extra information showing which teachers are causing the clashes. It is normal to refer to teachers by identifying numbers. Two clashes are worse than the others because they both involve two teachers rather than one. Option 2 in Year 10 could be timetabled at the same time as Option 3 in Year 11 providing that teacher 7 is removed from one of the two options. If the subject in question is, for instance, geography then another geography teacher is needed as a replacement.

Your Tasks

1 Study the staff planning information for Year 10 and Year 11 option pools. To simplify matters, the subjects have not been listed, only the teachers by number.

2 Construct a conflict matrix of Year 10 options against Year 11 options. Indicate the teachers, by number, involved in clashes.

3 Write down which option pool causes most concern and why.

4 Write down which option pool causes least concern and why.

5 If one Year 10 option pool must, in each case, be timetabled at the same time as one Year 11 option, decide which pairings you would select.

6 Explain the easiest way to arrive at a solution so that each of the five Year 10 options is paired with an option in Year 11 for timetabling at the same time.

7 Explain why it is impossible for one Year 10 option to be timetabled at the same time as another Year 10 option.

The staff planning information

Year 10	Option 1	Teachers 2, 4, 12, 26, 5, 32 and 28
	Option 2	Teachers 13, 11, 27, 34, 22, 23 and 30
	Option 3	Teachers 1, 29, 33, 21, 24, 41 and 53
	Option 4	Teachers 50, 35, 31, 3, 7, 6 and 20
	Option 5	Teachers 36, 37, 24, 25, 8, 9 and 58

Year 11	Option 1	Teachers 13, 9, 15, 10, 38, 8 and 59
	Option 2	Teachers 47, 16, 39, 25, 60, 12 and 29
	Option 3	Teachers 40, 27, 24, 25, 1, 54 and 33
	Option 4	Teachers 58, 42, 45, 57, 1, 14 and 43
	Option 5	Teachers 28, 17, 24, 22, 36, 5 and 53

Come on, get down to work.
You want to avoid problems don't you?
Stop Years 10 and 11 being in conflict!

LESSON FOUR: 'STEERING WHEEL'

Sarah Schedule is the timetabler at Clockwork High School. She uses a computer to sort out most of the placements before looking at the problems that still remain. In preparation for the work, Sarah went on a computer timetabling course. Among other things, she learned that you can

---

Problem-solving and Thinking Skills Resources for Able and Talented Children
© Barry Teare (Network Continuum Education, 2006)

program the computer to give an order of priority to the placements for the various years. If, for instance, you believe that Year 9 has the greatest difficulties and the highest priority, then that year would be given preference. This process is called 'steering'. Now put yourself in Sarah Schedule's place.

Your Tasks

1 Study the information below about the organization of lessons in the different years at Clockwork High School.

2 Write down how you believe the computer should be 'steered', starting with the year of top priority and finishing with the year of least priority.

3 Give an explanation as to why you have placed the years in that particular order.

Organization of timetable year by year

Year 7 All lessons are taught in mixed ability classes. PE groups the classes together to allow different activities to take place but, otherwise, each class is timetabled on its own, with a single teacher.

Year 8 Mathematics and modern foreign languages set children by ability. In these two subjects three classes are taught at the same time. Otherwise the position is as it is in Year 7.

Year 9 English and science are also set by ability so that in these two subjects, and in mathematics and modern foreign languages, three classes are taught at the same time. PE is run for all Year 9 pupils at the same time. Other subjects are timetabled as individual classes.

Year 10 Most subjects are taught in option blocks where pupils have chosen from a list of subjects. As a result, large teams of teachers operate with pupils across the year.

Year 11 The position is the same as Year 10, but now pupils are into the second year of their courses for external examinations. Where possible, teachers, in teams, continue to teach the groups that they had in Year 10. Occasionally changes have to be made when, for instance, a member of staff leaves but the disruption is kept to a minimum.

Year 12 There are fewer pupils than in Years 10 and 11 but subjects are again taught in option blocks. Teacher teams operate but they are not as large as in Years 10 and 11.

Year 13 Option blocks from the previous year continue as pupils go into the second year of their courses for external examinations. Every effort is made to keep the same teacher with their groups as in Year 12, as continuity is important. Some changes are inevitable because of staff leaving or being on long-term leave.

LESSON FIVE: 'QUALITY CONTROL'

Even when all the classes, teachers and rooms have been placed, the job is not quite over. All timetables have problems in them. The task is so complex that there is never a perfect solution. A good timetabler tries to reduce the number of placements that are far from ideal. The fewer of these unfavourable placements there are, the higher is the quality of the timetable and, therefore, the better it is for teachers and pupils in their daily routine.

Timetable

Mrs Perfectionist is a very good timetabler. She cares passionately about the quality of her work and its impact on other people. When she has 'finished' the timetable, in the sense that all placements have been made, Mrs Perfectionist takes another look to see if she can improve situations that work but that are not ideal. She goes into her 'quality control' mode. Are you able to do the same?

Your Tasks

1 Study the list of features that Mrs Perfectionist looks out for when trying to improve the details of the final timetable.

2 Take into account the information about the buildings of Rigley High School, where Mrs Perfectionist works.

3 Also study the information on the school day at Rigley High School.

4 Look at the separate sheets that contain the completed timetables of three classes and three teachers.

5 Identify a problem feature for each of the six timetables shown.

6 Explain why, at this stage, it might not be possible to improve on these problems, even for Mrs Perfectionist.

Features that Mrs Perfectionist tries to avoid

1 A bad spread of lessons during the week in one particular subject.

2 Subjects of too similar a nature occurring on the same day.

3 A teacher travelling too much between buildings, either in total or on any particular day.

4 A subject always having its lessons at an unfavourable time of day.

5 A bad balance of subjects from day to day.

6 All of a teacher's non-teaching time being bunched together.

The buildings at Rigley High School
Rigley High School is what is known as a 'split-site' school. There are two buildings, one mile apart. Years 7, 8 and 9 are taught in the Lower School on Langer Road. Years 10 and 11 are taught in the Upper School on Sedley Lane. Pupils leave at the age of 16.

The school day at Rigley High School
There are eight lessons or periods in the day, divided into twos by a morning break of 20 minutes, lunchtime of 50 minutes and an afternoon break of 15 minutes. Using two lessons together as a 'double' is a normal practice although some lessons are singles.

Problem-solving and Thinking Skills Resources for Able and Talented Children
© Barry Teare (Network Continuum Education, 2006)

THE SIX TIMETABLES

NOTE
For the three forms, the subjects are named together with initials of the teachers. No rooms have yet been added.

Timetable One   8F

	MON.	TUES.	WED.	THURS.	FRI.
1	MUSIC FD	ENGLISH MR	GEOGRAPHY PY	HISTORY AM	SCIENCE ED
2	MUSIC FD	DRAMA LT	PE RC/JL	FRENCH SL	THINKING SKILLS BT
3	ENGLISH MR	SCIENCE ED	RE PB	ENGLISH MR	TECHNOLOGY JE
4	INFORMATION TECHNOLOGY NW	SCIENCE ED	RE PB	ENGLISH MR	TECHNOLOGY JE
5	HISTORY AM	FRENCH SL	TECHNOLOGY MO	SCIENCE ED	GAMES RC/JL
6	FRENCH SL	FRENCH SL	TECHNOLOGY MO	SCIENCE ED	GAMES RC/JL
7	MATHS LS	ART BH	ENGLISH MR	MATHS LS	GEOGRAPHY PY
8	MATHS LS	ART BH	MATHS LS	INFORMATION TECHNOLOGY NW	MATHS LS

Timetable Two   Mr Hardy

	MON.	TUES.	WED.	THURS.	FRI.
1	9Y ENGLISH	YEAR 10 ENGLISH	7S ENGLISH	YEAR 10 ENGLISH	8C ENGLISH
2	9Y ENGLISH	YEAR 10 ENGLISH	7S ENGLISH	FREE	9G ENGLISH
3	8C ENGLISH	7N ENGLISH	FREE	8K ENGLISH	7N ENGLISH
4	8C ENGLISH	8K ENGLISH	FREE	8K ENGLISH	7N ENGLISH
5	7N ENGLISH	9G ENGLISH	YEAR 10 ENGLISH	9Y ENGLISH	8K ENGLISH
6	7N ENGLISH	9G ENGLISH	YEAR 10 ENGLISH	9Y ENGLISH	8K ENGLISH
7	7S ENGLISH	8C ENGLISH	FREE	9G ENGLISH	7S ENGLISH
8	7S ENGLISH	8C ENGLISH	FREE	9G ENGLISH	9Y ENGLISH

© Barry Teare (Network Continuum Education, 2006)

Timetable

Timetable Three   Miss Tennyson

	MON.	TUES.	WED.	THURS.	FRI.
1	7K SCIENCE	8S SCIENCE	FREE	YEAR 10 OPTION 4 PHYSICS	9O SCIENCE
2	7K SCIENCE	8S SCIENCE	FREE	YEAR 10 OPTION 4 PHYSICS	8F THINKING SKILLS
3	YEAR 11 OPTION 3 PHYSICS	8N SCIENCE	9O SCIENCE	7K SCIENCE	8S SCIENCE
4	YEAR 11 OPTION 3 PHYSICS	8N SCIENCE	9O SCIENCE	FREE	7K THINKING SKILLS
5	8N SCIENCE	FREE	8S SCIENCE	YEAR 11 OPTION 3 PHYSICS	8N SCIENCE
6	8N SCIENCE	FREE	8S SCIENCE	YEAR 11 OPTION 3 PHYSICS	FREE
7	YEAR 10 OPTION 4 PHYSICS	9O SCIENCE	7K SCIENCE	YEAR 7 GAMES	YEAR 8 GAMES
8	YEAR 10 OPTION 4 PHYSICS	9O SCIENCE	7K SCIENCE	YEAR 7 GAMES	YEAR 8 GAMES

Timetable Four   Form 9O

	MON.	TUES.	WED.	THURS.	FRI.
1	ENGLISH MR	TECHNOLOGY BR	ENGLISH MR	MATHS YT	SCIENCE BT
2	PE PR/HT	TECHNOLOGY BR	ENGLISH MR	MATHS YT	INFORMATION TECHNOLOGY NW
3	MATHS YT	FRENCH SL	SCIENCE BT	GEOGRAPHY GC	MUSIC FD
4	MATHS YT	FRENCH SL	SCIENCE BT	GEOGRAPHY GC	MUSIC FD
5	HISTORY OW	MATHS YT	FRENCH SL	RE PB	TECHNOLOGY JE
6	HISTORY OW	THINKING SKILLS AS	INFORMATION TECHNOLOGY NW	RE PB	TECHNOLOGY JE
7	GAMES PR/HT	SCIENCE BT	ART BH	ENGLISH MR	FRENCH SL
8	GAMES PR/HT	SCIENCE BT	ART BH	ENGLISH MR	DRAMA NM

Timetable Five — Miss Cordiale

	MON.	TUES.	WED.	THURS.	FRI.
1	YEAR 10 OPTION 2 FRENCH	7S FRENCH	7D FRENCH	7B FRENCH	YEAR 11 OPTION 5 GERMAN
2	YEAR 10 OPTION 2 FRENCH	7S FRENCH	7D FRENCH	9G FRENCH	YEAR 10 OPTION 1 GERMAN
3	7B FRENCH	YEAR 10 GAMES	YEAR 11 OPTION 5 GERMAN	7D FRENCH	9G FRENCH
4	7B FRENCH	YEAR 10 GAMES	YEAR 10 OPTION 1 GERMAN	FREE	9G FRENCH
5	YEAR 11 OPTION 5 GERMAN	7D FRENCH	FREE	YEAR 10 OPTION 2 FRENCH	7S FRENCH
6	YEAR 11 OPTION 5 GERMAN	FREE	FREE	YEAR 10 OPTION 2 FRENCH	FREE
7	9G FRENCH	YEAR 10 OPTION 1 GERMAN	7S FRENCH	8H FRENCH	7B FRENCH
8	8H FRENCH	YEAR 10 OPTION 1 GERMAN	7N THINKING SKILLS	8H FRENCH	8H FRENCH

Timetable Six — Form 7L

	MON.	TUES.	WED.	THURS.	FRI.
1	MATHS TW	FRENCH SL	ART BH	SCIENCE ED	ENGLISH MR
2	MATHS TW	ENGLISH MR	ART BH	SCIENCE ED	ENGLISH MR
3	SCIENCE ED	INFORMATION TECHNOLOGY NW	TECHNOLOGY BR	GEOGRAPHY PY	MATHS TW
4	SCIENCE ED	PE RC/JL	TECHNOLOGY BR	GEOGRAPHY PY	FRENCH SL
5	HISTORY RR	MATHS TW	MUSIC FD	FRENCH SL	RE PB
6	HISTORY RR	MATHS TW	MUSIC FD	ENGLISH MR	RE PB
7	FRENCH SL	THINKING SKILLS AS	DRAMA UF	GAMES BT/PR	TECHNOLOGY JE
8	ENGLISH MR	SCIENCE ED	INFORMATION TECHNOLOGY NW	GAMES BT/PR	TECHNOLOGY JE

Timetable

Teaching Notes

This is a major piece of problem solving, set in a world very close to the pupils themselves. 'Timetable' cannot follow the whole process, but the five challenges here are representative of problems to be solved along the way. A host of key skills are involved.

Key Elements

- ❖ problem solving
- ❖ logical thinking
- ❖ lateral thinking
- ❖ analysis
- ❖ synthesis
- ❖ evaluation
- ❖ close engagement with data
- ❖ decision making
- ❖ use of a combing chart
- ❖ use of a conflict matrix
- ❖ mental agility
- ❖ mathematical dexterity.

Contexts

'Timetable' can be used in a variety of ways:

- ❖ as extension work in mathematics lessons
- ❖ as an enrichment activity in mathematics lessons
- ❖ as part of a thinking skills course
- ❖ as an enrichment task for those who have completed other tasks
- ❖ as an activity during an enrichment day, weekend or summer school
- ❖ as material for a team tournament
- ❖ as an activity for the Mathematics Club or Problem-solvers' Club.

The Solutions

LESSON ONE: 'TEACHERS' TIME'

The number of history periods taught is calculated as follows:

Year 7	eight classes with one period each	=	8
Year 8	eight classes with one period each	=	8
Year 9	eight classes with one period each	=	8
Year 10	four groups with three periods each	=	12
Year 11	four groups with three periods each	=	12
Year 12	one group with six periods	=	6
Year 13	one group with six periods	=	6
		TOTAL	**60**

The staff, therefore, need to be able to cover 60 periods. The staffing availability is as follows:

Mrs Disraeli as head of faculty has	19
Mr Gladstone as an NQT has	20
Miss Palmerston's teaching load is 25 – 3 = 22,	
however six periods of politics must be deducted leaving	16
TOTAL	**55**

The history teachers can, therefore, cover 55 periods only of the 60 needed. There is a deficit of five periods.

Solution

A full extra teacher is not required. There are three likely ways forward:

1. When appointing new staff, look for somebody whose main subject is not history but who is capable of teaching five periods to younger pupils.

2. Find existing members of staff in other departments, with spare capacity on their timetable, who are capable of teaching five periods to Years 7 or 8.

3. Transfer Miss Palmerston's commitment in politics to a new or existing member of staff.

LESSON TWO: 'COMBING OUT THE KNOTS'

From the data the combing chart can be constructed:

PERIODS

TEACHERS	4	8	12	16	20	24	25	28
1	Year 7	Year 7	Year 8	Year 8	Year 8			
2	Year 7		Year 8	Year 9		Year 10	Year 11	
3	Year 7		Year 9			Year 10	Year 11	
4		Year 7	Year 9	Year 9		Year 10	Year 11	
5	Year 9	Year 7			Year 8	Year 10	Year 11	
6	Year 9			Year 8		Year 10	Year 11	
7						Year 10	Year 11	

In the plan, all the teachers have used their own correct individual allocation of periods. The 120 mathematics lessons have been covered by the seven teachers. However, as the combing chart shows, this plan cannot fit into less than 28 periods and there are only 25 periods in the week. Teacher teams must be changed. If, for instance Teacher 1 comes out of the second Year 7 team and is replaced by Teacher 6, then both Year 7 teams can operate at the same time. Teacher 1 could then replace Teacher 6 in either Year 10 or Year 11. This has not affected the total of teaching lessons to be taught by each teacher. However, the mathematics department may not normally use Teacher 1 in Year 10 or Year 11. In this case a complete re-shuffle of Years 8 and 9 would be needed.

LESSON THREE: 'YEARS 10 AND 11 IN CONFLICT'

Tasks 1 and 2

The data produce the following conflict matrix:

YEAR 11

YEAR 10	OPTION 1	OPTION 2	OPTION 3	OPTION 4	OPTION 5
OPTION 1		12			5, 28
OPTION 2	13		27		22
OPTION 3		29	1, 24, 33	1	24,53
OPTION 4					
OPTION 5	8, 9	25	24, 25	58	24, 36

Task 3

Year 10 Option 5 causes the most concern as it clashes with every one of the Year 11 options.

Task 4

Year 10 Option 4 causes the least concern as it has no clashes with any of the Year 11 options.

Task 5

The pairings cannot be final due to problems with Year 10 Option 5 but the best pattern is:
Year 10 Option 1 with Year 11 Option 3
Year 10 Option 2 with Year 11 Option 2 or Year 11 Option 4

Timetable

Year 10 Option 3 with Year 11 Option 1
Year 10 Option 4 with Year 11 Option 5
Year 10 Option 5 with Year 11 Option 2 or Year 11 Option 4
Year 10 Option 2 has no clashes with Year 11 Option 2 or Year 11 Option 4, so either can be the final choice. Year 10 Option 5 has clashes with all Year 11 options but the clash is restricted to one teacher only in Year 11 Option 2 and Year 11 Option 4.

Task 6

Attention needs to be paid to teachers 25 and 58. What subjects do they take? Is there any easier replacement for teacher 25 or 58? If teacher 25 is the easier route to replace, without a new clash taking place, then Year 10 Option 5 would be paired with Year 11 Option 2. As a result, Year 10 Option 2 would be paired with Year 11 Option 4. If, however, teacher 58 is the easier route to replace, again without a new clash taking place, then Year 10 Option 5 would be paired with Year 11 Option 4. As a result, Year 10 Option 2 would be paired with Year 11 Option 2.

Task 7

The same pupils are involved in all the option pools for a particular year. If, for instance, Year 10 Option 1 was timetabled at the same time as Year 10 Option 5, all the pupils would be expected to be in two different lessons at the same time!

LESSON FOUR: 'STEERING WHEEL'

'Steering Wheel' puts top priority with the years that are more difficult because teacher teams are in use. The more subjects that are taught in single classes, the easier it is to find solutions, as you are looking for only one teacher at a time. Therefore Years 10, 11, 12 and 13 are given priority. Where two-year courses are being followed, there is an additional pressure to keep the same teacher with a group throughout the course. As a result, Years 11 and 13 become even more important to place.

The most probable order of preference to be included in the steering process is:

Year 11 – there are large teams of teachers, and pupils are in the second year of the course.
Year 13 – the teams are smaller than Year 11 but teacher continuity is very important.
Year 10 – large teams have to be placed but some changes can be made as the courses are just starting.
Year 12 – the same reasoning as for Year 10 but the teams are smaller.
(An alternative pattern: it could be argued that the order should be Year 11 – Year 10 – Year 13 – Year 12. To some extent this depends on the size of the post-16 group in the school.)
Year 9 – several subjects involve small teams of teachers.
Year 8 – there are fewer subjects taught with classes in teams.
Year 7 – apart from PE, all subjects are taught as individual classes. These are the easiest problems to resolve.

LESSON FIVE: 'QUALITY CONTROL'

Solutions

In each case, a major weakness has been identified. However credit should be given for any other observations by pupils that fit the features identified by Mrs Perfectionist.

Timetable One: Form 8F

Problem: maths lessons are placed very unfortunately. They take place on Monday 7 and 8, Wednesday 8, Thursday 7 and Friday 8. Last lessons of the day have to be used but they tend to be not as productive. At least some of 8F's maths should come earlier in the day.

Timetable Two: Mr Hardy

Problem: the main difficulty is the distribution of his free time. He has five non-teaching lessons but four of them come on Wednesday with the other one on Thursday 2. That is not good for preparation of lessons and marking work.

Timetable

Timetable Three: Miss Tennyson

Problem: having just two groups in the Upper School, with four lessons for each group, complete morning or afternoon sessions would have been extremely helpful. The toing-and-froing on Mondays and Thursdays is going to cause problems. On those two days Miss Tennyson has to move buildings three times. This is compounded on Thursdays by taking Year 7 games for periods 7 and 8. When does she change? The travelling pattern certainly needs attention.

Timetable Four: Form 90

Problem: there is less to worry about here than the three previous timetables. However, there is one flaw that jumps out. To have both PE and games on Monday is not helpful. They should be on different days. As well as the demands on pupils, it may cause problems with kit.

Timetable Five: Miss Cordiale

Problem: with almost equal time spent in the two buildings, the teacher has a very heavy travel pattern. There are 11 moves, three on Monday, three on Tuesday, two on Wednesday, two on Thursday and one on Friday. There is also a very poor allocation of French lessons for Form 8H. Their lessons fall on Monday 8, Thursday 7 and 8, and Friday 8.

Timetable Six: Form 7L

Problem: there is nothing very dramatic here but the placement of lessons on Wednesday is questionable. With so much practical activity it could be argued that there is not enough variety on that particular day.

The chance of improvement

Mrs Perfectionist does not like what she has discovered on these six timetables. However, movement at this stage is very difficult, especially for teams of teachers in option pools. The worst scenario is that concerning Miss Cordiale but that is also where movement is most difficult as the 'solution space' will be very small.

Section 2

Wordplay

It is a truism to say that language is important not only in English but in every area of the curriculum. All sections of the National Curriculum 1999 stress the central place of subject-specific vocabulary. Edward de Bono in *Teaching Thinking* (Penguin, 1978) states that 'language provides the handles with which we grasp the world' (page 37). The Literacy Framework has a major strand called 'vocabulary extension'.

A good proportion of this section on wordplay is concerned with the teaching of English. The National Curriculum 1999 exhorts teachers to encourage children to 'use adventurous and wide-ranging vocabulary'. However, wordplay can be applied to other subjects and this is reflected in these materials.

The first four pieces can be termed word games. Not everybody appreciates their value but they can be very useful indeed. Tony Augarde says in his introduction to *The Oxford Guide to Word Games* (1986):

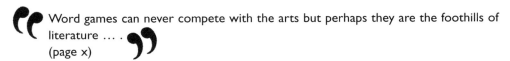 Word games can never compete with the arts but perhaps they are the foothills of literature … .
(page x)

- 'Merlin' requires students to identify 20 words that contain the letters 'LIN' at the start, in the middle or at the end. This is achieved through cryptic clues and the correct number of letters for each word. In this, and the other pieces, word humour is used – an important commodity for many able children. It was Gyles Brandreth in *Everyman's Word Games* (J.M. Dent, 1986) who stressed the richness of our language and said 'I believe we would value our language more if we enjoyed it more …' ('Foreword').

- In 'Grateful for the Ghost' the central feature is that many words contain smaller words as, indeed, within the title – 'rate', 'or', 'he' and 'host'. There are 20 examples to solve by using cryptic clues; the number of letters for the answer (the larger word) and for the smaller word enclosed are given. This method is also used in 'The Avid Diva', but here we deal with what some people label 'semordnilap' – 'palindromes' spelled backwards. Two words are identified from clues, where one word has the order of letters in reverse order to the other – as, indeed, with 'avid' and 'diva' in the title.

- The fourth word game is more cross-curricular as it contains sections on science, geography and history as well as an English/general group. Two words have to be identified from clues where the last letter of one word is the first letter of the second word in the pair. This gives the title for the piece 'The Last Shall Be First'.

- The next two pieces concern the origins of words, an area stressed in English curriculum guidelines and the Literacy Framework. 'Gremlin' promotes creative writing to explain the origin of ten unusual words or phrases. There are some parameters but there is also much open-endedness to stimulate the imagination. 'Dictionary Delia' results from the fact that the *Collins Dictionary* included Delia Smith's name with a definition. Children are asked to write similar definitions for some of the 40 other people quoted from many walks of life.

- The section then moves on to two pieces that play to a particular curriculum area outside English. 'Turning the Corner: A Mathstory' has a short account with 36 spaces in it. These spaces have to be filled by mathematical terms that make sense in the story but also fit the mathematical definitions that are given on a separate sheet. Here is an unusual way of dealing with mathematical terms as requested by the Cockcroft Report some years ago and the Numeracy Framework more recently.

- 'Hide and Seek Solve a Problem' also uses a story format, indeed, a detective story. Twenty-one British towns and cities have to be identified by means of cryptic clues. As homographs or homophones they then make sense within the detective story. As well as wordplay there are strong geographical links.

- 'The Name of the Game' is the final exercise in this section. It is based upon the fact that many people's first names have other meanings. Again, homographs and homophones are involved. The spoof setting and puzzle format will appeal to many able children.

merlín

'King Arthur's bird of prey' (6) is a clue that would lead you to 'Merlin' where (6) indicates the number of letters in the word. Here, 'LIN' is at the end of the word, as it is on a number of occasions, although sometimes 'LIN' appears at the start of, or in the middle of, words.

Your Task

Identify the 20 words below from the clues, some of which are straightforward definitions and others are cryptic. Each word contains the letters 'LIN' at the beginning, in the middle or at the end.

see if you can fly to the solutions like a wizard; just like merlín!

clues

1	A large ship.	(5)
2	An important antibiotic.	(10)
3	A place for medical treatment.	(6)
4	Harry Potter's process for writing out words.	(8)
5	To break into small, sharp fragments.	(8)
6	The weakest may bring about the damage or downfall of a larger unit.	(4)
7	A bird of the finch family.	(6)
8	A musical instrument.	(6)
9	Relating to salt.	(6)
10	Cricketers and artists like this oil.	(7)
11	A container that is useful for storing rolled-up posters.	(8)
12	A syrupy medicinal preparation.	(7)
13	The antonym of the floor.	(7)
14	For writing rather than blank for drawing.	(5)
15	Tearful or sentimental.	(7)
16	The base of a column or statue.	(6)
17	A mischievous troublemaker.	(7)
18	To trace the shape or outline of; to sketch; to represent pictorially.	(9)
19	A horizontal beam over a door or window.	(6)
20	You may do this to the edge of a cliff to avoid falling!	(5)

Extension Tasks

1. Collect another 15 words that contain 'LIN': five at the start of a word (very easy with a dictionary!), five in the middle and five at the end.
2. Write clues for your 15 words, making some of them cryptic. Give them to somebody to try to identify.

Problem-solving and Thinking Skills Resources for Able and Talented Children
© Barry Teare (Network Continuum Education, 2006)

merlin

Teaching Notes

Key Elements

- ❖ wordplay
- ❖ word humour
- ❖ vocabulary extension
- ❖ use of a dictionary.

Contexts

'Merlin' could be used in the following ways:

- ❖ as extension work to other exercises on vocabulary
- ❖ as an enrichment activity for those who have completed other tasks
- ❖ as a differentiated homework
- ❖ as an activity during an enrichment day, weekend or summer school
- ❖ as an activity for the English Club or Society.

Solution

1 Liner

2 Penicillin

3 Clinic

4 Spelling

5 Splinter

6 Link

7 Linnet

8 Violin

9 Saline

10 Linseed

11 Cylinder

12 Linctus

13 Ceiling

14 Lined

15 Maudlin

16 Plinth

17 Gremlin

18 Delineate

19 Lintel

20 Cling

Grateful for the Ghost

Some words contain smaller words. In fact all four words in the title have this feature. They could be identified by means of cryptic clues, as follow:

1 Thankful for the amount for the job (4 within 8) → g**rate**ful
2 An alternative in the place of (2 within 3) → f**or**
3 A male definite article (2 within 3) → t**he**
4 This spirit looks after you (4 within 5) → g**host**

Your Task

Identify 20 words from the cryptic clues below. Also name the shorter word that is included within the longer word. The shorter word can be at the beginning, in the middle or at the end of the longer word. The order of the cryptic clue also varies with regard to whether the longer word or the shorter word is referred to first.

The Clues

1   A means of catching fish and attracting metal.   (3 within 6)
2   A piece of stone proves to be a missile.   (4 within 6)
3   A facial feature is part of an engine.   (4 within 7)
4   This animal enclosure might occur.   (3 within 6)
5   Has the alcoholic drink caused complaint?   (3 within 7)
6   This reptile has eaten a fish.   (3 within 9)
7   Rule out everything.   (3 within 8)
8   A human limb causes a disadvantage.   (4 within 8)
9   Not a high deer.   (3 within 6)
10 You have the power of means to take this medicine.   (4 within 6)
11 A single band.   (3 within 4)
12 A rodent who is an eloquent speaker.   (3 within 6)
13 The side of the room is where we find a migratory bird.   (4 within 7)
14 A small portion of the whole is large enough.   (5 within 6)
15 The breakfast food has a raised strip.   (5 within 8)
16 A mathematical diagram is part of somebody's life story.   (5 within 9)
17 The atmospheric conditions are there to digest.   (3 within 7)
18 Unlock the problems of this four-legged animal.   (3 within 6)
19 The farmer's work could include excessive admiration or belief.   (4 within 11)
20 A long seat proves to be a faulty structure.   (4 within 12)

Extension Tasks

1 Find 15 more words that fit the principles behind 'Grateful for the Ghost'. Try to mix up the examples so that the shorter words occur at the beginning, the middle and at the end of the longer words.
2 Write cryptic clues for your 15 words and give them to somebody else to try to identify.

Problem-solving and Thinking Skills Resources for Able and Talented Children
© Barry Teare (Network Continuum Education, 2006)

Grateful for the Ghost

Teaching Notes

Key Elements

- ❖ wordplay
- ❖ vocabulary extension
- ❖ dictionary work
- ❖ close engagement with text.

Contexts

'Grateful for the Ghost' can be used in the following ways:

- ❖ as extension work to other exercises on vocabulary
- ❖ as an enrichment activity for those who have completed other work quickly and well
- ❖ as a differentiated homework
- ❖ as an activity during an enrichment day, weekend or summer school
- ❖ as an open-access competition where the extension tasks could be used as a discriminator if more than one entry identifies all 20 words in the main task correctly.

Solution

1	MAG**NET**	net
2	**ROCK**ET	rock
3	MA**CHIN**E	chin
4	HAP**PEN**	pen
5	G**RUM**BLE	rum
6	CRO**COD**ILE	cod
7	DIS**ALL**OW	all
8	**HAND**ICAP	hand
9	FAL**LOW**	low
10	T**ABLE**T	able
11	Z**ONE**	one
12	O**RAT**OR	rat
13	S**WALL**OW	wall
14	S**AMPLE**	ample
15	POR**RIDGE**	ridge
16	BIO**GRAPH**Y	graph
17	W**EAT**HER	eat
18	DON**KEY**	key
19	AGRI**CULT**URE	cult
20	MAL**FORM**ATION	form

The Avid Diva

If you look carefully at the title, you will see that there is a particular connection between the words 'avid' and 'diva'. One word has been reversed in letter order to produce the other. Some people refer to them as 'mirror words', for obvious reasons. Others give them the strange label 'semordnilap' because that spells 'palindromes' backwards (palindromes being words that spell the same word backwards and forwards, for example 'deed'). Words like 'avid' and 'diva' are used in crosswords and they are known as 'reversals'. In the spirit of crosswords, the two words can be identified by means of a cryptic clue such as 'the keen and famous opera singer' (4), where (4) refers to the number of letters.

Your Task   Work out the mirror words or reversals from the clues below.

The Clues

1	Doze off while removing the skin.	(5)
2	The track for wheels doesn't tell the truth.	(4)
3	The bottom of the boat is a vegetable.	(4)
4	The puddings are under pressure.	(8)
5	Comfortably fitting weapons.	(4)
6	William Shakespeare is dull.	(4)
7	The cooking utensils finish.	(4)
8	Led one's life as a wicked person.	(5)
9	The flavour of the small insect.	(4)
10	The base of the teeth are complacent.	(4)
11	The working instrument takes the plunder.	(4)
12	The roofing expert got the fire going again	(5)
13	To distribute or hand over the bitterly abused.	(7)
14	Get ready for publication the flow of the sea.	(4)
15	Swallow hard the stopper.	(4)
16	Negative off.	(2)
17	Make merry with the method to move something with a bar.	(5)
18	A small tag on the cricket equipment.	(3)
19	The cart is in the enclosed, paved area.	(4)
20	An atmosphere of foreboding.	(4)

Extension Tasks

1   Find at least ten more examples of your own. You may wish to use a dictionary. What clues are there as to where it is best to look in the dictionary?

2   Write cryptic clues and ask somebody else in your class to try to decipher the pairs of words.

Problem-solving and Thinking Skills Resources for Able and Talented Children
© Barry Teare (Network Continuum Education, 2006)

The Avid Diva

Teaching Notes

'The Avid Diva' provides an interesting example of wordplay and vocabulary extension.

Key Elements

- ❖ use of a dictionary
- ❖ wordplay
- ❖ word humour
- ❖ vocabulary extension
- ❖ application (in the extension task).

Contexts

'The Avid Diva' can be used in the following ways:

- ❖ as a feature of dictionary work
- ❖ as part of vocabulary extension work
- ❖ as an enrichment activity for those who have completed other work
- ❖ as a differentiated homework
- ❖ as an activity during an enrichment day, weekend or summer school
- ❖ as an activity for the English Club or Society.

Solution

1	sleep and peels	11	tool and loot
2	rail and liar	12	tiler and relit
3	keel and leek	13	deliver and reviled
4	desserts and stressed	14	edit and tide
5	snug and guns	15	gulp and plug
6	bard and drab	16	no and on
7	pots and stop	17	revel and lever
8	lived and devil	18	tab and bat
9	tang and gnat	19	dray and yard
10	gums and smug	20	mood and doom

Extension Task

Some words are much more likely to reverse than others, for example ending in 'ed'. Pupils can save time by understanding the possibilities.

The Last Shall Be First

'The Last Shall Be First' is not a religious nor philosophical message, as it might sound, but rather a word game. This is based upon the fact that the last letter of one word is the first letter of the second word in a pair. The two words are identified through a cryptic clue.

An example is:

'The present time 24 hours back' [5 and 9] where the numbers give the number of letters in each word. The two words are 'today' and 'yesterday'.

YOUR TASK

From the cryptic clues and the number of letters, work out the pair of words in each case, following the rule that the last letter of the first word is the first letter of the second word. You may wish to attempt all the sections or perhaps choose particular areas.

THE CRYPTIC CLUES

Section One: English/General

1 Something advantageous in the set of rules enforceable by the courts (10 and 3).

2 Has this glass vessel the nerve to be correct in every detail (6 and 5)?

3 A secluded, sheltered place or narrow recess may be home for the dog (4 and 6).

4 A place for buying and selling is good for camping (6 and 4).

5 This large spider has a slight illness (9 and 7).

6 Your personal record of daily events normally covers this period of time (5 and 4).

7 An adhesive label, poster or paper leads to a conundrum or puzzle (7 and 6).

8 A form of music pleases this black-and-white striped animal (4 and 5).

9 Nothing for the coloured fruit (4 and 6).

10 A compulsory financial contribution to raise revenue by the government could pay for a musical instrument (3 and 9).

Section Two: Science

1 The point at which liquid turns to vapour causes the beginning of the growth of a seed (7 and 11).

2 Green pigment in plants makes an optical device made of glass (11 and 4).

3 Part of the eye becomes a yellow, non-metallic element (4 and 7).

4 The bending of a light ray shows us a new star or one that suddenly burns brighter (10 and 4).

5 This warming effect has the capacity to do work (10 and 6).

6 A protein acting as a biological catalyst leads to a position where a set of forces is completely balanced (6 and 11).

7 The flow of electrical charge produces a soft, malleable and ductile metal (7 and 3).

8 The smallest part of an element that can exist, that has all the properties of that element, is linked to the quantity of matter in a substance (4 and 4).

9 A gas becomes a liquid that is neither acidic nor alkaline (12 and 7).

10 A mixture of two metals leads to a single-celled fungus that releases carbon dioxide when it respires (5 and 5).

Section Three: Geography

1 The river leaves a fine soil when flooding, that might have resulted from a storm, with very strong winds and heavy rainfall (4 and 7).
2 Molten rock at the height above sea-level (4 and 8).
3 The layer of the earth below the crust and above the core won't be subject to wearing away by rivers, sea, ice or wind (6 and 7).
4 A part of the coastline that juts out into the sea may be near a flat area of alluvium at the mouth of the river, with Greek connections (8 and 5).
5 A type of fuel from the remains of plants or ancient life that tells you how far a place is north or south of the Equator (6 and 8).
6 A long spell of dry weather might affect a small river flowing into a bigger river (7 and 9).
7 The boundary between two river basins is near a weather system with low pressure at its centre (9 and 10).
8 A pattern of routes that are linked together helps to explain the map (7 and 3).
9 People go on holiday to a place where this type of migrant might be working before returning home (6 and 9).
10 A volcano that has not erupted for so long that it is not expected to erupt again will not lead to a tidal wave from an undersea earthquake (7 and 7).

Section Four: History

1 Franz Ferdinand's demise brings into play British fighting strength (13 and 4).
2 George VI was king as a result of a bird that played an important medical role in the Crimean War (10 and 11).
3 Flowers at war in the Middle Ages lasted longer than Britain's capitulation in Singapore during the Second World War (5 and 9).
4 Trouble brewing in Boston Harbour was a long way from Philip II of Spain's fleet (3 and 6).
5 Nazi Germany's lightning strike was a shock, which is what Fawkes hoped his explosive substance would cause (10 and 9).
6 Norman violated our privacy, which some wish to protect by strong loyalty or devotion to their country (8 and 11).
7 The addictive cause of dispute between Britain and China in the nineteenth century is linked to an area protected against the enemy (5 and 9).
8 She chained herself to the railings to make a point more forcefully than a friendly understanding between political powers, such as that between Britain, France and Russia before the First World War (11 and 7).
9 Townshend's favourite vegetable leads on to a person who refuses military service (6 and 8).
10 Humphry Davy might shed illumination on the system of government in the Roman Catholic Church that Henry VIII clashed with (4 and 6).

Extension Tasks

1 Write your own cryptic clues to pairs of words that will fit in the sections above.
2 Choose a different subject area and write the clues to the pairs of words that follow the principle that 'The Last Shall Be First'.

The Last Shall Be First

Teaching Notes

This word exercise involves solving cryptic information while dealing with subject-specific vocabulary, a key component in all areas of the National Curriculum.

Key Elements

- wordplay
- vocabulary extension
- handling cryptic data
- dictionary work
- subject-specific vocabulary in science, history and geography.

Contexts

'The Last Shall Be First' can be used in the following ways:

- as vocabulary extension work in English lessons
- as subject-specific vocabulary work in science, history and geography
- as an open-access competition where the extension tasks act as a discriminator
- as a differentiated homework
- as an enrichment activity for those who have completed other work
- as an activity during an enrichment day, weekend or summer school
- as an activity for the English Club or Society, History Club, Science Club or Geography Society.

NOTE: The teacher can choose an individual section to fit in with a particular curriculum area or pupils could be asked to tackle the piece more generally.

The Solution

Section One: English/General
1 beneficial and law
2 bottle and exact
3 nook and kennel
4 market and tent
5 tarantula and ailment
6 diary and year
7 sticker and riddle
8 jazz and zebra
9 zero and orange
10 tax and xylophone

Section Two: Science
1 boiling and germination
2 chlorophyll and lens
3 iris and sulphur
4 refraction and nova
5 greenhouse and energy
6 enzyme and equilibrium
7 current and tin
8 atom and mass
9 condensation and neutral
10 alloy and yeast

Section Three: Geography
1 silt and typhoon
2 lava and altitude
3 mantle and erosion
4 headland and delta
5 fossil and latitude
6 drought and tributary
7 watershed and depression
8 network and key
9 resort and temporary
10 extinct and tsunami

Section Four: History
1 assassination and navy
2 abdication and Nightingale
3 roses and surrender
4 tea and armada
5 blitzkrieg and gunpowder
6 invasion and nationalism
7 opium and minefield
8 suffragette and entente
9 turnip and pacifist
10 lamp and papacy

NOTE: Alternative answers that fit the clues should be given credit.

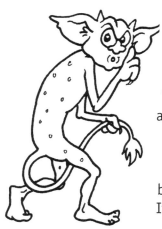

Gremlin

The origin of words is a fascinating subject. There are many different sources – foreign languages, real people, the Bible and other religious texts, characters from literature, and so on. However, some words and phrases have no definite sources but, instead, only tentative explanations are given. It is interesting to speculate as to how these words and phrases came into existence.

Your Task

Choose one, or more, of the ten words and phrases listed below. Write a story that explains how your choice came into use in the English language. You can be very creative, but do remember to take note of the little that is known, including the historical context.

The Words and Phrases

1 **Gremlin**: an imaginary gnome or goblin that is blamed for something that goes wrong. Gremlin was first used, probably, at the end of the First World War or during the 1920s. The word was certainly in use by Royal Air Force personnel abroad in the 1930s.
How was this wonderful word created?

2 **Smart Alec**: a person regarded as a conceited know-all or one who is too clever for their own good. The source suggested is the United States of America and the phrase goes back to at least the 1860s.
Who was the original Alec?

3 **Square**: a slang term for a person of boringly traditional outlook, especially in matters of music or dress. Square came into use in the later years of the twentieth century.
Why should square have come to be used in this way?

4 **Oops-a-daisy**: this is an expression of sympathy, especially to a child, when he or she falls over or has an accident. Tentative suggestions have been made about a combination of variations of 'up' and 'lackaday', an expression of misfortune.
How did this strange combination come into existence?

5 **Half-Nelson**: a wrestling hold in which an arm is passed under the opponent's arm from behind while simultaneously pressing on the opponent's neck.
Who was the Nelson who gave a name to this hold?

Gremlin

6 Billy: in Australia or New Zealand, a metal pot or can for boiling water over a campfire. It is thought that the word may be of Aboriginal origin. In North American use 'billy' is a policeman's truncheon.
How did the name come to be used in either case?

7 Boffin: a research scientist, especially one employed by the armed services or government. 'Boffin' was a nickname used by Royal Air Force personnel during the Second World War. The term passed into general use in the 1940s.
What led to the creation of this eccentric name?

8 Skimmington: the name given to an old custom in rural areas of Britain in which a strange procession takes place to ridicule either an unfaithful husband or a nagging wife. Descriptions appear in literature as early as 1663.
How did this old custom get named 'skimmington'?

9 The real McCoy: a term now in general use for 'the genuine article'. There are several suggestions as to its origin. An American boxer, 1873–1940, had the nickname but in Scotland, where Mackay is often substituted for McCoy, the term was applied to whisky, or other goods, of the highest quality.
What is your explanation for 'the real McCoy'?

10 Scrimshaw: a sailor's spare-time handicraft, such as carving or engraving designs on shells, bone or ivory, in order to pass away the time. The word goes back to sailing-ship days but its origin is unclear.
How does the activity come to have this name?

Extension Tasks

1 Use a good dictionary, either general or the *Brewer's Dictionary of Phrase & Fable*, to construct a list of other words or phrases for which the origin is uncertain.

2 Write down your own explanations of the origin.

Problem-solving and Thinking Skills Resources for Able and Talented Children

Gremlin

Teaching Notes

'Gremlin' gives an unusual opportunity for creative writing, which also deals with the request in literacy schemes to consider the origin of words. There are some parameters but with a high level of open-ended opportunities to display individual understanding and interpretation.

Key Elements

- deduction and inference
- hypothesizing
- use of the imagination
- creative writing
- research
- use of different forms of dictionaries in the extension tasks.

Contexts

'Gremlin' can be used in a variety of ways:

- as extension work to literacy tasks
- as enrichment work for those ahead in normal lessons
- as a general classroom activity where differentiation by outcome will result in able pupils producing outstanding responses
- as differentiated homework
- as an activity during an enrichment day, weekend or summer school
- as an open-access competition.

Success Criteria

However the piece of work is used, 'Gremlin' is likely to produce very varied outcomes. Assessing the writing will need to take account of:

- the quality of the writing
- the creativity and imagination displayed
- the regard paid to the information provided, including the historical context
- the suitability of the genre and style chosen.

Dictionary Delia

Cookery expert Delia Smith made history when her first name was used in the *Collins Dictionary*.

A 'Delia' is defined as 'a recipe or style of cooking of

British cookery writer Delia Smith'.

Perhaps that entry might start a trend.

You can help to create it!

Your Tasks

1 Explain why the dictionary had to use the first name, Delia, rather than the surname.

2 Look at the list of famous names below. Some are the first name but many are surnames for clear identification. Most are real people but there are a few fictional characters as well.

3 Write a suitable definition either using the word as a noun like 'a Delia' or as a verb like 'to Delia'. Look for the essential qualities that you are trying to convey. You may need to do a little research in reference books or on the internet.

SPECIAL NOTE: try to be rather more adventurous than the definition of a 'Delia'. Capture the spirit of a person but use flair and imagination. Do not be afraid to display a creative sense of humour.

THE LIST OF NAMES

1	Columbus	11	Beethoven	21	Dickens	31	Merlin
2	Titchmarsh	12	Houdini	22	Bradman	32	Nureyev
3	Picasso	13	Potter	23	Archimedes	33	Olivier
4	Victoria	14	Churchill	24	Elton	34	Gandhi
5	Christie	15	Nightingale	25	Wordsworth	35	Blyton
6	Tiger	16	Fawkes	26	Mandela	36	Lennon
7	Bond	17	Thatcher	27	Ayckbourn	37	Austen
8	Einstein	18	Plato	28	Kylie	38	Bart
9	Sherlock	19	Napoleon	29	Brunel	39	Leonardo
10	Beckham	20	Greer	30	Attenborough	40	Garbo

Extension Task

Construct a list of your own of names that could produce interesting dictionary definitions. Either write the definitions yourself or get a friend to try.

Problem-solving and Thinking Skills Resources for Able and Talented Children

Dictionary Delia

Teaching Notes

'Dictionary Delia' is an unusual exercise that combines a variety of contrasting features. Teachers can limit the number to be defined if 40 seem to need too much time. Then, the choice made by pupils would offer an interesting insight into their thinking.

Key Elements

- ❖ dictionary work
- ❖ research
- ❖ succinct writing of a most particular kind
- ❖ creativity and imagination
- ❖ cross-curricular
- ❖ analysis of essential qualities
- ❖ sense of humour.

Contexts

'Dictionary Delia' would give a splendid opportunity for an open-access competition but it could also be used in other ways:

- ❖ as differentiated homework
- ❖ as enrichment work when other tasks are completed
- ❖ as classwork where differentiation by outcome would apply
- ❖ as an activity during an enrichment session, cluster day or summer school.

Answers

Very different types of responses can be expected. There are no set answers but success criteria are likely to be:

- ❖ the degree to which essential features have been captured
- ❖ the quality of the writing
- ❖ the imagination and flair displayed
- ❖ the sense of humour in some responses
- ❖ the evidence of appropriate research.

Turning the Corner: A Mathstory

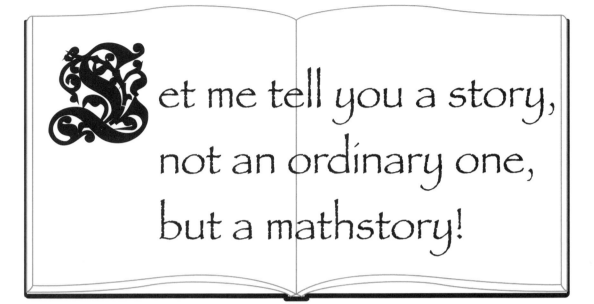

et me tell you a story, not an ordinary one, but a mathstory!

Many mathematical terms have a meaning in common use that is different, to some extent, to the specialized meaning within mathematics itself. 'Common denominator' in mathematics means specifically 'a number that is a multiple of each of the denominators of a set of fractions, especially the least'. In general use, the same phrase refers to something that allows agreement between people to take place. With some terms, the difference between mathematical use and more general use is less marked. A 'cube' is 'a solid figure bounded by six square faces' and the term is applied to examples in everyday life, such as sugar cubes or dice.

Now, can you find the right mathematical terms to complete the 'mathstory', 'Turning the Corner'.

Your Tasks

1 Work out the 36 mathematical terms you need by looking at their definitions on the separate sheet. The order has been mixed up. In other words, this is not the correct chronological order of how they appear in the 'mathstory'.

2 Fill in the 36 spaces in the story by the inclusion of a suitable mathematical term. The number of letters is indicated, to give you help.

Problem-solving and Thinking Skills Resources for Able and Talented Children

Turning the Corner

As the Managing Director began her end-of-year speech, there was considerable gloom in the audience. Mrs Douglas ignored the * (4) looks and the * (8) attitudes. She intended to raise spirits. By the time that Mrs Douglas' delivery came to a conclusion, the atmosphere had improved.

'On the * (7) this has certainly been a very difficult year. A * (6) of things have gone wrong. What is now needed is for employees of the company to take a * (8) view and then, in all * (11), our fortunes will start to improve. We need to keep a sense of * (10). To * (3) up, this unfortunate * (8) is unlikely to continue. I am sure that we are * (5) to the tasks that lie ahead.'

Much applause greeted Mrs Douglas as she sat down. Company results had been the worst for a * (7) but with an exciting new * (7) ready for the market, there was an * (4) chance that progress could be made. The * (6) of sales was likely to rise, especially in the Midlands, an * (4) where results had been particularly disappointing.

In the months that followed, the Managing Director's optimism was seen to be justified. Three * (11) sets of figures showed better-than- * (7) results. Several new * (5) were rented as business began to * (8). At the * (6) of the improvements was strong teamwork. The * (6) of success surprised everybody, although the company had maintained a strong underlying * (4). The * (9) of telephone calls involving new orders increased. Results plotted in a * (5) form showed a * (4) of steep * (8).

Wales was the region that remained the * (3) one out, where sales remained depressingly low. Mrs Douglas called a meeting of her senior advisers. As she walked around the * (9) of the room, she listened to their views. There was a * (8) of opinion, as the advisers made comments in a * (9) direction. One * (4) of the argument concerned the smaller * (10) of funds that had been spent on advertising in Wales. Another * (6) that was suggested was the strength of a rival company in that region. One adviser said that he looked at the situation from a different * (5). He felt that there had been a * (8) situation some five or six years ago in the north-east of England. For the * (9) of the meeting, Mrs Douglas congratulated her team on the way that the company had turned the corner.

Extension Task

Write your own 'mathstory' on a different theme. Use a mathematics dictionary to select appropriate words. Include at least 20 of them in your story. Create a separate page that defines the mathematical terms. Ask somebody else to try to complete your 'mathstory' by filling in the blanks with the correct words.

Turning the Corner: A Mathstory

Definitions of
The 36 Mathematical Terms
(in mixed-up order)

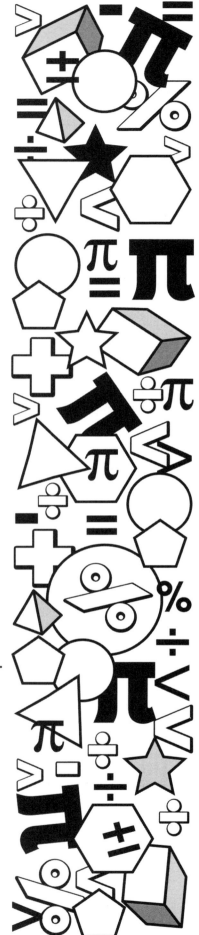

1 A hundred years.
2 A quantity obtained by multiplying other numbers together.
3 That which is left after division takes place.
4 Following in unbroken regular order.
5 Divisible by two without a remainder.
6 A measure of turn.
7 The average of a set of numbers calculated by adding up the numbers and dividing by the number of numbers.
8 Lines that run in exactly the same direction but which never meet.
9 A number by which a larger number can be divided exactly.
10 A number that has a remainder of one when divided by two.
11 How many times something occurs.
12 Numbers that are greater than zero.
13 The chance of something happening.
14 The distance around the outside of a shape or object.
15 The unit used to measure angles.
16 The point within a circle that is equidistant from any point on the circumference.
17 That by which single things are counted.
18 The amount of space inside an object.
19 The side or face on which a geometrical figure is regarded as standing.
20 The steepness of a line or hill.
21 The measure of centralness.
22 In the direction that the hands of a clock rotate.
23 When straight, it is the shortest distance between two points.
24 A diagram depicting the relationship between two or more variables.
25 One of five in a pentagon, or of six in a hexagon.
26 Identical in quantity; of the same value.
27 To the right of thousands, hundreds and tens.
28 Numbers that are less than zero.
29 Splitting a number up into smaller parts.
30 A relationship between quantities, also known as ratio.
31 A set of numbers with a pattern.
32 A number expressed as part of 100.
33 A flat two-dimensional figure that has length and breadth but no thickness; the outer boundary or face of anything.
34 The result of adding numbers together.
35 The size of a surface; the amount of space a shape covers.
36 To increase the number of; to obtain the product.

Problem-solving and Thinking Skills Resources for Able and Talented Children

Turning the Corner: A Mathstory

Teaching Notes

Subject-specific language is important throughout the curriculum. This is certainly true in mathematics as the Cockcroft Report and the Numeracy Framework have stressed. 'Turning the Corner: A Mathstory' provides an unusual way of looking at mathematical terms.

Key Elements

- ❖ wordplay
- ❖ mathematical terms
- ❖ use of a mathematical dictionary
- ❖ deduction
- ❖ inference
- ❖ engagement with text
- ❖ allocation by a process of elimination.

Contexts

'Turning the Corner: A Mathstory' can be used in the following ways:

- ❖ as extension work on mathematical terms
- ❖ as an enrichment activity for those who have completed other work
- ❖ as a differentiated homework
- ❖ as an activity during an enrichment day, weekend or summer school
- ❖ as an activity for the Mathematics Club.

Solution

The 36 mathematical terms are:

1	century	19	base
2	product	20	gradient
3	remainder	21	average
4	consecutive	22	clockwise
5	even	23	line
6	angle	24	graph
7	mean	25	side
8	parallel	26	equal
9	factor	27	units
10	odd	28	negative
11	frequency	29	division
12	positive	30	proportion
13	probability	31	sequence
14	perimeter	32	percentage
15	degree	33	surface
16	centre	34	sum
17	number	35	area
18	volume	36	multiply

Turning The Corner: A Mathstory

The completed story is therefore:

'Turning the Corner'

As the Managing Director began her end-of-year speech, there was considerable gloom in the audience. Mrs Douglas ignored the **mean** looks and the **negative** attitudes. She intended to raise spirits. By the time that Mrs Douglas' delivery came to a conclusion, the atmosphere had improved.

'On the **surface** this has certainly been a very difficult year. A **number** of things have gone wrong. What is now needed is for employees of the company to take a **positive** view and then, in all **probability**, our fortunes will start to improve. We need to keep a sense of **proportion**. To **sum** up, this unfortunate **sequence** is unlikely to continue. I am sure that we are **equal** to the tasks that lie ahead.'

Much applause greeted Mrs Douglas as she sat down. Company results had been the worst for a **century** but with an exciting new **product** ready for the market, there was an **even** chance that progress could be made. The **volume** of sales was likely to rise, especially in the Midlands, an **area** where results had been particularly disappointing.

In the months that followed, the Managing Director's optimism was seen to be justified. Three **consecutive** sets of figures showed better-than-**average** results. Several new **units** were rented as business began to **multiply**. At the **centre** of the improvements was strong teamwork. The **degree** of success surprised everybody, although the company had maintained a strong underlying **base**. The **frequency** of telephone calls involving new orders increased. Results plotted in a **graph** form showed a **line** of steep **gradient**.

Wales was the region that remained the **odd** one out, where sales remained depressingly low. Mrs Douglas called a meeting of her senior advisers. As she walked around the **perimeter** of the room, she listened to their views. There was a **division** of opinion, as the advisers made comments in a **clockwise** direction. One **side** of the argument concerned the smaller **percentage** of funds that had been spent on advertising in Wales. Another **factor** that was suggested was the strength of a rival company in that region. One adviser said that he looked at the situation from a different **angle**. He felt that there had been a **parallel** situation some five or six years ago in the north-east of England. For the **remainder** of the meeting, Mrs Douglas congratulated her team on the way that the company had turned the corner.

HIDE AND SEEK
SOLVE A PROBLEM

Can you match the investigatory skills of our two great detectives, Hide and Seek? As well as an appreciation of the way in which criminal cases are solved, you will need to employ your geographical knowledge and keep your wits about you to handle the cryptic wordplay.

Your Tasks

1 Read the detective story below, which contains the names of 21 British towns and cities – either spelled the same way as the word needed to complete the sentence or spelled differently but sounding the same.

2 By use of the clues, and also the general sense of the passage, identify all 21 towns and cities.

 THE DETECTIVE STORY

When Inspector Hide was put in charge of the case he successfully requested that Sergeant Seek should work with him. The early '***battery connections in Yorkshire***' concerned threads from a '***garment on the estuary of the River Teifi***' and footprints in the wet soil. When the neighbours were questioned, the police got an interesting statement from Mr '***famous English sailor turns a blind eye in Lancashire***' who said that he had heard '***canine communication in London***' in the early hours of the morning. Another witness said that she had seen a '***Cleveland's coloured vehicle***' in the lane earlier that same evening and she did not recognize it.

Inside the house a thorough search was made. Inspector Hide was interested in a damp patch on the wall halfway up the '***method of elevation in Bleak House, Kent***' but it turned out to be an area of '***decaying Flintshire***' caused by a '***Staffordshire vegetable***' from a pipe. Of greater significance were the marks on the side of the '***clean Roman remains***', which indicated where the intruder had stepped after climbing in through the window.

HIDE AND SEEK SOLVE A PROBLEM

The owner Miss *'male participant in TT races'* was upset at the loss of her valuable necklace but she believed that the burglar had been disturbed and may very well have been forced to hide the jewellery with the intention of returning later to collect it. One possibility was that the burglar had tried to *'underground activity in Lancashire'* the necklace. Sergeant Seek carried out a detailed search of the grounds and particular interest was paid to the old *'watering holes in Somerset'*. During the investigation the remains of a *'Kent snack'* were found behind a tree in a nearby field in which the farmer kept his *'yachting quadrupeds'*. Hide suggested that the house might have been watched prior to the burglary.

Just when the two detectives had given up hope, the necklace was found in its case, hidden under a large stone in the rockery. Hide and Seek made a great show of packing up their things and leaving, making it look as though they had completed their investigation. That evening they returned to the house but by a back door and inconspicuous route. They took a great *'preliminary to card game in Kent holiday resort'* of care in keeping out of sight.

Nothing happened for some time. Hide and Seek were glad of the hot coffee they had brought, for the night *'breathe in a holiday town in the heart of Burns' country'* was chilly. Just before midnight, a dark shadow crossed the lawn towards the rockery. The detectives waited until the man removed a large stone in his search for the abandoned necklace. Then quickly they moved in and arrested the intruder. A car was summoned. During the *'Isle of Wight journey'* to the police station the suspect sat sullen and quiet but later on he was more co-operative. He gave his name as Henry *'local football match but much further north than Epsom'* and explained that he was a member of the *'Cheshire railway team row in'* of a merchant vessel currently loading at the docks. While Hide was *'leisure and education pursuit in Berkshire'* the arrested man his rights, Seek gave the news of the capture to his superiors. Both detectives were commended for their *'currency where Highlands and Lowlands meet'* work.

Extension Task

Write a story of your own. This can be a detective case or involve a different genre. Include a number of British towns and cities by means of cryptic clues. You may find that an atlas of the British Isles will help.

Problem-solving and Thinking Skills Resources for Able and Talented Children
© Barry Teare (Network Continuum Education, 2006)

HIDE AND SEEK SOLVE A PROBLEM

Teaching Notes

This is an entertaining piece to challenge able pupils but which exercises a number of useful skills.

Key Elements

- ❖ wordplay
- ❖ word humour
- ❖ homographs
- ❖ homophones
- ❖ use of an atlas of Britain
- ❖ geographical knowledge of Britain
- ❖ deduction
- ❖ inference
- ❖ creative writing of a particular type (in the extension task).

Contexts

'Hide and Seek Solve a Problem' can be used in a variety of ways:

- ❖ as extension work in literacy or vocabulary extension
- ❖ as extension work in geography
- ❖ as an enrichment activity for those who have completed other work
- ❖ as a differentiated homework
- ❖ as an activity during an enrichment day, weekend or summer school
- ❖ as an open-access competition, where the extension task acts as a discriminator
- ❖ as an activity for the English Club or Society, or the Geography Club.

Solution

1	Leeds (leads)	12	Wells
2	Cardigan	13	Sandwich
3	Nelson	14	Cowes (cows)
4	Barking	15	Deal
5	Redcar (red car)	16	Ayr (air)
6	Broadstairs (broad stairs)	17	Ryde (ride)
7	Mold (mould)	18	Derby
8	Leek (leak)	19	Crewe (crew)
9	Bath	20	Reading
10	Douglas	21	Stirling (sterling)
11	Bury		

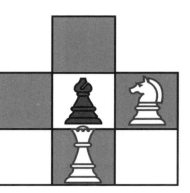

The Name of the Game

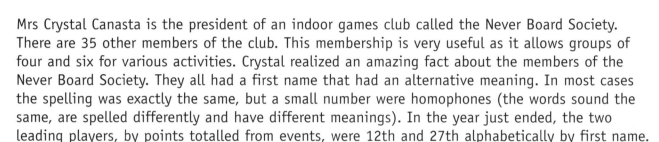

Mrs Crystal Canasta is the president of an indoor games club called the Never Board Society. There are 35 other members of the club. This membership is very useful as it allows groups of four and six for various activities. Crystal realized an amazing fact about the members of the Never Board Society. They all had a first name that had an alternative meaning. In most cases the spelling was exactly the same, but a small number were homophones (the words sound the same, are spelled differently and have different meanings). In the year just ended, the two leading players, by points totalled from events, were 12th and 27th alphabetically by first name.

Your Tasks

1 Work out the first names of the other 35 members from the clues below.

2 Place the 36 names into alphabetical order.

3 Work out the names of the two leading players for last year's events.

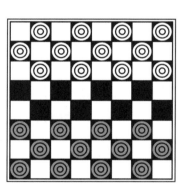

THE CLUES

1 There are two herbs, one male and one female, making 13 letters in total.

2 Both ends of the day are represented by two women.

3 There are two birds (both male and comprising of 11 letters) and three months (all female and whose positions in the year add up to 15).

4 You may get an allowance to meet the cost of something. It also gives you two men of five letters and four letters respectively.

5 The pilot signs off.

6 A professor gives a backward nod.

7 The five-letter man might fade out.

8 It sounds like one woman is blowing hard.

9 Three women, whose names collectively have the same number of letters as a baker's dozen, have the theme of a Christmas song, both specifically and generally.

10 This five-letter man has a long way to go.

Problem-solving and Thinking Skills Resources for Able and Talented Children
© Barry Teare (Network Continuum Education, 2006)

11 Be absolutely honest with this man.

12 This foreign invader might have made a point of using such a weapon, thereby giving a man of six letters and a man of five letters.

13 A useful man for cards and bowls.

14 Two precious jewels give two women, each of five letters and both containing the 5th, 12th and 18th letters of the alphabet.

15 You might take legal action if you got a stain on your clothing, producing one woman and one man of seven letters in total.

16 She comes before meals.

17 He is often by the sea.

18 Two men sound like they complete to the top in the exercise area.

19 You may go forth to meet this cat, thus identifying a five-letter woman and a three-letter man.

20 If you move up and down, you might not see this small point (a man and woman, both of three letters).

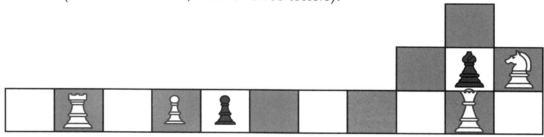

Extension Tasks

1 Find some other first names that have alternative meanings.

2 Write clues for them.

3 Get somebody else to work out the names of these additional people.

The Name of the Game

Teaching Notes

'The Name of the Game' is a piece that is light in tone but involves a number of important skills.

Key Elements

- wordplay
- homographs
- homophones
- logical thinking
- lateral thinking
- engaging with cryptic information
- alphabetical order
- following instructions.

Contexts

'The Name of the Game' can be used in the following ways:

- as extension material to vocabulary work
- as differentiated homework
- as an activity during an enrichment day, weekend or summer school
- as an activity for the English Club or Society.

Solution

Answers are given below that fit the clues exactly. From that, the names have been ordered alphabetically. This may not be a unique solution and credit should be given for alternative answers, so long as they answer all the details of the clues.

The Clues

1 Basil and Rosemary
2 Dawn and Eve
3 The birds are Robin and Martin. The months are April, May and June (the 4th, 5th and 6th months of the year).
4 Grant and Bill
5 Roger
6 Don
7 Peter
8 Gail (gale)
9 Holly, Ivy and Carol
10 Miles
11 Frank
12 Norman and Lance
13 Jack
14 Pearl and Beryl (containing E the 5th letter, L the 12th letter and R the 18th letter)
15 Sue and Mark
16 Grace
17 Cliff
18 Phil (fill) and Jim (gym)
19 Sally and Tom
20 Bob and Dot

Remembering to include Crystal, the alphabetical order is:

1 April	9 Dawn	17 Holly	25 May	33 Rosemary
2 Basil	10 Don	18 Ivy	26 Miles	34 Sally
3 Beryl	11 Dot	19 Jack	27 Norman	35 Sue
4 Bill	12 Eve	20 Jim	28 Pearl	36 Tom
5 Bob	13 Frank	21 June	29 Peter	
6 Carol	14 Gail	22 Lance	30 Phil	
7 Cliff	15 Grace	23 Mark	31 Robin	
8 Crystal	16 Grant	24 Martin	32 Roger	

The leading two players for last year's events were therefore **Eve** (12th alphabetically) and **Norman** (27th alphabetically).

Section 3

Logical Thinking

'Logic' is described as the science of reasoning correctly. 'Logical' is characterized by clear or valid reasoning and is described as following necessarily from facts or events. Conversely, illogical is regarded as senseless and unreasonable. Given those definitions, it is easy to see why logical thinking is regarded so highly in life, at work and in school subjects. Even Edward de Bono, who made famous lateral thinking, was not opposed to logical thinking but rather the exclusivity of logical thinking.

Robert Fisher in *Teaching Children to Think* (Nelson Thornes, 1995) puts this skill at the heart of two particular subjects:

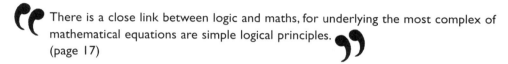
There is a close link between logic and maths, for underlying the most complex of mathematical equations are simple logical principles.
(page 17)

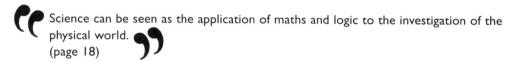
Science can be seen as the application of maths and logic to the investigation of the physical world.
(page 18)

Professor Ian Stewart in *The Magical Maze* (Phoenix, 1998), having said that 'logic is the study of valid deductions' (page 169) goes on to comment upon the importance in information and communications technology:

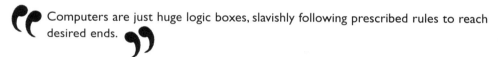
Computers are just huge logic boxes, slavishly following prescribed rules to reach desired ends.

Among many comments in the National Curriculum 1999 that can be selected are:

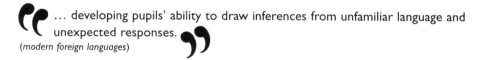
… developing pupils' ability to draw inferences from unfamiliar language and unexpected responses.
(*modern foreign languages*)

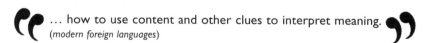
… how to use content and other clues to interpret meaning.
(*modern foreign languages*)

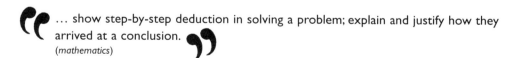
… show step-by-step deduction in solving a problem; explain and justify how they arrived at a conclusion.
(*mathematics*)

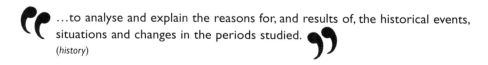
…to analyse and explain the reasons for, and results of, the historical events, situations and changes in the periods studied.
(*history*)

Solving logic problems has also become a popular pastime. Writers such as Raymond Smullyan, Professor of Mathematical Logic, have produced entertaining and often amusing challenges. Among Smullyan's intriguing titles are *What is the Name of this*

Book? (Penguin, 1981), *To Mock a Mockingbird* (Oxford University Press, 2000), *Alice in Puzzle-Land* (Penguin, 1984), *The Lady or the Tiger?* (Pelican, 1983), *The Chess Mysteries of Sherlock Holmes* (Hutchinson, 1980) and *The Chess Mysteries of the Arabian Knights* (Hutchinson, 1983).

The Japanese puzzle, Sudoku, has swept the country, turning many people into addicts. There are a number of variations from the straight 1–9 digits once, and once only, in every row, every column and in every 3 × 3 square. Some include the diagonals, others have introduced letters in Wordoku. *The Times* newspaper has presented its readers with 'Killer Sudoku' (no numbers included at all, just totals of certain groups of squares) and 'Samurai', the devilish linking of five overlapping squares. The *Guardian* newspaper has responded with 'Kakuro' puzzles, in some ways similar to 'Killer Sudoku' but without the discrete 3 × 3 squares.

- Books of matrix puzzles have been around for much longer. The author has used this technique in his various publications of resources for Network Continuum Education. '**Key to the Room**' asks children to place guests at the Enigma Hotel in their correct rooms by way of a number of clues. This does not have direct curriculum content but does employ thinking skills more generally, including synthesis, as the clues have to be used together.

- '**Fit the Bill**' has as its two variables the names of eight men and women and the forms of exercise that they use to keep fit. Its only curriculum content is very basic knowledge of sport. The solution, as with other matrix problems in this section, can be achieved through a written method, by the use of pieces of paper or by a matrix itself.

- '**Larry Literacy's Love of English**' follows the same principles but there is strong curriculum content. Understanding of a number of figures of speech is essential – similes, metaphors, alliteration, onomatopoeia, euphemisms, proverbs, hyperbole and oxymorons. Parts of speech also play an important role – nouns, interjections, conjunctions, prepositions, verbs and adverbs.

- '**Willowmere**' is a much longer logical thinking problem. There is substantial data about 20 wildfowl together with more basic information about the 26 children in Mrs Andoh's class. The task is to match the 20 ducks, geese and swans with the children who adopted them, and name the six children who did not adopt a bird. As well as the many information sheets, there are 26 cryptic clues. Not only are thinking skills, such as synthesis, logical thinking and analysis involved, there is also science content, namely life processes and living things. The amount of information demands span of concentration.

- '**Suit Yourself**' is subtitled '*A short excursion into the wonderful world of Bridge*'. It is even longer than the previous piece. There is considerable mathematical interest through calculation, handling data and problem solving. Again, span of concentration is a vital element. The piece ends with a logic problem called 'In Hand' where students work out the 13 cards in Alison's hand, from clues requiring synthesis of every section previously covered – a suitable and challenging finale to the section.

Key to the Room

The Enigma is a small hotel that has just 12 rooms (1–12). On one particular night, half the rooms were occupied. Those in residence that night were three married couples – Mr and Mrs Haller (German), Mr and Mrs Dupont (French), and Mr and Mrs Davies (English) – and three people on their own – Ms Silver (American), Mrs Holgrove (English) and Mr Conti (Italian).

Can you say who was staying in which room from the information given below?

A   Only two even-numbered rooms were in use.

B   The two odd numbers not in use add up to 16, as do the two even numbers that were in use.

C   A married couple was in Room 11.

D   Room 6 was empty.

E   Residents of the same nationality were in Rooms 3 and 5.

F   Room 4 was occupied by one person only.

G   Although they had not planned a joint visit, the French couple knew the couple in Room 11 from a previous engagement.

H   The American had to borrow some coffee from the resident of Room 4 when she got no answer at the door of Room 1.

I   The numbers of the rooms occupied by married couples added up to 17.

Key to the Room

Teaching Notes

Key Elements

- ❖ simple arithmetic
- ❖ logical thinking
- ❖ odd and even
- ❖ alternative methods of working
- ❖ synthesis.

Contexts

'Key to the Room' can be used in a number of ways:

- ❖ as an item in a thinking skills course
- ❖ as enrichment work for those ahead in other work
- ❖ as differentiated homework
- ❖ as an activity during an enrichment day, weekend, summer school or cluster day.

Alternative Methods of Working

1 A written account.
2 A matrix (remembering to take account of six unoccupied rooms).
3 A kinesthetic method, moving around slips of paper.
4 A plan on which information is recorded and crossed off.

Solution

A Four odd-numbered rooms were in use.
B The two odd numbers not in use were either 5 and 11, or 7 and 9, and the two even numbers in use were either 4 and 12, or 6 and 10.
C Room 11 was in use and, from B, Rooms 7 and 9 were not in use and, therefore, Rooms 1, 3, 5 and 11 were used.
D From B, the two even numbers in use were 4 and 12. (If the matrix method is used, we can now construct a matrix using Rooms 1, 3, 4, 5, 11 and 12.)
E Mrs Holgrove and Mr and Mrs Davies were in Rooms 3 and 5 but we do not know which way around.
F The occupant of Room 4 was either Ms Silver or Mr Conti.
G Mr and Mrs Dupont were not in Room 11, which must have been occupied by Mr and Mrs Haller.
H Ms Silver was not in Room 4, which was therefore occupied by Mr Conti, nor was she in Room 1, which must have been Mr and Mrs Dupont's room. Ms Silver therefore occupied Room 12.
I The rooms of the married couples known so far add up to 12 and, therefore, Mr and Mrs Davies were in Room 5 and Mrs Holgrove was in Room 3.

The complete matrix (if used).

1	3	4	5	11	12	
X	X	X	X	✓	X	Mr and Mrs Haller
✓	X	X	X	X	X	Mr and Mrs Dupont
X	X	X	✓	X	X	Mr and Mrs Davies
X	X	X	X	X	✓	Ms Silver
X	✓	X	X	X	X	Mrs Holgrove
X	X	✓	X	X	X	Mr Conti

Problem-solving and Thinking Skills Resources for Able and Talented Children

FIT THE BILL

Many people understand that regular exercise is an important part of keeping fit and healthy. This is certainly true of a group of people who live in the seaside resort of Exquay:

PATRICK, CARMEN, LISA, IVAN, MAGGIE, GREG, LOUIS AND LEAH

(the first two named are married to each other).

They all try to keep fit but they each prefer different forms of exercise.

Your Task

Read the information below, which describes the methods of keeping fit. Use that information and the clues to work out the choice of exercise for the eight men and women.

THE FORMS OF EXERCISE

1 Swimming in the pool at Exquay Leisure Centre on Wednesdays and Saturdays.
2 Running on the long beach in Exquay, normally three times a week.
3 Playing badminton at Exquay Leisure Centre on Monday evenings and Thursday evenings.
4 Playing women's five-a-side football, once a week, at Exquay Leisure Centre.
5 Walking on the moors that are inland from Exquay, twice a week.
6 Playing squash on Tuesday evenings and Sunday afternoons at Exquay Leisure Centre.
7 Cycling on Wednesdays and Sundays along various coastal routes out of Exquay.
8 Playing golf, on Wednesdays and Saturdays, at Tormouth, ten miles west of Exquay.

THE CLUES

1 The activities at Exquay Leisure Centre are undertaken by members of the same gender.
2 Maggie had to give up swimming due to shoulder problems. Her unmarried friend still relies on swimming to keep fit.
3 Ivan does not need anything other than clothing for his exercise.
4 Patrick normally exercises three times more per week than his wife.
5 Lisa has bought a new racquet for her activity.
6 Greg always travels in the same direction for his sport.
7 Lisa looks forward to her regular Sunday exercise.

FIT THE BILL

Teaching Notes

'Fit the Bill' is a short, logical thought problem with two variables. Very basic knowledge of sport is required. It can be solved by a written method, by the use of pieces of paper or by the matrix method. Some synthesis is involved, as clues need to be used in conjunction with other information.

Solution

CLUE 1 Together with the information about the forms of exercise, this eliminates swimming, badminton, five-a-side football and squash for the four men. This also means that the other four activities must be ruled out for the four women.

CLUE 2 Neither Maggie nor Carmen (married to Patrick) swims and therefore swimming can only be the activity of either Lisa or Leah.

CLUE 3 This clue rules out cycling and golf for Ivan.

CLUE 4 Patrick runs (normally three times a week) and his wife, Carmen, plays five-a-side football (once a week). It must, by process of elimination, be Ivan who goes walking.

CLUE 5 Lisa plays badminton or squash and, therefore, Leah is the swimmer.

CLUE 6 Greg plays golf and, therefore, Louis cycles.

CLUE 7 Lisa plays squash and, therefore, Maggie plays badminton.

	SWIMMING	RUNNING	BADMINTON	FIVE-A-SIDE	WALKING	SQUASH	CYCLING	GOLF
PATRICK	X	✓	X	X	X	X	X	X
CARMEN	X	X	X	✓	X	X	X	X
LISA	X	X	X	X	X	✓	X	X
IVAN	X	X	X	X	✓	X	X	X
MAGGIE	X	X	✓	X	X	X	X	X
GREG	X	X	X	X	X	X	X	✓
LOUIS	X	X	X	X	X	X	✓	X
LEAH	✓	X	X	X	X	X	X	X

LARRY LITERACY'S LOVE OF ENGLISH

INTRODUCTION

Larry Literacy is an eccentric English teacher who likes to use unusual and interesting ways of delivering his subject. On one occasion, Larry Literacy devised a puzzle so that his pupils could revise their knowledge of figures of speech and parts of speech, while, at the same time, deploy more general thinking skills See if that exercise makes you 'as happy as a lark'.

THE PUZZLE

Eight lovers of English played a game in which they drew cards that had upon them a phrase or sentence. The players had to construct a story in which their cards were used. At the start of the game, each of the eight players drew their first card.

Your Task

After studying the information above, the list of players and the clues, work out which card was drawn by each of the eight lovers of English in the first round

THE PLAYERS OR 'LOVERS OF ENGLISH'

Simon Simile	Alison Alliteration	Elizabeth Euphemism	Henrietta Hyperbole
Megan Metaphor	Orson Onomatopoeia	Paul Proverb	Olive Oxymoron

THE CARDS DRAWN IN ROUND ONE

1 A big, black book.
2 Carpet on the stairs.
3 They wanted a drink of tea or coffee.
4 I heard the buzz of the insects.

5 The doctor passed away quietly in the night.
6 Oops! That hurt.
7 Call frantically.
8 A dreary, dull day.

THE CLUES

1 The person, whose name illustrated by example at the end of the Introduction, drew a card with four words written on it.
2 None of the players picked a card where the words contained an example of their own name.
3 The lover of English most likely to have complained that she warned someone millions of times, drew a card upon which two nouns were separated by a conjunction.
4 The card where the words include an interjection was picked by a man.
5 The person who is likely to have advised to 'strike while the iron is hot' or to 'make hay while the sun shines' picked a card involving a large, dark example of alliteration.
6 The woman whose name brings opposites together (for example – 'be cruel to be kind' or 'bitter sweet') drew a card with four words including a preposition.
7 A verb and adverb comprise the phrase on the card picked by the woman whose name refers to the application of a descriptive term to an object to which it is imaginatively but not literally applicable, such as 'a glaring error'.

Teaching Notes

This short, logical thinking problem involves only two variables but, even so, it requires very careful reading indeed. Thinking skills have been combined with English and literacy content, which is included within curriculum guidelines and literacy frameworks.

Key Elements

- logical thinking
- figures of speech
- parts of speech
- careful analysis of data
- vocabulary extension
- synthesis.

Contexts

'Larry Literacy's Love of English' can be used in a number of ways:

- as extension material to vocabulary work
- as enrichment work for those ahead on other tasks
- as differentiated homework
- as an activity during an enrichment session, cluster day or summer school
- as an activity for the English Club or Society.

Solution

Pupils can use a written method, pieces of paper or a matrix method.

Clue 1 'As happy as a lark' is a simile and, therefore, it was Simon Simile who drew **Card 1, 2** or **8**.

Clue 2 This needs particularly careful interpretation. **Cards 1** and **8** are obvious examples of alliteration and were not, therefore, picked by Alison Alliteration. **Card 4** has 'buzz' written on it and, therefore, could not have been drawn by Orson Onomatopoeia. 'Passed away' is a euphemism for died and, therefore, **Card 5** cannot have been chosen by Elizabeth Euphemism.

Clue 3 Warning somebody 'millions of times' is hyperbole or exaggeration and so Henrietta Hyperbole chose **Card 3** where the two nouns 'tea' and 'coffee' are separated by the conjunction 'or'.

Clue 4 'Oops' is an interjection or exclamation and, therefore, **Card 6** is eliminated for Megan Metaphor, Alison Alliteration, Elizabeth Euphemism and Olive Oxymoron.

Clue 5 'Strike while the iron is hot' and 'Make hay while the sun shines' are proverbs. Paul Proverb picked **Card 1** as 'a large, dark example of alliteration' refers to the book that is big and black. By process of elimination, this also means that Orson Onomatopoeia picked **Card 6**.

Clue 6 An oxymoron involves putting opposites together. **Card 2** has four words including the preposition 'on'. Therefore it was Olive Oxymoron who drew **Card 2**. By process of elimination, **Card 8** was chosen by Simon Simile.

Clue 7 This definition refers to a metaphor. Therefore Megan Metaphor picked **Card 7** which has the verb 'call' and the adverb 'frantically'. By process of elimination, **Card 4** was chosen by Elizabeth Euphemism and **Card 5** was drawn by Alison Alliteration.

	CARD 1	CARD 2	CARD 3	CARD 4	CARD 5	CARD 6	CARD 7	CARD 8
SIMON SIMILE	X	X	X	X	X	X	X	✓
MEGAN METAPHOR	X	X	X	X	X	X	✓	X
ALISON ALLITERATION	X	X	X	X	✓	X	X	X
ORSON ONOMATOPOEIA	X	X	X	X	X	✓	X	X
ELIZABETH EUPHEMISM	X	X	X	✓	X	X	X	X
PAUL PROVERB	✓	X	X	X	X	X	X	X
HENRIETTA HYPERBOLE	X	X	✓	X	X	X	X	X
OLIVE OXYMORON	X	✓	X	X	X	X	X	X

Willowmere

Each year it is the normal practice for every class at Millstream Primary School to go on a day out, which is intended to be both enjoyable and educational. This year Mrs Andoh decided to take her class to Willowmere – a centre for wildfowl. As Willowmere is close to the coast it attracts birds who frequent inland waters and those who like to be near the sea. As a result of the visit, the class became involved in a scheme whereby you 'adopt' a bird of your choice by payment of a sum of money that helps to protect wildfowl as part of a conservation programme. Of the 26 children in Mrs Andoh's class, 20 children each chose a different bird to adopt and six children did not want to be involved in the scheme.

Your Task

Can you match the 20 ducks, geese and swans with the children who adopted them, and name the six children who did not adopt a bird?

Information to Help You

1 There are 26 clues.
2 You are given information about the 26 children in Mrs Andoh's class.
3 The 20 ducks, geese and swans that could be 'adopted' are listed, with information about all of them.

You will need to read the information about the wildfowl and the children, and then use them both in conjunction with the clues. Some clues give you information that you cannot use fully immediately. You will have to extract and store information carefully in order to complete the task successfully.

NOTE: if you have enjoyed this puzzle and are interested in some of the birds described, why not find out more about the Wildfowl and Wetland Trust, which has nine visitor centres, like Willowmere (which is, of course, an imaginary place), in real life in the UK. Their website is www.wwt.org.uk

The Clues

1 The two swans were chosen by the only two children who had the same initials for both parts of their names.
2 The girl who has already left the class realized that she could not adopt one of the wildfowl.
3 A small, red-haired boy thought that it was appropriate for him to choose a duck with plumage on its body of the same colour as his hair. He was also fascinated by the duck's name, as he thought that it sounded somewhat naughty!

Willowmere

4   It was a girl who chose a bird with the greatest length.

5   One boy, whose initials suggest that he is very old, did not adopt a bird, perhaps because he was reluctant to push himself forward.

6   The new girl chose a duck particularly noted for its long, thin tail.

7   Of the two children particularly noted for their mathematical ability, one did not adopt a bird and one chose a bird with a crest.

8   Two 'sawbills' were chosen by two children whose interests were fishing and stamp collecting.

9   Susan Bridge chose a diving duck.

10 Martin Hince did not like the bird that is blamed for taking quite large fish and spoiling the quality of the angling in some places.

11 The bird with the shortest average length was adopted by the girl who had returned recently to school after a long illness.

12 The two boys with the same first name as the boy who chose the smew, did not adopt a wildfowl.

13 The girl who chose the great crested grebe is the best friend of the girl who adopted the mute swan.

14 The girl who adopted the tufted duck was very pleased with her choice.

15 Farmers are not very happy about the goose that was chosen by the girl who travels furthest to school each day.

16 The most common of our wild ducks was adopted by one of the best artists in the class.

17 Brian Allen chose a bird that lays its eggs in hollow trees in the British Isles. It is one of the few of its kind that is resident.

18 It was ironic that the girl who got on so well with everybody (she quite often did short sketch portraits to entertain the class) chose an aggressive bird that perhaps needed its white 'shield' for protection.

19 Two diving birds were adopted by the two girls who were very good at sport.

20 One boy was too interested in practising his music in order to achieve his ambition, for him to bother with the adoption scheme.

21 The teacher's daughter chose a bird with a distinctive white patch between its eye and bill.

22 A girl who was interested in flight chose one of the types of geese.

23 A girl chose a bird who lays 8–12 yellowish eggs.

24 One boy made his choice because he was fascinated that the male and female were coloured similarly. He looked at books to read up on his adopted bird on his frequent visits to the library.

25 One boy travelled better than normal and enjoyed his day enormously. His one complaint was that the photographs in the souvenir shop were very expensive. He joked that the distinctive feature of the bird he chose fitted perfectly with his complaint about the cost.

26 If you have worked carefully through the clues, you should now be able to make the last pairing.

Problem-solving and Thinking Skills Resources for Able and Talented Children
© Barry Teare (Network Continuum Education, 2006)

The Children in Mrs Andoh's Class

Brian Allen Brian is a tall thin boy who wears glasses. He loves swimming and outdoor activities, such as camping, walking and canoeing.

Michael Barber A short, stocky boy with red hair and a mass of freckles. The loves of his life are his dog, Sandy, and football.

Susan Bridge A new girl who has recently joined the class after a move from Birmingham. She is medium height and has long, blonde hair.

Bernard Cooper A shy, retiring boy who finds it difficult to make friends. His main interest in life is his computer and he spends many hours every week using it.

Jennifer Darlington A strong, athletic girl who is an excellent swimmer and runner. She represents the area in the 100 metres and 200 metres. Her father is a teacher in the local secondary school.

Elizabeth Denton The only girl in the class who wears glasses. She is a very popular child and gets on well with nearly everyone in the class. She is a good artist and enjoys painting and drawing.

Jane Earle Jane is a small frail-looking girl whose appearance is extremely misleading as she is very good at sport. Her ambition is to become a Physical Education teacher.

Ruth Fairfax Ruth has only fairly recently returned to school after a long illness. She loves birds and animals and it was she who suggested to Mrs Andoh that the class might visit Willowmere.

David France David is a fine musician who plays both the piano and the violin to a high standard. He hopes to join the local Youth Orchestra in the near future.

Sally Gates Sally has just left Mrs Andoh's class as her family have moved home. She was very keen to go on the visit and permission was given for her to return for the one day.

Michael Gray Michael is a lively and energetic boy who throws himself into everything with great enthusiasm.

Jean Hall Jean enjoys life in the class so much that she still attends, even though her new home is five miles from school. This means that she is brought to school by car each day.

Willowmere

Martin Hince Martin's favourite activity is fishing. He hopes that for his next birthday he will be given a new rod.

Paul Hooper Mrs Andoh is always concerned when Paul goes on a visit by coach, as he is not a good traveller and very often is sick.

Julie Jones Julie has recently won a camera in a competition in the local paper. She looked forward to taking some photographs of the wildfowl at Willowmere.

Robert Kelly Robert is a good artist and he enjoys making things at home. He is particularly interested in learning about the incubators at Willowmere.

Martin Lostock Because of his red hair, Martin is nicknamed 'Ginger', a description that he encourages. He is one of the smallest children in the class.

Kerry Lundy Kerry is perhaps the best mathematician in the class. She loves compiling facts and figures.

Julie Mason A tall, thin girl with a great interest in making and flying model aeroplanes.

John Millington John is very good at writing stories that display great imagination. He also loves reading and he visits the local library regularly.

Martin Norton Martin's particular friend is Michael Barber. They enjoy exchanging football stickers and programmes.

Christine Parker Christine loves travelling and she is looking forward to the coach journey as much as the time to be spent at Willowmere.

Richard Ralston Richard was delighted when he knew that the class was going to visit Willowmere. His elder brother had been there in the past and he had thoroughly enjoyed the trip.

Dorothy Smith Dorothy's main concern was that she could get a seat on the coach next to her best friend, Julie Jones.

Hilary Turton Hilary's hobby is stamp-collecting. She thought it was rather a coincidence when a new set of stamps depicting wildfowl was issued shortly before the visit to Willowmere.

Ben Williams Ben is an excellent mathematician. He uses figures very naturally.

Problem-solving and Thinking Skills Resources for Able and Talented Children
© Barry Teare (Network Continuum Education, 2006)

Description of the Wildfowl

(**NOTE:** Colouring described is for the male, unless stated otherwise.)

MALLARD *Anas platyrhynchos*

The mallard is our most common wild duck and it is seen in many locations. The male has a dark, bottle-green head with a white collar. The underparts are grey and the tail feathers are black. The female is a mottled brown colour. The average length is 58cm. The nest is normally found on the ground in dense vegetation although holes in trees are sometimes used. The hen lays 10–12 eggs. In the wild, mallards are mainly vegetarian, but they also eat insects, worms and crustaceans. They feed by dabbling or up-ending in shallow water. The mallard is resident in the British Isles, although numbers increase during the winter.

LONG-TAILED DUCK *Clangula hyemalis*

This long-tailed duck is a winter visitor. It is normally found on the sea but it does also inhabit inland waters. The average length is 51cm. It is only the male that has the long tail. The females are darker in colour. This diving duck is able to reach 30 metres underwater. Favourite foods are shellfish and crustaceans. The long-tailed duck has the typically round body which is associated with diving.

MUTE SWAN *Cygnus olor*

This UK resident is a well-known sight on many lakes, ponds and rivers. It has a graceful curved neck and an orange bill with a black knob and patch at its base. The length is 150cm. The nest is made from sticks and reeds or a large platform of vegetation and down. Something in excess of 5 eggs are laid. Food consists mainly of water plants and grasses but small animals, such as frogs, are also eaten.

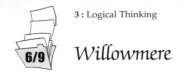
TUFTED DUCK *Aythya fuligula*

This resident averages 43cm in length. The male is black and white, the female is more a dark brown. The drooping black crest is very distinctive. Many inland waters are populated by this duck. The nest, which is near to the water, is made from vegetation and down. Food consists of water plants, insects, shellfish and frogs. The female lays 8–11 olive-coloured eggs.

GREAT CRESTED GREBE *Podiceps cristatus*

This resident is found on inland stretches of water in the summer but the winter home is normally on the coast. The average length is 48cm. The bird is easy to spot because of its black ear-tufts. Other striking features are the long, thin white neck and the long bill. The nest is built at the water's edge, made from reeds and other vegetation in which 3–4 eggs are laid. The bird is a diver and favourite foods are fish, insects and shellfish.

GREYLAG GOOSE *Anser anser*

Most greylag geese come to Britain in the winter but some breed in north Scotland. There the large nest holds 4–6 eggs. The plumage is grey, the feet are pink and the bill is orange. Grain and grasses form the diet, and this is why farmers worry about the greylag goose. The average length is 82cm.

BEWICK'S SWAN *Cygnus columbianus*

At an average length of 120cm, Bewick's swan is smaller than the mute swan. The neck is straighter and the bill (which is shorter) is black and yellow rather than orange. Locations include both inland waters and coastal areas.
This is a winter visitor.
Food includes water plants and shellfish.

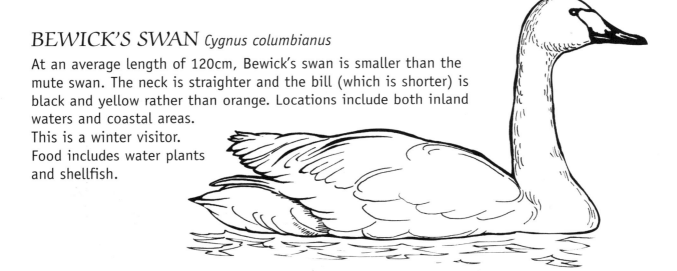

MANDARIN DUCK *Aix galericulata*

This very colourful duck originally comes from Asia. The sail-like fan is a very distinctive orange. Blue, black, orange, brown, white and pink are displayed on different parts of the body. A small number are present all the year. The diet consists of both vegetable matter and small creatures. The nests are normally found in hollow trees and they contain 9–12 eggs. The average length is 42cm.

Problem-solving and Thinking Skills Resources for Able and Talented Children
© Barry Teare (Network Continuum Education, 2006)

BARNACLE GOOSE *Branta leucopsis*

This winter visitor averages 62cm in length. The plumage is black and white, and the underparts are grey. The barnacle goose grazes on grassland. The most likely locations to see this goose are to be found on the north-west coast of Britain.

PINTAIL *Anas acuta*

The origin of the name is clear when one looks at the long, sharply pointed tail. The head and neck of the male are chocolate brown, and the plumage is grey. Its main foods are seeds, plants, insects, molluscs and worms. The pintail is one of the dabbling ducks – that is, upending in the water.

The nest is made by lining a hollow in the ground with grasses, leaves and down. The female lays 7–9 eggs and these are coloured pale olive-green or pale blue. This resident has an average length of 55cm.

GOLDENEYE *Bucephala clangula*

A large number visit the British Isles in winter but the goldeneye is not resident. The body is black and white. The head is black with a green sheen and there is a round white patch between the eye and the bill. The goldeneye likes estuaries and sheltered coastal waters, but it also settles on inland lakes, reservoirs and rivers. Feeding is done by diving and the diet consists of small water animals, mostly shellfish and insects. The average length is 45cm.

COOT *Fulica atra*

Coots are black, except for a white patch over the bill that resembles a shield in shape. The toes are lobed with webbing. This resident lays 6–9 eggs, buff with black spots, in a large nest of reeds. The coot is an aggressive bird and has a territory which it defends. It is a diving bird and sometimes stays under the water for half a minute.

Food includes the shoots of plants, seeds, small fish, newts, tadpoles and insects. The favourite haunts are lakes, meres and river-flats. The average length is 38cm.

Willowmere

GOOSANDER *Mergus merganser*

This, the largest of the British saw-billed ducks (average length 65cm), has a dark-green head and back, pale salmon-pink underparts and a scarlet bill and legs. Goosanders have a long, thin hooked bill with sharp teeth. Some are resident but they are joined by winter visitors. The nest, which is positioned in a hole in a bank, rock or tree, is lined with rotten wood, leaves and feathers. The female lays 7–13 creamy white eggs. The goosander lives off fish for which it swims under water. It is unpopular with anglers for this reason.

COMMON SCOTER *Melanitta nigra*

A few are resident in the British Isles but the great majority are winter visitors. Identification of the male is easy as this is our only black duck. There is a distinctive orange mark on the bill. The female is dark brown, with pale buff cheeks. The common scoter likes the sea but it does also frequent inland lakes and meres. It dives for food, which includes mussels, shrimps, crabs, worms and insects. The average length is 47cm.

GADWALL *Anas strepera*

This British Isles' resident nests in a hollow lined with dead leaves and down. The female lays 8–12 yellow-buff eggs. The average length is 50cm. The male is dull brownish-grey with a black rear end. The gadwall is a surface-feeding or dabbling duck, finding its food on or near the surface.

The diet includes water plants, and small snails and worms. The gadwall is one of our scarcer breeding ducks.

SMEW *Mergus albellus*

Like the goosander, this is a saw-bill but it is smaller – average length 41cm. On the water, the male looks mainly white with just a few black markings. In the air it appears darker. The female is grey on the back, with chestnut on the crown and back of the neck. The smew is a winter visitor. Feeding is done by diving. The diet includes small fish, shrimps, snails and water-beetles.

TEAL *Anas crecca*

This duck is a resident but it is most common in the winter. It is the smallest of our ducks. Movement is very rapid. The quick reaction to any danger is important as they live in well-wooded areas where there is little warning of impending problems.

The male has a white stripe above the wing, a chestnut head and a curved, green stripe around each eye. The female is mottled buff and brown. The teal is a surface-feeding duck and it eats

Problem-solving and Thinking Skills Resources for Able and Talented Children
© Barry Teare (Network Continuum Education, 2006)

water plants, insects, crustaceans and grain. The female lays 8–10 pale buff eggs in a hollow in the ground lined with dead leaves, bracken and down. The average length is only 35cm.

SHOVELER *Spatula clypeata*

This resident is found in varying numbers over most of Britain. Its average length is 50cm. The male has a bottle-green head, a white breast and a chestnut body. The female is mottled brown. The large, heavy bill is very distinctive and it is that which gives the duck its name, which is particularly suitable for feeding on the surface of ponds and lakes.

Food consists of water insects, weeds, frogs and shellfish. The nest is in a deep hollow in dry ground and it is lined with grass and down. The female lays 8–12 greenish-white eggs.

RUDDY DUCK *Oxyura jamaicensis*

The real home of the ruddy duck is North America, but some birds have escaped from wildfowl collections and there is now a reasonably sized population in central and southern England. The ruddy duck is smallish – the average length being 39cm. The male is noted for its rich chestnut red body. The top of the head is black but the face is white and the bill is bright blue. The female is coloured dark brown. The female lays 6–15 eggs in a nest which resembles a basket. The ruddy duck is a diving bird, feeding mainly on water plants. Another unusual feature is the stiff tail, which acts as a rudder under the water.

SHELDUCK *Tadorna tadorna*

This is the largest British duck, averaging 65cm in length. It is found around all the coasts of the British Isles, and it is a resident. The shelduck is an exception to the rule that the females are more drably coloured than the males. Both sexes have greenish-black heads. The plumage is black, white and chestnut. The bill is bright red, but there is a difference because the male has a knob at the base of the bill which the female does not have.

The female lays 8–14 creamy white eggs in a nest of moss and down that is usually positioned in a rabbit burrow. When the tide retreats, the shelduck searches the shore and pools for shellfish, sand-worms, small crabs and shrimps.

Willowmere

Teaching Notes

This lengthy, logical thought exercise combines higher-order thinking skills and content that is applicable to some aspects of life processes and living things in science.

Key Elements

- synthesis of data
- information processing
- logical thinking
- span of concentration

- science content (life processes and living things)
- wordplay
- careful recording.

Contexts

'Willowmere' can be used in a number of ways:

- as extension work on life processes and living things
- as enrichment work for those ahead on other tasks
- as differentiated homework
- as an activity during an enrichment day, weekend, cluster day or summer school
- as an activity for the Science Club or Ornithology Club.

When handling the feedback on this exercise, it is very beneficial to demonstrate one method of recording the information to assist the children to develop effective working practices (while stressing that this is only one method and others, which suit the children, may be equally effective). One method that the author has found very useful is to divide a sheet of paper vertically into four. In the first column, the children are listed, in the second the birds are listed, in the third information is held when there are options to be resolved. The final column lists definite solutions. Once a child is linked to a bird the names are deleted from columns one and two. In this way the information that needs to be referred to for later clues is greatly reduced.

Solution

1. Julie Jones and Richard Ralston chose the mute swan and Bewick's swan but we do not yet know which was which.
2. Sally Gates did not adopt a bird.
3. There are two boys who fit the description – Michael Barber and Martin Lostock. One of them chose the ruddy duck – 'noted for its rich chestnut red body' and with a name that sounds like swearing.
4. The greatest length (150cm) belongs to the mute swan and, therefore, from **Clue 1** it was Julie Jones who adopted the mute swan and Richard Ralston who chose Bewick's swan.
5. No bird was adopted by Bernard Cooper, 'a shy retiring boy' whose initials make BC!
6. The new girl is Susan Bridge. She chose either the pintail or the long-tailed duck.
7. The two noted mathematicians are Kerry Lundy and Ben Williams. One did not adopt a bird, the other chose either the tufted duck or the great crested grebe.
8. The two sawbills are the goosander and the smew; the two children are Martin Hince (fishing) and Hilary Turton (stamp-collecting). At this stage we cannot say which is which.
9. In **Clue 6** we know that Susan Bridge chose either the pintail or the long-tailed duck. We now know the choice was definitely the long-tailed duck which is a diving bird whereas the pintail is a dabbling duck.

Willowmere

10   In **Clue 8** we know that Martin Hince chose either the goosander or the smew. It is the goosander which is blamed for spoiling angling by taking fair-sized fish. Therefore Martin Hince's choice was the smew and Hilary Turton adopted the goosander.

11   The shortest bird is the teal (35cm) and it was adopted by Ruth Fairfax.

12   Martin Hince chose the smew so we are now concerned with Martin Lostock and Martin Norton. Neither of them adopted a bird. Therefore, from **Clue 3**, Michael Barber chose the ruddy duck.

13   The mute swan was chosen by Julie Jones. Her best friend is Dorothy Smith who therefore adopted the great crested grebe. This also helps **Clue 7**, as it eliminates the great crested grebe and means that Kerry Lundy and Ben Williams between them chose the tufted duck and no bird.

14   From **Clues 7** and **13** it must be Kerry Lundy who chose the tufted duck and, therefore, Ben Williams did not adopt a bird.

15   The girl who travels furthest to school each day is Jean Hall and it is the greylag goose that upsets farmers because of its appetite for grain and grasses.

16   The bird is the mallard but the child could be either Elizabeth Denton or Robert Kelly.

17   Three birds are mentioned as using trees for nests. Two of them, the mallard and the goosander, have been linked with other children. Therefore Brian Allen adopted the mandarin duck.

18   The girl who is noted for both her popularity and her artistic skill is Elizabeth Denton. The bird is the coot, which is aggressive and has a white patch on the front of its head in a shield shape. This also means, from **Clue 16**, that the mallard was adopted by Robert Kelly.

19   The two girls who are noted for their sporting prowess are Jennifer Darlington and Jane Earle. The only two diving birds not already placed are the goldeneye and the common scoter. At this stage we do not know which is which.

20   The musician is David France and he did not adopt a bird.

21   The teacher's daughter is Jennifer Darlington. From this clue and **Clue 19** it was she who chose the goldeneye and, therefore, Jane Earle who adopted the common scoter.

22   The girl who likes making and flying model aeroplanes is Julie Mason. The only goose remaining is the barnacle goose.

23   Of the four children remaining, the only girl is Christine Parker. Of the four birds remaining, the eggs are the wrong colour for the pintail (olive-green or pale blue) and for the shoveler (greenish-white). 'Yellowish' suits the gadwall rather better than the 'creamy white' description of the shelduck's eggs. A small additional point is the inclusion of '8–12 eggs', which fits the gadwall better than the shelduck (8–14 eggs).

24   The boy who goes to the library a great deal is John Millington. The bird where male and female are both brightly coloured is the shelduck.

25   This boy is Paul Hooper. The distinctive feature is the 'large heavy bill' of the shoveler, and this is an alternative description of 'expensive'.

26   The final pairing must therefore be Michael Gray and the pintail.

The final list is:

BRIAN ALLEN	mandarin duck	PAUL HOOPER	shoveler
MICHAEL BARBER	ruddy duck	JULIE JONES	mute swan
SUSAN BRIDGE	long-tailed duck	ROBERT KELLY	mallard
BERNARD COOPER	none	MARTIN LOSTOCK	none
JENNIFER DARLINGTON	goldeneye	KERRY LUNDY	tufted duck
ELIZABETH DENTON	coot	JULIE MASON	barnacle goose
JANE EARLE	common scoter	JOHN MILLINGTON	shelduck
RUTH FAIRFAX	teal	MARTIN NORTON	none
DAVID FRANCE	none	CHRISTINE PARKER	gadwall
SALLY GATES	none	RICHARD RALSTON	Bewick's swan
MICHAEL GRAY	pintail	DOROTHY SMITH	great crested grebe
JEAN HALL	greylag goose	HILARY TURTON	goosander
MARTIN HINCE	smew	BEN WILLIAMS	none

Suit Yourself

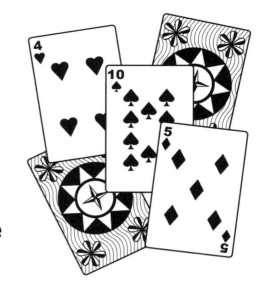

A short excursion into the wonderful world of BRIDGE

Most people enjoy playing games of one sort or another. Card games are particularly popular and, to many enthusiasts, Bridge is the greatest of them all. Successful players need skill, judgement and concentration. They draw heavily on simple but crucial mathematical calculations. Playing Bridge well has many similarities to the demands required in skills-based exercises in a variety of school subjects. The players have to sort out information, solve problems, plan strategies, make decisions and work closely with their partners.

Some features of this marvellous game are described below and there are questions and problems for you to answer.

Pit your wits against the cards

The Pack

Bridge is played with one pack of 52 cards.
There are four suits, each containing 13 cards: 2, 3, 4, 5, 6, 7, 8, 9, 10, jack, queen, king, ace in ascending value, with the ace being the highest card.
The suits are ranked in order, as follows, with spades having the greatest value and clubs the least.

♠	SPADES	BLACK
♥	HEARTS	RED
♦	DIAMONDS	RED
♣	CLUBS	BLACK

That order is important in the bidding which is explained later and it is also used to indicate the cards in a particular hand, for instance:

K J 4 3
J 7 6
A 10 3
K Q 9

> The player with this hand would hold:
> king, jack, 4 and 3 of spades,
> jack, 7 and 6 of hearts,
> ace, 10 and 3 of diamonds,
> king, queen and 9 of clubs.

Problem-solving and Thinking Skills Resources for Able and Talented Children

The Players

In some matches the players have already chosen their partners before they sit down at the table. On other occasions, the four players take a card each from the pack and the two highest cards play as partners against the two lowest cards. Thus a 6 beats a 5. If two 5s are drawn then the higher-ranking suit wins; for example, the 5 of spades beats the 5 of diamonds.

The players are known by their 'compass positions' around the table.

NORTH

WEST   EAST

SOUTH

Partners sit opposite to each other.

The Deal

The player who drew the highest card is the dealer for the first hand. The player to his or her left shuffles the cards (mixes them up). The dealer can give them a final shuffle if required before passing them to the player to his or her right who 'cuts' the pack. This means that the cards are divided into two portions, face downwards, and the dealer now puts them back together by placing the lower section onto the top pile. The dealer then deals the cards one at a time, starting with the player to his or her left, going clockwise to each player in turn, until each player has 13 cards. The last card dealt, therefore, is the dealer's.

After one complete 'hand' the cards are prepared for the next hand. The dealer is now the person to the left (or clockwise) of the previous dealer.

Let us look at an example. South is the dealer. West therefore shuffles the cards and returns them to South who gets East to cut them. South then deals the cards starting with West. The 52nd and final card is dealt by South to himself or herself. When that hand has been played the next dealer is West.

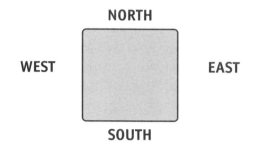

Suit Yourself

Section One Questions

You have read a lot of information and the game has not yet got going properly! See if you can answer these questions:

1 In each case say which people will play as partners and who the first dealer will be when the four players draw the cards indicated at the start of a game.

a) Mr Avenue   10 of clubs   Mr Pan   jack of diamonds
    Miss Crescent   ace of diamonds   Miss Dish   5 of spades
    Mrs Road   4 of spades   **c)** Miss Sprout   ace of hearts
    Mr Drive   6 of diamonds   Mr Onion   10 of diamonds
b) Mrs Kettle   5 of hearts   Mrs Carrot   7 of spades
    Mrs Pot   7 of clubs   Mrs Bean   10 of hearts

2 At the local Bridge Club, four members sat down to play a rubber (a complete game). Their positions at the table were North – Mr Leigh, South – Mrs Brown, East – Mr Grout, West – Mrs Hall. The cards for the first hand were held as follows:

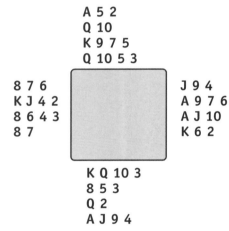

```
            A 5 2
            Q 10
            K 9 7 5
            Q 10 5 3
876                      J 9 4
K J 4 2                  A 9 7 6
8 6 4 3                  A J 10
8 7                      K 6 2
            K Q 10 3
            8 5 3
            Q 2
            A J 9 4
```

a) The dealer of this first hand was Mrs Brown. Who dealt the third hand? For that third hand, who shuffled the cards and who cut the cards?

b) Which player held the following cards in the first hand that is illustrated above?

   (i) ace of spades   (v) queen of hearts   (ix) jack of spades
   (ii) 9 of diamonds   (vi) 3 of diamonds   (x) 4 of hearts
   (iii) king of clubs   (vii) ace of clubs
   (iv) 8 of hearts   (viii) king of diamonds

3 The four Grey sisters sat down for a game of Bridge. When they drew for partners their cards were Lisa – 10 of hearts, Maggie – 5 of diamonds, Barbara – 4 of clubs, Joan – 5 of hearts. At the table Maggie was East. Who was West?

    Problem-solving and Thinking Skills Resources for Able and Talented Children

Playing the Game

TRICKS
The four cards played in one round of the table, with one card coming from each player, make a trick. The winner is the player who plays the card of highest value.

FOLLOWING SUIT
Each player must follow suit if he or she is able to do so. Thus, if a spade is played by North, then East, South and West, in turn, must also play a spade if they have one in their hand.

TRUMPS
One suit is normally made trumps as a result of the bidding (this is explained below). If the game is played in a hearts contract, for example, then hearts are trumps and they beat the other three suits as the cards are played. The 2 of hearts would beat even an ace of another suit and win the trick. Remember, however, that you cannot play a trump to win a trick if you are breaking the 'following suit' rule. In a game where clubs are trumps and an opponent plays a diamond, you cannot win the trick by playing a club if you have a diamond in your hand.

NO TRUMPS
Sometimes the bidding results in a game being played in a 'No Trumps' contract. This time no suit beats the other suits and the trick is won by the highest card of the suit led by the first player.

SOME EXAMPLES

	Trumps	Cards Played	Trick Won
1	Spades	North – 3 of diamonds East – 4 of diamonds South – queen of diamonds West – ace of diamonds	West – ace of diamonds
2	Hearts	South – 3 of clubs West – 5 of clubs North – king of clubs East – 5 of hearts	East – 5 of hearts (East did not have a club left and was able to play a trump to win the trick)
3	No Trumps	East - king of spades South – 4 of spades West – 3 of diamonds North – 5 of spades	East – king of spades (West did not have a spade left and had to play a card from another suit. This did not win the trick because it was not a trump)

ORDER OF PLAY
You will have also realized that the cards are played in a clockwise direction. The first player is the one who has won the last trick. This does not, of course, work for the very first card of the hand as a trick has not yet been won. This is decided rather differently as you will see later below.

Suit Yourself

Section Two Questions

Name the player who won the trick in the following examples:

	TRUMPS	CARDS PLAYED	
1	Diamonds	West – 4 of spades	North – jack of spades
		East – 7 of spades	South – 6 of spades
2	Spades	South – 3 of hearts	West – 7 of hearts
		North – 4 of spades	East – 5 of hearts
3	No trumps	North – 5 of clubs	East – 4 of clubs
		South – jack of clubs	West – ace of clubs
4	Hearts	East – 6 of diamonds	South – queen of diamonds
		West – 4 of clubs	North – 7 of diamonds
5	No trumps	West – 8 of clubs	North – 6 of clubs
		East – 5 of hearts	South – 7 of clubs
6	Spades	South – 4 of hearts	West – 7 of hearts
		North – 5 of spades	East – 7 of spades
7	Hearts	South – 3 of spades	West – 2 of spades
		North – king of spades	East – 9 of spades
8	Clubs	West – 6 of diamonds	North – 10 of diamonds
		East – jack of diamonds	South – 4 of hearts

BIDDING

Before the cards are played, an auction takes place. The players make bids in which they say how many tricks they will make, either with No Trumps or with one suit named as trumps. There are 13 tricks to be won (52 cards in groups of 4) and, therefore, a partnership needs at least seven tricks to secure more than the opponents. For this reason the first six tricks are taken for granted when a bid is being made. Thus 'one club' means that you expect to make seven tricks (6 + 1) with clubs as trumps. 'Three hearts' means that you expect to make nine tricks (6 + 3) with hearts as trumps and 'three No Trumps' means nine tricks (6 + 3) with no suit as trumps.

HIGH-CARD POINTS

Before bidding, a player needs to be able to value his or her hand. Obviously, the more strong cards held, the more likely it is that tricks will be won. The system used is to score high-card points as follows: 4 points for each ace, 3 points for each king, 2 points for each queen and 1 point for each jack.

Example: A 10 5 2   The hand is valued at 14 points.
K J 3
Q 4 2
A 9 7

Problem-solving and Thinking Skills Resources for Able and Talented Children

Suit Yourself

Section Three Questions

1 What do the following bids mean?

a) 2 hearts   **c)** 3 No Trumps   **e)** 5 diamonds   **g)** 6 No Trumps
b) 1 spade   **d)** 4 spades   **f)** 1 club   **h)** 7 hearts

2 When the following final bids have been made, what is the maximum number of tricks that the declarer (the person who plays the cards) could afford to lose if the contract is to be made?

a) 3 diamonds   **c)** 3 No Trumps   **e)** 2 spades   **g)** 6 spades
b) 1 heart   **d)** 4 hearts   **f)** 5 clubs   **h)** 7 No Trumps

3 What is the high-card points value of the following hands?

a) 9 7 6 / A K Q 5 / A J 3 / Q 10 7
b) J 4 / A 5 3 / K Q J 7 2 / J 10 9
c) Q J 6 5 3 / 9 7 / 5 4 3 2 / J 2
d) Q J 7 3 / A Q / K J 8 / J 8 7 6
e) 6 / Q J / A K Q 9 7 / A Q J 8 4

Some Simple Opening Bids

There are many systems for bidding. Some of the features of one of them are used here. It is based upon the need to communicate information to your partner as accurately as possible. There are 40 high-card points in the pack, so an average hand will contain ten points. Anything more than that is better than average. An opening bid is one that is made in the first round. Players with a weak hand are unlikely to take part in the auction and they indicate this by saying 'no bid'.

Let us see what we need, in our designated system, to make an opening bid. Normally we require at least 12 high-card points. To bid a suit it must contain at least four cards. We can open one of a suit with 12–19 points and four cards in a suit.

Example: A K 7 5 / Q 9 6 / K J 2 / A 8 7

> The player can open 1 spade because the hand is worth 17 points and there are four spades.

If there are more than four cards in a suit we can open the bidding with fewer points because, in a game played with that suit as trumps, the extra cards are important.

Thus, we can also open one of a suit with 11–19 points with five cards in the suit and with 9+ points with six cards in the suit.

Sometimes there are two suits containing at least four cards. If one is longer than the other (five to four, for instance) that suit should be the opening bid. Where there are two four-card suits the higher ranking should be bid first. Remember, from the section on the pack, that the

Suit Yourself

spade suit is the highest ranking, followed in order by hearts, diamonds and clubs. There is one exception – with both clubs and spades in the hand, 1 club is bid before 1 spade.

One problem with bidding 1 of a suit for such a wide range of points is that your partner is unsure how strong you are. A bid with a much smaller range would therefore be helpful. Such a bid is 1 No Trump. This is used for a hand worth 12–14 points but only where there is balance. This means that the hand has a reasonable distribution of cards between the suits. Remember that, in a game played with No Trumps, no suit is stronger than another and, unless you have fair cards in each suit, the opponents could make too many tricks in a suit in which you are weak. A balanced hand can be 4 – 3 – 3 – 3 or 4 – 4 – 3 – 2 or 5 – 3 – 3 – 2. A No Trumps bid is not suitable for a hand that contains a suit with none or one card, or that contains two suits of two cards. Where it can be bid, 1 No Trump is very useful as it gives precise information to a partner. (There are many other opening bids but it would be too complicated to deal with them here.)

NOTE: this is one particular bidding system. Other players follow different routes. Use the information here only to answer the following questions.

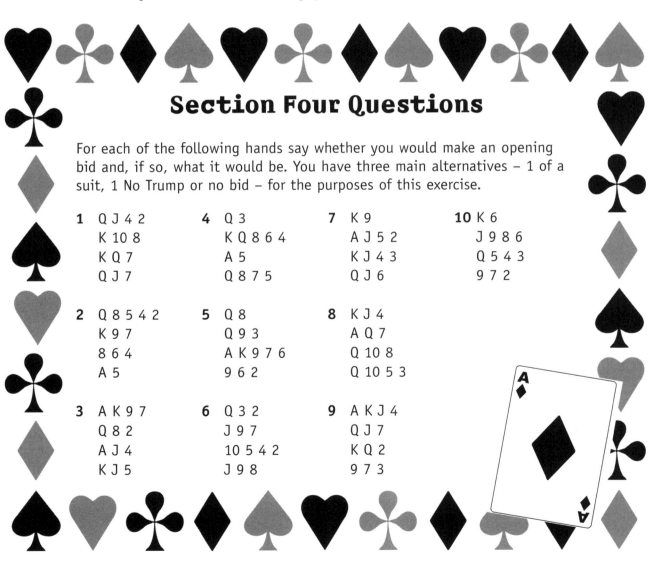

Section Four Questions

For each of the following hands say whether you would make an opening bid and, if so, what it would be. You have three main alternatives – 1 of a suit, 1 No Trump or no bid – for the purposes of this exercise.

1	Q J 4 2	4	Q 3	7	K 9	10	K 6
	K 10 8		K Q 8 6 4		A J 5 2		J 9 8 6
	K Q 7		A 5		K J 4 3		Q 5 4 3
	Q J 7		Q 8 7 5		Q J 6		9 7 2

2	Q 8 5 4 2	5	Q 8	8	K J 4
	K 9 7		Q 9 3		A Q 7
	8 6 4		A K 9 7 6		Q 10 8
	A 5		9 6 2		Q 10 5 3

3	A K 9 7	6	Q 3 2	9	A K J 4
	Q 8 2		J 9 7		Q J 7
	A J 4		10 5 4 2		K Q 2
	K J 5		J 9 8		9 7 3

Problem-solving and Thinking Skills Resources for Able and Talented Children
© Barry Teare (Network Continuum Education, 2006)

Suit Yourself

The Cards are Played

The bidding continues until three players in succession have said no bid. Sometimes this involves several bids (which increase each time) until the final contract is made. To go through all the many routes is impossible here, but one example is quoted to show how complicated the process can be.

NORTH	EAST	SOUTH	WEST
No bid	1 heart	No bid	1 spade
No bid	3 No Trumps	No bid	4 No Trumps
No bid	5 hearts	No bid	5 No Trumps
No bid	6 hearts	No bid	7 No Trumps
No bid	No bid	No bid	

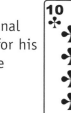

This is an extreme case as East–West have made a grand slam bid, thus saying that they intend to win all 13 tricks. We must now leave the bidding, after a cursory glance, and move to the playing of the hand.

The person who first mentioned the suit or No Trumps in which the final contract is made is known as the declarer. He or she plays the cards for his or her partnership. In the example above, East is the declarer because of the bid of 3 No Trumps when the final contract was 7 No Trumps. Here is another example:

SOUTH	WEST	NORTH	EAST
1 spade	No bid	1 heart	No bid
4 spades	No bid	3 spades	No bid
		No bid	No bid

Declarer is North because of the 1 spade bid when the final contract is 4 spades.

The opening lead (the first card) is played by the person next to the declarer in a clockwise position. If North is the declarer, East makes the opening lead. Once that first card has been played, the declarer's partner lays all the cards from his or her hand face-up on the table. This hand is now known as the dummy. The declarer plays both the cards from the dummy and his or her own hand. All the other three players are fully aware what cards there are in the dummy. Each round of cards is played in a clockwise direction as was explained earlier.

Problem-solving and Thinking Skills Resources for Able and Talented Children
© Barry Teare (Network Continuum Education, 2006)

Suit Yourself

Section Five Questions

The bidding for a number of hands is given below. In each case you are asked to name a) the declarer, b) the person to play the opening lead and c) the dummy.

1	NORTH	EAST	SOUTH	WEST
	1 diamond	No bid	1 spade	No bid
	3 spades	No bid	4 spades	No bid
	No bid	No bid		

2	WEST	NORTH	EAST	SOUTH
	No bid	No bid	1 club	No bid
	1 spade	No bid	2 clubs	No bid
	3 clubs	No bid	No bid	No bid

3	SOUTH	WEST	NORTH	EAST
	No bid	1 No Trump	No bid	3 No Trumps
	No bid	No bid	No bid	

4	EAST	SOUTH	WEST	NORTH
	1 heart	No bid	4 hearts	No bid
	4 No Trumps	No Bid	5 diamonds	No bid
	5 No trumps	No Bid	6 diamonds	No bid
	7 hearts	No bid	No bid	No bid

5	EAST	SOUTH	WEST	NORTH
	No bid	1 No Trump	No bid	2 clubs
	No bid	2 hearts	No bid	3 hearts
	No bid	4 hearts	No bid	No bid
	No bid			

Scoring

This section is long and detailed. You will need to concentrate very hard on a number of items before you reach the next set of questions.

Before the scoring system is looked at, two more bids need explanation.

a) **DOUBLE:** if a player believes that the opponents will not succeed in making a bid they have called, a bid of double can be made. This has the effect of increasing the penalties when a contract goes down.

b) **REDOUBLE:** one of the players in a partnership trying to make the contract feel confident that they will be successful and will therefore respond to a call of double by redouble. If the contract fails, the penalties are further increased, whereas if the contract succeeds the trick scores and bonuses are greater.

Problem-solving and Thinking Skills Resources for Able and Talented Children

Suit Yourself

THE SCORECARD

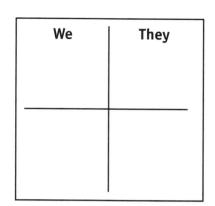

('The line')

The card is divided down the middle to separate the score of your own partnership from that of your opponents. You will also notice a dividing line across the middle. Below the line are placed the points gained by contracts bid and made. As in the bidding, only tricks above six are considered. Thus, if eight tricks are made, two are counted for scoring purposes. The points values vary as indicated below:

20 points for each trick (above 6) in clubs and diamonds.
30 points for each trick (above 6) in hearts and spades.
40 points for the first trick (above 6) in No Trumps and then 30 points for each additional trick.

Example:	**a)** 2 clubs is bid and made (8 tricks)	Score = 40 points
	b) 3 hearts is bid and made (9 tricks)	Score = 90 points
	c) 2 No Trumps is bid and made (8 tricks)	Score = 70 points

NOTE: it is important to realize that points for scoring purposes are quite distinct from those used in assessing hands when high cards are valued.

When a contract is bid and made, and the opponents have doubled it, the trick score below the line is doubled.

In the case of a redoubled bid the trick score below the line is multiplied by 4.

GAME
A game consists of scoring 100 points below the line. This can be achieved in one hand.

Example:	**a)** 3 No Trumps (40 + 30 + 30)
	b) 4 hearts (30 + 30 + 30 +30)
	NOTE: 3 hearts scores 90 points and does not reach 'game'.
	c) 5 clubs (20 + 20 + 20 + 20 + 20)

Game can also be made in part scores. If one partnership has bid and made 2 spades they will have 60 below the line. Game can now be achieved by the addition of 40 points which could be a successful 2 diamonds contract.

When one partnership has reached game, a line is drawn across the scoring card. A second game starts, in which a part score of the partnership that lost the previous game cannot be counted towards the new game.

Suit Yourself

11/17

RUBBER
A rubber is won by the first partnership to score two games. A rubber can therefore be won by two games to nil or two games to one.

ABOVE THE LINE
Scores are made above the line for the following items:

1 rubber

2 slam bonuses

3 overtricks

4 bonus for doubled and redoubled contracts

5 undertricks

6 honours.

These scores are now explained in turn.

RUBBER POINTS
If you win a rubber by two games to nil, 700 bonus points are scored above the line. If the winning score is two games to one then 500 bonus points are scored.

SLAM BONUSES
You now need to know what the terms vulnerable and not vulnerable are. When you have won one game towards the rubber you are called 'vulnerable'. Any penalties that you incur are increased but, to compensate for that, certain bonuses are also bigger. Of course, both pairs can be vulnerable in a rubber if they have won a game each. It goes without saying, therefore, that a pair is not vulnerable when they have not yet won a game in that particular rubber.

A small slam means that you have won 12 tricks and have therefore bid and made a contract in 6 of a suit or No Trumps. The bonuses above the line are 500 points when not vulnerable and 750 points when vulnerable.

A Grand Slam means that you have won all 13 tricks and have, therefore, bid and made a contract of 7 of a suit or 7 No Trumps. The bonuses above the line are 1,000 points when not vulnerable and 1,500 points when vulnerable.

Overtricks
Any tricks made above what has been bid are still scored but they are placed above the line and therefore do not count towards game. The normal trick values are used as explained above in the scorecard section.

Examples: **1** A pair bids 3 hearts but makes 4 hearts. Heart tricks are valued at 30 points. Below the line would be scored 90 points (30 + 30 + 30) and above the line 30 points for the overtrick. The partnership would not get the benefit of the extra trick to score 100 and reach game but the 30 points would still be scored.

2 A pair bids 3 No Trumps but makes 5 No Trumps. Below the line they would score 100 points (40 + 30 + 30) and above the line 60 points (30 + 30) for the two overtricks.

The position changes when doubles and redoubles are involved. When the contract has been doubled you score 100 points for each overtrick when not vulnerable; 200 when vulnerable. When the contract has been redoubled, overtricks are scored at 200 not vulnerable; 400 vulnerable.

NOTE: it is important to realize that in a doubled or redoubled contract, the tricks bid and made are scored below the line but at increased value. Three hearts bid and made would normally score 90 points below the line. In a doubled contract the score would be 180 points below the line and in a redoubled contract 360 points below the line. In both these cases, a part score of 90 points has been made into a game score by the double or redouble.

It is also important to understand that, no matter how much the game total of 100 points is passed in one contract, it still only counts to that game. The example given above, where 3 hearts redoubled was successfully made, scored 360 points below the line but that was still only one game. The extra 260 points cannot be put to another game score.

Thus doubled and redoubled contracts, bid and made, are scored below the line and overtricks are scored above the line.

Example: In the first game of the rubber, Pair A bid 2 No Trumps. One player in Pair B believes strongly that the contract will go down and therefore doubles. The player in Pair A who called 2 No Trumps is equally confident that the contract will be made and, therefore, redoubles. The tension mounts as the cards are played and Pair A's confidence is shown to be justified when they win 9 tricks, one more than the 2 No Trumps that was bid.

The normal score below the line for 2 No Trumps is 70 points (40 + 30). Doubled that becomes 140 and redoubled 280. Thus 280 points are scored below the line. There was also an overtrick in a redoubled contract which is scored as 200 points above the line (it would have been 400 if the partnership had already won a game in the rubber and had therefore been vulnerable).

The card would look like this (written by Pair A):

We	They	
50		
200		('The line')
280		('Game line')

A line has been drawn across to show that a game was won at this point. The 50 points above the line are explained in the next section.

Of course, Pair B's scorecard would show the reverse.

We	They	
	50	
	200	('The line')
	280	('Game line')

Suit Yourself

This was an expensive hand for Pair B. The original score would have been a part score of 70 points but doubled and then redoubled it results in 280 points below the line and game, and 250 points above the line (200 + 50).

So, beware of doubling without good reason!

BONUS FOR DOUBLED AND REDOUBLED CONTRACTS

As well as the additional points scored above, there is also a bonus of 50 points above the line for any doubled or redoubled contract that is made. This is compensation for the 'insult' that has been made by one pair doubting that their opponents could make their contract. This explains the mysterious 50 points which appeared on the scorecards above.

UNDERTRICKS

If you bid a contract but fail to make it, there are penalties to be paid. This is to stop a player over-bidding stupidly in an attempt to prevent the other side from making a contract. The penalty for each undertrick is normally 50 points when not vulnerable, 100 when vulnerable. Just as the value of overtricks was increased in a doubled or redoubled contract, so the penalties for undertricks also get bigger!

When the contract has been doubled, the penalty for the first undertrick not vulnerable is 100 and for every other undertrick 200. If vulnerable, the penalties are 200 for the first undertrick and 300 for every other undertrick. If the contract has been redoubled, all these amounts are doubled again. Thus, not vulnerable the first undertrick is penalized at 200 and others at 400 and, when vulnerable, the first undertrick is penalized at 400 and the others at 600 points.

Example: Petula and Paul have allowed themselves to be swept away by false confidence and have bid 3 No Trumps when they are vulnerable. The opponents have doubled their contract. Not content with overbidding, Petula has taken up the challenge and redoubled – so now she and Paul are in 3 No Trumps redoubled! They make only 7 tricks and therefore go 'two off'. There are two undertricks redoubled when vulnerable. The penalty is 1,000 points – 400 for the first undertrick and 600 points for the second – an expensive business. Petula and Paul have scored nothing as they did not make their contract and the opponents have scored 1,000 points above the line.

HONOURS

Scoring for honours has been abandoned in some circumstances but it is still used in normal rubber bridge. The five trump honours are ace, king, queen, jack and ten. In a suit contract, any player holding all five honours in his or her hand scores 150 points above the line. If four of the five honours are held in one hand, the score is 100 points. In a No Trumps contract, any player holding all four aces scores 150 points above the line. This applies to any of the four players but it is much more likely to apply to the declarer or dummy, as he or she should have a stronger hand than the defenders in most cases.

Suit Yourself

INTERPRETING THE SCORECARD

Your head must be spinning by now with all the information about scoring. Take heart (sorry about the pun), only one more section left to mention before you can try some more questions. Below there is a specimen scorecard – let us see what it means.

WE	THEY
500	
30	
30	200
500	50
60	100
100	
120	80
1340	430

- ♣ **WE** bid and made 2 hearts, giving us 60 points below the line.

- ♣ In the next hand, **THEY** bid and made 3 No Trumps giving them 100 points and game – therefore a line was drawn across.

- ♣ **THEY** then bid 4 spades which **WE** doubled. **THEY** made only eight tricks, thus going two off. **THEY** were vulnerable and therefore paid 500 penalty points to us for the two undertricks doubled (200 for the first and 300 for the second).

- ♣ In the next hand **WE** bid 3 No Trumps and actually made ten tricks. This gave us 100 points below the line and game. **WE** also scored 30 above the line for the overtrick.

- ♣ Each pair now had one game towards rubber and both were vulnerable.

- ♣ At the start of the third and deciding game, **THEY** bid 2 clubs which **WE** doubled and **THEY** in fact made nine tricks. The 40 points for 2 clubs was doubled to an 80 part score below the line. **THEY** scored 50 above the line as the bonus for making a doubled contract. Their one overtrick, doubled when vulnerable, gave them 200 points above the line.

- ♣ **WE** then bid 4 hearts and made 11 tricks. This gave us 120 points below the line for the 4 hearts. The one overtrick scored 30 above the line. As **WE** had now won the rubber by two games to one, **WE** also scored 500 bonus points.

- ♣ Then all the points were totalled up both above and below the line to give the final score for the rubber.

Suit Yourself

Section Six Questions

1   Calculate the scores below and above the line in the following hands, indicating if game is reached.

   a) Bid 3 No Trumps, 9 tricks made
   b) Bid 2 clubs, 10 tricks made
   c) Bid 4 hearts, 10 tricks made
   d) Bid 1 No Trump, 7 tricks made
   e) Bid 5 clubs, 11 tricks made
   f) Bid 4 spades, 11 tricks made
   g) Bid 3 diamonds, 9 tricks made
   h) Bid 2 No Trumps, 9 tricks made

2   In each of the following hands the opponents doubled the contract. As in the previous question, calculate the scores below and above the line and indicate if game is reached. **WE** were not vulnerable.

   a) Bid 2 diamonds, 8 tricks made
   b) Bid 3 hearts, 9 tricks made
   c) Bid 1 No Trump, 8 tricks made
   d) Bid 2 spades, 8 tricks made
   e) Bid 2 clubs, 10 tricks made

3   Repeat the examples given in question 2 but this time the contracts have been **redoubled**. Again **WE** were not vulnerable.

4   At the start of a game you have bid and made 2 diamonds. In the next hand you have reached 2 No Trumps. Why are you happy to leave the bidding there even though you have sufficient strength in your hand to attempt 3 No Trumps?

5   Before you answer these questions, remind yourself about the scoring of slams. What would you score above and below the line in the following situations?
   a) Bid 6 No Trumps, not vulnerable, 12 tricks made
   b) Bid 7 hearts, vulnerable, 13 tricks made
   c) Bid 4 spades, not vulnerable, 12 tricks made
   d) Bid 6 diamonds, vulnerable, 12 tricks made
   e) Bid 7 clubs, not vulnerable, 13 tricks made

6   Having read the information on scoring, explain, in your own words, why double and redouble have been included in the game.

7   Each of the following hands were played by your opponents. What would **WE** have marked on the scorecard?
   a) Bid 3 No Trumps, not vulnerable, 7 tricks made
   b) Bid 4 hearts, vulnerable, 9 tricks made
   c) Bid 5 clubs, doubled, not vulnerable, 10 tricks made
   d) Bid 4 spades, redoubled, vulnerable, 9 tricks made
   e) Bid 3 clubs, doubled, vulnerable, 7 tricks made

8   The opponents have bid 2 hearts in the first hand of a game. You think you may be able to put the contract down but you have some doubts. What considerations might prevent you doubling the opponents' contract?

© Barry Teare (Network Continuum Education, 2006)

Suit Yourself

9 Would you place any score above the line in the following situations? If so, what?

a) Bid 4 spades	North's hand	A K Q 10 K J 3 Q 6 2 J 9 8
b) Bid 3 No Trumps	East's hand	A J 7 10 4 2 A 9 7 3 A 10 5
c) Bid 5 clubs	South's hand	J 9 2 J 7 Q 9 8 A K Q J 10
d) Bid 3 hearts	North's hand	J 8 A K J 9 A Q 9 J 9 7 3
e) Bid 6 No Trumps	West's hand	A Q 3 A K 4 A Q J 9 A K 8
f) Bid 4 hearts	East's hand	7 6 2 J 9 8 A K Q J 4 J 7

10 Draw a blank scorecard. Now follow through the rubber described below. Complete the scorecard. (Don't forget to consider vulnerable and not vulnerable.)

a) **WE** bid 2 No Trumps and made 8 tricks.
b) **THEY** bid 4 hearts which we doubled. They made 10 tricks.
c) **THEY** bid 3 No Trumps and made 8 tricks.
d) **WE** bid 7 No Trumps and made 13 tricks.
e) **THEY** bid 4 spades and made 11 tricks.

Section Seven: In Hand

'Suit Yourself' finishes with a substantial logic problem that draws upon many of the items you have already considered.

Your Task

Can you pull together all the knowledge that you have gained to discover the identity of the hidden cards? Think back to all that you have learned in this short excursion into the wonderful world of Bridge. Now study the 15 clues and then work out the 13 cards that formed Alison's hand.

Suit Yourself

THE CLUES

a) These cards were drawn for partners.

Alison – king of spades   Mary – 6 of clubs
June – 10 of hearts   Christine – 9 of diamonds

b) Dealer sat in the South position and Christine was on her left.

c) The bidding was as follows:

South	West	North	East
1 No Trump	No bid	2 No Trumps	No bid
3 No Trumps	No bid	No bid	No bid

South went to a game bid of 3 No Trumps because she had the maximum points in the range in her opening bid.

d) The cards were now in place. The person who shuffled the cards got the ace of diamonds and the player who cut the cards held the ace of clubs.

e) West led the 5 of hearts, which was the fourth card in her longest suit. At that point, June placed the cards in dummy on the table. The dummy contained these cards:

K Q 5
J 9
K 10 7 2
K 10 8 6

f) Alison planned out her campaign. She had the same number of spades as the dummy and between the two hands the top three cards in spades were held and there were three definite tricks in that suit.

g) Counting her hand and dummy, Alison had 7 diamonds, including two of the three strongest cards in that suit.

h) Between dummy and her own hand, Alison also had 7 clubs but this time they contained four of the five strongest cards in that suit.

i) By now you should know how many cards there were in each suit in Alison's hand, the identity of four particular cards, the high-card points total of the hand and how many high-card points are still to be identified.

j) After playing the cards, Alison and June scored 100 points below the line and 30 above.

k) During the hand Alison got the 3 spades tricks she expected. She played the 10 and 7 from her own hand against the dummy's king and queen.

l) Declarer made three tricks in clubs after losing one early in the hand when she led out the 7 of clubs to the dummy's king but the trick was taken by East's ace.

m) Declarer made two tricks in diamonds. She played the 8 from her own hand in the round won by dummy's king. She could equally well have led the 9 of diamonds in that round.

n) The remaining tricks were made in hearts. This included a trick won with the dummy's jack when the declarer played a heart one more in value than the number of tricks won in total in hearts. The next lowest heart in declarer's hand had the same value as a card in both the spades and clubs suits in her hand.

o) You should now be able to identify the last two cards and write out Alison's hand in total.

FOOTNOTE

Although 'Suit Yourself' is lengthy, it has only scratched the surface in looking at the wonderful game of Bridge. You have had a taste of procedures, bidding, playing and scoring but there is much, much more.

Perhaps you will be encouraged to develop your interest further in the future.

Suit Yourself

Teaching Notes

Bridge is far too complicated to explain fully in anything less than a lengthy book. There are many different bidding systems. However, many features have been illustrated and they provide interesting material of an information-processing and problem-solving nature. There is a strong mathematical content and there is also emphasis on clear and logical thought, and on following instructions. The qualities of Bridge fit the needs of a skills curriculum. There is, too, an emphasis upon concentration, as 'Suit Yourself' is lengthy and complicated.

Key Elements

- ❖ information processing
- ❖ analysis of data
- ❖ synthesis (especially in Section Seven: In Hand)
- ❖ logical thinking
- ❖ mathematics – calculation, handling data and problem solving
- ❖ following instructions
- ❖ span of concentration
- ❖ strategy.

Contexts

'Suit Yourself' can be used in a number of ways:

- ❖ as extension material in mathematics (one school used 'Suit Yourself' for GCSE coursework)
- ❖ as an enrichment activity for those ahead in mathematics
- ❖ as material within a thinking skills course
- ❖ as differentiated homework
- ❖ as an activity during an enrichment session, cluster day or summer school
- ❖ as an activity for the Mathematics Club or the Games Society.

Answers

SECTION ONE

1 a) Miss Crescent and Mr Avenue played against Mr Drive and Mrs Road. Miss Crescent had the highest card and was therefore the dealer.

   b) Mr Pan and Mrs Pot played against Miss Dish and Mrs Kettle. Mr Pan had the highest card and was therefore the dealer.

   c) Miss Sprout and Mrs Bean played against Mr Onion and Mrs Carrot. (The 10 of hearts is stronger than the 10 of diamonds.) Miss Sprout had the highest card and was therefore the dealer.

2 a) The third hand was dealt by Mr Leigh (North). The cards were shuffled by the player on Mr Leigh's left who was Mr Grout (East). The cards were cut by the player on Mr Leigh's right who was Mrs Hall (West).

   b) (i)   ace of spades   Mr Leigh
       (ii)   9 of diamonds   Mr Leigh
       (iii) king of clubs   Mr Grout
       (iv)   8 of hearts   Mrs Brown
       (v)   queen of hearts   Mr Leigh
       (vi)   3 of diamonds   Mrs Hall
       (vii) ace of clubs   Mrs Brown
       (viii) king of diamonds   Mr Leigh
       (ix)   jack of spades   Mr Grout
       (x)   4 of hearts   Mrs Hall

3 Lisa and Joan played against Maggie and Barbara. Maggie's partner was Barbara who was, therefore, West.

Suit Yourself

SECTION TWO

1 Trick won by North with the jack of spades.

2 Trick won by North with the 4 of spades, as spades were trumps. This meant that North did not have any hearts left.

3 Trick won by West with the ace of clubs.

4 Trick won by South with the queen of diamonds. The unwary might have nominated the 4 of clubs but that was not a trump, just a discard because West had no diamonds left.

5 Trick won by West with the 8 of clubs. There are no trumps and the 5 of hearts was just a discard.

6 Trick won by East with the 7 of spades. This is a case where North tried to win the trick with a trump but East, who also had no hearts, played a higher trump.

7 Trick won by North with the king of spades.

8 Trick won by East with the jack of diamonds. The 4 of hearts was just a discard as trumps were clubs.

SECTION THREE

1 a) 2 hearts means to make eight tricks with hearts as trumps.
   b) 1 spade means to make seven tricks with spades as trumps.
   c) 3 No Trumps means to make nine tricks with no suit as trumps.
   d) 4 spades means to make ten tricks with spades as trumps.
   e) 5 diamonds means to make 11 tricks with diamonds as trumps.
   f) 1 club means to make seven tricks with clubs as trumps.
   g) 6 No Trumps means to make 12 tricks with no suit as trumps.
   h) 7 hearts means to make 13 tricks with hearts as trumps.

2 There are 13 tricks in total.

a)	3 diamonds	= 9 tricks	therefore 4 could be lost
b)	1 heart	= 7 tricks	therefore 6 could be lost
c)	3 No Trumps	= 9 tricks	therefore 4 could be lost
d)	4 hearts	= 10 tricks	therefore 3 could be lost
e)	2 spades	= 8 tricks	therefore 5 could be lost
f)	5 clubs	= 11 tricks	therefore 2 could be lost
g)	6 spades	= 12 tricks	therefore 1 could be lost
h)	7 No Trumps	= 13 tricks	therefore none can be lost

3 a) 16 points
   b) 12 points
   c) 4 points
   d) 14 points
   e) 19 points

SECTION FOUR

1 14 points. An opening bid of 1 No Trump is best. 1 spade is also possible, but less good as it could be bid up to 19 points.

2 Only 9 points and no opening bid is possible.

3 18 points. An opening bid of 1 spade.

4 13 points. The opening bid is 1 heart. Although the points are in the 1 No Trump range that should not be bid as the balance is wrong with two suits of two cards.

5 11 points but a five-card suit, therefore 1 diamond can be bid.

6 Only 4 points and no opening bid is possible.

7 15 points and two four-card suits. 1 heart should be bid as it is the higher-ranking suit.

8 14 points and a balanced hand. 1 No Trump is the opening bid.

9 16 points. An opening bid of 1 spade.

10 Only 6 points and no opening bid is possible.

Suit Yourself

SECTION FIVE

1   Declarer is South (1 spade bid resulting in a final contract of 4 spades); therefore West makes the opening lead and North is dummy.

2   Declarer is East (1 club bid resulting in a final contract of 3 clubs); therefore South makes the opening lead and West is dummy.

3   Declarer is West (1 No Trump bid resulting in a final contract of 3 No Trumps); therefore North makes the opening lead and East is dummy.

4   Declarer is East (1 heart bid resulting in a final contract of 7 hearts); therefore South makes the opening lead and West is dummy.

5   Declarer is South (2 hearts bid resulting in a final contract of 4 hearts); therefore West makes the opening lead and North is dummy.

SECTION SIX

1   a)   100 points below the line. Game reached.
    b)   40 points below the line, 40 points above the line for two overtricks. No game.
    c)   120 points below the line. Game reached.
    d)   40 points below the line. No game.
    e)   100 points below the line. Game reached.
    f)   120 points below the line, 30 points above the line for one overtrick. Game reached.
    g)   60 points below the line. No game.
    h)   70 points below the line, 30 points above the line. No game.

2   a)   40 points, doubled to 80 points, below the line. No game. 50 points above the line bonus for making a doubled contract.
    b)   90 points doubled to 180 points, below the line. Game reached. 50 points bonus above the line.
    c)   40 points, doubled to 80 points, below the line. No game. 50 bonus points above the line. Also above the line 1 overtrick, doubled, not vulnerable scores 100 points.
    d)   60 points, doubled to 120 points, below the line. Game reached. 50 bonus points above the line.
    e)   40 points, doubled to 80 points, below the line. No game. Two overtricks, doubled, not vulnerable score 200 points above the line. 50 bonus points above the line.

3   a)   40 points, redoubled to 160 points, below the line. Game reached. 50 bonus points above the line.
    b)   90 points, redoubled to 360 points, below the line. Game reached. 50 bonus points above the line.
    c)   40 points, redoubled to 160 points, below the line. Game reached. 50 bonus points above the line. One overtrick, redoubled, not vulnerable scores 200 points above the line.
    d)   60 points, redoubled to 240 points, below the line. Game reached. 50 bonus points above the line.
    e)   40 points, redoubled to 160 points, below the line. Game reached. 50 bonus points above the line. Two overtricks, redoubled, not vulnerable score 400 points above the line.

4   2 diamonds gives a part score of 40 points. 2 No Trumps would score 70 points and make a game. Going to 3 No Trumps is unnecessary for game purposes and will make the contract more difficult.

5   a)   190 points below the line. Small slam, not vulnerable scores 500 points above the line.
    b)   210 points below the line. Grand slam, vulnerable scores 1,500 points above the line.
    c)   120 points below the line. 60 points are scored above the line for two overtricks. There is no slam bonus because a slam was not bid.
    d)   120 points below the line. Small slam, vulnerable scores 750 points above the line.
    e)   140 points below the line. Grand slam, not vulnerable scores 1,000 points above the line.

Suit Yourself

6   Without the heavy penalties that can result from a contract doubled, many players would be tempted to make false bids simply to prevent the opponents making a successful contract. With the double bid available a player has to think carefully before making an unwise bid. This, in turn, necessitates a call to prevent contracts being doubled unnecessarily. Redouble allows a massive score to be gained by successfully completing a contract. Both calls are part of a 'checks and balances' system so that there are always consequences to bear in mind. It is possible to lose a rubber two games to nil but still win on points total because of the penalties in operation.

7 a)   Under **THEY** nothing is scored as the contract went down. **WE** score 100 points above the line for two undertricks, not vulnerable.
    b)   Nothing under **THEY**. **WE** score 100 points above the line for one undertrick, vulnerable.
    c)   Nothing under **THEY**. **WE** score 100 points above the line for one undertrick, doubled, not vulnerable.
    d)   Nothing under **THEY**. **WE** score 400 points above the line for one undertrick, redoubled, vulnerable.
    e)   Nothing under **THEY**. **WE** score 500 points above the line for two undertricks, doubled, vulnerable.

8   If they make 2 hearts they will score 60 points below the line but as this is the first hand of the game they will not have already made another part score. This means that they will not have the 100 points necessary for a game. If you double the contract and you are proved wrong, not only will they score penalties above the line but they will also be doubled into game below the line.

9 a)   100 points for North's partnership for four of the five honours in the trump suit, spades.
    b)   No points to score for honours as all four aces are needed in a No Trumps contract.
    c)   150 points for South's partnership for all five honours in the trump suit, clubs.
    d)   No points to score for honours.
    e)   150 points for West's partnership for all four aces in a No Trumps contract.
    f)   No points to score. The high cards are held in diamonds, which are not trumps.

10

WE	THEY
	500
1,000	30
100	50
70	240
220	
	120
1,390	940

  a)   **WE** get 70 points below the line for a successful contract of 2 No Trumps.
  b)   **THEY** make 4 hearts doubled giving them 240 points below the line and a 50 points bonus above the line. Game line is drawn.
  c)   **THEY** go one off in 3 No Trumps. **THEY** score nothing. **WE** score 100 points for one undertrick, vulnerable.
  d)   **WE** score 220 points below the line for 7 No Trumps. Game line is drawn. **WE** also score 1,000 points above the line for a Grand Slam not vulnerable.
  e)   They score 120 points below the line for 4 spades and 30 points above the line as an overtrick. This gives them rubber by two games to one so that 500 points are scored above the line.

It is interesting to see that **THEY** win the rubber by two games to one but **WE** win on points.

Suit Yourself

SECTION SEVEN: IN HAND

a) The cards drawn meant that Alison and June were partners, and Mary and Christine formed the other pair.

b) Dealer for the first hand is the person who draws the highest card – this was Alison. We now know the positions around the table: South – Alison, West – Christine, North – June, East – Mary.

c) South – Alison, bid 1 No Trump showing a balanced hand with 12–14 points. She went to 3 No Trumps, because of a maximum in the range, which means that she had 14 points. We also know that Alison is the declarer so it is the declarer's hand that we are trying to work out.

d) West shuffled the cards and therefore West had the ace of diamonds. East cut the cards and therefore East had the ace of clubs.

e) We can also eliminate the 5 of hearts and the 13 cards in dummy from Alison's hand.

f) Alison's hand contains three spades, one of which is the ace of spades because the king and queen are in dummy.

g) Alison's hand contains three diamonds, one of which is the queen of diamonds, as the ace is held by West and the king is in dummy.

h) Alison's hand contains three clubs, two of which are the queen of clubs and jack of clubs, as the ace is held by East and the king and 10 are in dummy.

i) The distribution is 3 spades, 3 diamonds, 3 clubs and therefore 4 hearts. The four cards definitely identified are the ace of spades, the queen of diamonds, the queen of clubs and the jack of clubs. The high-card points total is 14 and the four cards identified account for 9 of them. There are 5 points still to place.

j) Alison and June made their contract plus one overtrick. They therefore made ten tricks in total.

k) Three of the ten tricks are accounted for and we can place the 10 and 7 in Alison's hand as the two spades not identified so far.

l) Three more of the ten tricks are accounted for and we know that the third club in Alison's hand was the 7.

m) The other two diamonds in Alison's hand are the 9 and 8. Eight of the ten tricks are accounted for, so the other two tricks were made in hearts.

n) The low heart must be the 3 (2 tricks + 1). The only card value appearing in both spades and clubs is 7 and therefore the next lowest heart is the 7.

o) The two remaining cards are hearts. We have still to identify 5 of the 14 high-card points. Therefore these last two cards are the king of hearts and the queen of hearts (the jack is in the dummy).

Alison's hand can now be written down:

A	10	7	
K	Q	7	3
Q	9	8	
Q	J	7	

Section 4

Lateral Thinking

Einstein might, in some people's mind, be the very personification of logic, yet he believed that the key to learning was, in fact, flexible thinking. A quote from Einstein, spotted in the programme of the Royal Shakespeare Company's production of *Beauty and the Beast*, might surprise many readers:

 If you want your children to be intelligent, read them fairy tales. If you want them to be very intelligent, read them more fairy tales.

It was Edward de Bono who made 'lateral thinking' famous. In *Po: Beyond Yes and No* (Pelican, 1973) he said:

The word lateral implies moving sideways from established ways of looking at things to find new ways. … Lateral thinking is not for building on ideas but for restructuring them.
(page 72)

Edward de Bono was frustrated by the limitations of logical thinking but still recognized its strong merits. What he was against was the exclusivity of logical thinking. More tools were needed in the thinking armoury. In recent years, Edward de Bono likened the situation to a car with four wheels. One wheel, or type of thinking, was not enough in itself. To function properly, the car needed four wheels all operating well.

At first he struggled with the phraseology, toying with the label of 'creative thinking', but felt that it was not quite right even though lateral thinking is creative.

To be able to think differently is important in solving problems. Designers and innovators need to plough a new furrow. Criminal investigations sometimes come to a dead end and a new approach is required. Mathematical and scientific problems often require a new line of direction. Crossword solvers often have to think laterally to work out the meaning of cryptic clues. Symbolism is often a linked feature. The English section of the National Curriculum 1999 talks of the need to 'look for meaning beyond the literal'.

- **'Life's Little Mysteries'** presents seven contrasting situations with a question to be answered. The given facts cannot be contradicted but pupils are encouraged to think laterally and 'fill in the gaps' with additional points that are not ruled out by the original data. They are also encouraged to look for several solutions and to prioritize them. 'Fluency', seeking more than a single answer, allows choice to follow. It is also highly beneficial in real-life situations where a problem is being tackled.

- It is appropriate that **'England Expects'** was written in 2005, the 200th anniversary of the Battle of Trafalgar, as the starting point is Horatio Nelson's famous statement 'England expects every man will do his duty'. Within the 40 very varied 'expects' children have a wide choice, with the opportunity for some creative thinking. They are urged not to be too literal in their responses.

As suggested above, Edward de Bono considered seriously the term 'creative thinking'. The three pieces that follow certainly fit into that category. They are also particularly suitable for those children who enjoy a visual thinking style.

- **'In My Mind's Eye'** asks students to work out the meanings of 45 sayings, expressions and terms by studying visual representations. They certainly need to think laterally. There is a wide cross-curricular spread with eight general expressions, nine mathematical terms or sayings that have a mathematical content, nine scientific examples, three terms from art, three examples from the Bible, four events in history, four examples from literature and five geographical terms. As the visual representations are in mixed-up order, the challenge is increased considerably. Flexible thinking and good working methods are very important to success.

- **'The Crustacean of Fashion'** has similar features with children looking at 11 pictures drawn by Carly Cartoon, working out which signs they represent and why they are misleading in their existing format. Many able children, with their particular sense of humour, will delight in the entertaining representations.

- The theme of pictorial representation is continued with **'No Words Needed'**. Logos are the central feature of this piece. First, children are asked to think laterally to interpret given, made-up logos and to suggest which group is likely to use such a logo. Then they have the chance to create ten of their own for stated groups, companies, charities and businesses.

LIFE'S LITTLE MYSTERIES

There are times when you come across situations that are puzzling and where the answer is not immediately obvious. More than that, there may well be more than one possible answer. Perhaps not all the facts are known. So, put your thinking caps on as you ponder 'Life's Little Mysteries'.

Your Tasks
1. Study the seven situations described below.
2. Find an answer or, better than that, more than one answer for each one. You must not contradict any of the given facts but you are entitled to add-in extra points. Be creative and imaginative but make your answers realistic.

A THEATRICAL CASE

It was a special day at the Theatre Royal. The visiting celebrity company was staging a trio of linked-theme plays in the one day. Duty manager, Jamila Darweish, was excited about the programme, even if it was going to be a tiring day.

The morning audience was only moderate in number, as you might expect. Among those in the dress circle was a middle-aged couple. Jamila noticed that the man carried a black document case. This caused some difficulty when the couple sat down in the front row. Eventually the man jammed the case under the protective rail.

The couple were back for the afternoon performance. Jamila was surprised to see the man struggle again with the document case. Why had he brought it again? Why had he not used the cloakroom to deposit the case?

Intrigued, Jamila waited for the evening to see if the couple would return. Yes they did, and so did the case, despite the obvious discomfort that it caused.

★ Why did the theatregoer bring his problem case three times in the day and keep it with him throughout the performances despite the nuisance value?

THE LIKELY VISIT

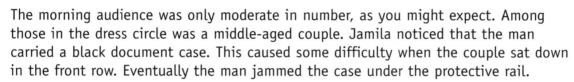

Janice looked anxiously down the list. She had already crossed off mustard and plum. So far she had not visited the kitchen nor seen the cook. Janice knew that she had yet to look in on the dining-room. 'Was the candlestick correctly placed?' she wondered. There was more work to do on the list she had before her.

★ Can you explain what Janice was doing?

MISSING HOUSES

Postwoman Lettice Mail looked at the houses in front of her on Dyson Avenue. On her right the houses started 2, 4, 6, 8, 10, 12, 14, 16 as she would have expected. As she looked at the row of houses on her left, Lettice's face had a frown upon it. In order, the numbers were 1, 5, 7, 9, 11, 15 and 17. Lettice looked at the rather different appearance of 1 Dyson Avenue and then at the identically looking buildings further along.

Problem-solving and Thinking Skills Resources for Able and Talented Children
© Barry Teare (Network Continuum Education, 2006)

★ Why was Lettice puzzled? Can you find an explanation as to what she saw along the odd-numbered side of Dyson Avenue?

THE TRAIN NOW STANDING AT PLATFORM FIVE

Mr Tucker arrived at the railway station carrying a small suitcase. He asked at the information desk about the train that was to arrive from Penzance and then journey on to London Paddington. He crossed the passenger footbridge and walked onto Platform Five. There he used the colour coding on the edge of the platform so as to be level with where coaches F and G would halt.

The train pulled into the station on time. Mr Tucker allowed three passengers to alight from the train. Then he entered Coach F, had a quick look around and then got off the train again. Mr Tucker made his way back to the main entrance to the station and left.

★ Can you explain Mr Tucker's rather strange behaviour?

SHORT AND SWEET

A hush settled over the hall. The Secretary of State for Education got up to address the conference of some 450 headteachers. You could feel the tension in the air. 'I have nothing to say' said the Secretary of State and then she sat down. After a short silence, wild applause broke out throughout the audience.

★ Why did such a short speech cause a very enthusiastic response?

TRY THIS FOR SIZE

The sales assistants on the counter at the famous store were trained to read out the sizes of clothes to the customers before a purchase was completed. This was to avoid customers buying the wrong size by mistake.

On one Tuesday in January, the sales assistant served a customer who handed over three pairs of trousers at the counter. To her surprise she found that the man had three identical pairs of trousers in terms of style, colour and material but the sizes were different. All three pairs were 31 inside leg but the waist sizes were 38, 40 and 42. The sales assistant pointed this out to the customer but he confirmed that he wanted to purchase the three differently sized pairs of trousers.

★ Can you explain why the customer should want to buy three pairs of trousers identical in every respect apart from the waist size?

BARGE IN

Lucy Weller was taking a walk alongside the canal in Wigan. As she approached the Waterside Centre along the tow path, she saw a barge on the canal, tied up by a rope. Lucy looked at the attractive barge and saw the name. She was somewhat surprised to see the name on the side of the barge – 'Viktoria'.

★ Why was Lucy surprised by the name? Have you an explanation as to why it was exactly that?

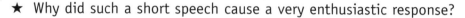

LIFE'S LITTLE MYSTERIES

Teaching Notes

These varied situations give the opportunity to exercise a number of thinking skills.

Key Elements

- ❖ lateral thinking
- ❖ alternative answers
- ❖ deduction
- ❖ inference
- ❖ fluency – seeking more than a single answer
- ❖ handling data accurately.

Contexts

'Life's Little Mysteries' can be used in the following ways:

- ❖ as 'icebreakers' at the start of a lesson, enrichment session or form period
- ❖ as part of a problem-solving/thinking skills course
- ❖ as an enrichment activity for those who have completed other tasks
- ❖ as differentiated homework
- ❖ as an activity during an enrichment day, weekend or summer school
- ❖ as an open-access competition
- ❖ as 'Question of the Week' on the classroom wall
- ❖ as an activity for the Problem-solvers' Club.

One Particular Working Method

The pupils discuss each situation in groups. They are encouraged to look for more than one answer. The teacher then asks for ideas. Once an idea has been suggested, other pupils are asked whether it works or if there are weaknesses. If weaknesses are identified, the person/group who made the original suggestion is encouraged to develop the idea so as to answer the criticisms. Everybody in the class is involved in thinking critically about the various suggestions. They are then asked to prioritize them in order of strength.

Additional Key Elements with this Method

- ❖ listening carefully
- ❖ thinking critically
- ❖ prioritizing.

Some Answers

For each situation at least one solution is put forward that answers the given facts. However, credit should be given for any suggestion that fits and is realistic.

A Theatrical Case

This is a real-life situation relating to the author himself. Some materials for a new book had been written but they had not, as yet, been put onto the computer. As a consequence, they were the only existing copies and were being carried for security reasons until they could be word-processed. Anything valuable would fit the bill but there may well be other good answers.

The Likely List

A number of details are given. This may lead to all sorts of ingenious solutions. However the facts certainly do fit Janice playing the game 'Cluedo'. The players eliminate suspects, weapons and rooms on a list. Colonel Mustard and Professor Plum are among the suspects as is Mrs White the cook. The kitchen and the dining-room are among nine possible rooms. The candlestick is one of six possible weapons.

MISSING HOUSES

Clearly the postwoman was puzzled because numbers 3 and 13 did not appear. It will be interesting to see whether pupils offer two separate explanations or link the two missing houses in their answers. One possibility is that 13 has not been used because the number is regarded as unlucky. The missing 3 might be for a separate reason. One pointer is that one house looks different from the others. A real-life situation known to the author is a road where there should have been two semi-detached houses numbered 1 and 3. However there was an old pond on that particular part of the land and it was decided that it was too swampy to be used. As a result a gap was left and the houses started with the house numbered 5. At a later date, a couple purchased the land, had it drained and special work was carried out for the foundations. A single, but larger, house was constructed and was given the number 1. As a consequence the numbering jumped from 1 to 5 with the 3 missing.

THE TRAIN NOW STANDING AT PLATFORM FIVE

Just four of a number of possibilities are:

1   Mr Tucker was supposed to be catching the train but something changed his mind. Perhaps he suddenly remembered that he had forgotten something important at home, such as not switching off the oven. Possibly he was to travel with somebody else in Coach F but the person was not there.

2   Mr Tucker was to meet a traveller getting off that particular train but he or she was not there. The small suitcase is then just a coincidence.

3   Mr Tucker is a railway inspector and he was carrying out part of his duties. The small suitcase might be a blind or a cover for his identity, or a coincidence.

4   Mr Tucker was carrying out a 'dummy run' for somebody else, perhaps an elderly mother so as to make sure of the arrangements.

SHORT AND SWEET

One likely possibility is that, after a period of many changes in education, it had been widely forecast that more were on the way. This was expected to be part of the Secretary of State's speech. When invited to tell the delegates about the next changes, she made the surprising announcement that came as welcome relief to the headteachers.

TRY THIS FOR SIZE

It will be very interesting to see what pupils make of this intriguing situation. Three possibilities are:

1   The customer has recently put on a lot of weight. He now wishes to diet and exercise to get back to his earlier size of 38-inch waist. At the moment he is a 42 and he needs a new pair of trousers. The 40 and the 38 are to add impetus to the attempt to lose weight.

2   The customer is now a 38, but he is facing a stomach operation in the future that will leave him very tender for some time. The larger sizes have been advised by the hospital until the operation wound heals and his body returns to its normal state.

3   The customer has family members with similar tastes but different waist sizes; so one pair is for the man himself and the other two are for other people.

BARGE IN

Lucy's surprise was that 'Viktoria' was spelled with a 'k' rather than a 'c' as would be expected. In that case, 'Victoria' might be named after the former queen. This spelling suggests a foreign origin or link. Heavy goods were transported by canal barge from other countries.

England Expects ...

During the Battle of Trafalgar, Viscount Horatio Nelson famously said – 'England expects every man will do his duty'. This has gone down in history as one of the most famous quotations.

Here is your chance to create fictional quotations.

Your Task

For each of the 40 'expects' below, write a suitable ending. The examples are very mixed and include objects, animals, real people and characters from literature. Make your answers appropriate but do not always be too literal. Some responses can be humorous; others might be unusual or, even, surreal. Let your imagination go to create some dramatic images and concepts.

The Starting Points

1 The tax inspector expects ...
2 Professor Dumbledore expects ...
3 The Poet Laureate expects ...
4 The train passenger expects ...
5 Paddington Bear expects ...
6 Picasso expects ...
7 Queen Victoria expects ...
8 Fantastic Mr Fox expects ...
9 The new day expects ...
10 The Martian expects ...
11 The city trader expects ...
12 Charles Dickens expects ...
13 Father Christmas expects ...
14 The hospital patient expects ...
15 The Man in the Moon expects ...
16 The cloned sheep expects ...
17 Beethoven expects ...
18 The negotiator expects ...
19 The Turner Prize judge expects ...
20 The woman on the Clapham omnibus expects ...

21 William Shakespeare expects ...
22 The prevailing wind expects ...
23 The spin doctor expects ...
24 Albert Einstein expects ...
25 Aslan expects ...
26 The child in Africa expects ...
27 The blank canvas expects ...
28 Mother Theresa expects ...
29 The civil servant expects ...
30 Sherlock Holmes expects ...
31 The arms manufacturer expects ...
32 The Asian black bear expects ...
33 The still of the night expects ...
34 Cinderella expects ...
35 The human spirit expects ...
36 The dictionary expects ...
37 The news announcer expects ...
38 The empty bottle expects ...
39 Mr Toad expects ...
40 The next generation expects ...

Extension Task

Create some of your own 'expects' examples. These can be starting points only or they can be complete statements. Try to make the subjects varied and certainly try to include some provocative examples.

Problem-solving and Thinking Skills Resources for Able and Talented Children
© Barry Teare (Network Continuum Education, 2006)

England Expects ...

Teaching Notes

'England Expects ...' covers a number of contrasting areas, including history, literature, art, music, politics and science. Some examples, like Paddington Bear, are light and are likely to produce amusing responses. Others are involved with real, and difficult, issues and are aimed to be thought provoking. The most unusual examples hope to promote imaginative, and even surreal, answers. Children should be encouraged to break away from the restrictions of 'tramlines' and, instead, to think freely and creatively.

Key Elements

- ❖ lateral thinking
- ❖ connections and associations
- ❖ creativity and imagination
- ❖ responding to issues
- ❖ deduction and inference
- ❖ wordplay (for some examples especially)
- ❖ succinct creative writing of a very particular type
- ❖ working in the abstract (for some examples more than others)
- ❖ cross-curricular material.

Extension Task

The examples created by pupils are likely to be even more powerful in illustrating their style of thinking than the original responses. Interesting themes can provide additional material for other children to discuss. At all times, this piece of work should allow the possibility of a number of equally valid answers to be developed from the original ideas.

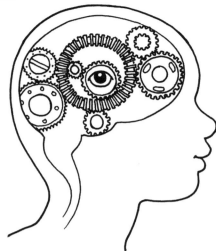

In My Mind's Eye

Information comes to us in many different ways. A good proportion of what we know is the result of visual interpretation. 'In My Mind's Eye' fits into that type of thinking.

Your Task

Work out the meaning of 45 sayings, expressions or terms by studying the visual representations below. You need to use subject knowledge, to look at the position of words and to think laterally about the information provided.

You are looking for (in mixed-up order):

1 Eight general expressions.
2 Nine mathematical terms, or sayings that have a mathematical context.
3 Nine scientific examples.
4 Three terms from art.
5 Three examples from the Bible.
6 Four events in history, one from the seventeenth century, one from the eighteenth century and two from the twentieth century.
7 From the world of literature, a play by William Shakespeare, a novel by Charles Dickens, a fantasy trilogy and a group of characters from a series of children's books.
8 Five geographical terms.

Go on – look at what is in your mind's eye

THE VISUAL REPRESENTATIONS

1   **rain   wind   sun**
         feel

2   *sound sound sound sound*

3   **atpollion**

4   **NOAH**

5   spring   plumber
     summer   nurse
     autumn   decorator
     winter   shop assistant

6   **sense 5 : 2**

7

DEPRESSION

8
well-known
well-known
well-known
well-known
well-known

9 **purple (3, 4)**

10 **carb**
dioxide

11 M5 M5 M5 M4 M4 M4 M4 M4 M4 M5 M5 M5

12
| GERMANYRUSSIA |
| GERMANYRUSSIA |
| GERMANYRUSSIA |
| GERMANYRUSSIA |
| GERMANYRUSSIA |
| GERMANYRUSSIA |
| GERMANYRUSSIA |

13 **mandogger**

14 ● **illism**

15 thefrenchthefrenchthefrenchthefrench

16 myself - - - & - - - ♀

17 6 (no) 23 (no) 57 (no)

18 **set → land**

19 give him
give him
give him
give him

20 **N ♥ S**

In My Mind's Eye

21

22
do	don't
don't	do
do	don't
don't	do
do	don't

23 **gniog**

24 **2379651 x**
   7182392
   _____
   _____

25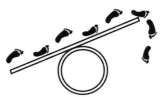

26

27   paying
   1 3 5 7 9

28 **li** _ _

29 **2kg 4 2kg**

30 chemical cmiehlac

31
| r   g |
| a |
| p   h |

32 showing l~~ies~~   red
                        blue
                        yellow
                        green

33 so nice to see you

hope you are well

34   _____
        stream

35

36 com   m   o
              o   c   m
          c

37 **computter**

38 **v biotics**

39

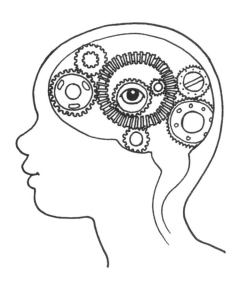

40 f o o d

41 **religious address**
   mount

42 **1 farmer**
   2 machine worker
   3 teacher

43 **s m l g**
   a i n p

44 **i s o**

45 **Caligula Nero inch pint pound**

Extension Task

Design some examples of your own.
You can concentrate upon a subject area that interests you or select items from a variety of subjects.

In My Mind's Eye

Teaching Notes

'In My Mind's Eye' will appeal to able pupils who like to think laterally and to interpret visual information. Flexible thinking is very important to success.

Key Elements

- ❖ lateral thinking
- ❖ interpretation of visual information
- ❖ analysis
- ❖ wordplay
- ❖ subject-specific vocabulary from English, mathematics, art, science, history, geography and religious education
- ❖ classification
- ❖ process of elimination
- ❖ imagination and creativity (in the extension task).

Contexts

'In My Mind's Eye' can be used in the following ways:

- ❖ particular examples in appropriate curriculum lessons
- ❖ as part of a study skills or thinking skills course
- ❖ as differentiated homework
- ❖ as an enrichment activity for those who have completed other work
- ❖ as an activity during an enrichment day, weekend or summer school
- ❖ as an open-access competition, with the extension task as a discriminator where necessary.

Solution

NOTE: latitude should be given for alternative, appropriate answers, so long as they fit the data.

1	feel under the weather	(general)
2	sound wave	(science)
3	pollination	(science)
4	Noah's Ark	(religious education/the Bible) (has mathematical connections)
5	seasonal jobs	(geography)
6	a sense of proportion	(mathematics)
7	the Great Depression	(history)
8	The Famous Five	(literature)
9	colour co-ordinated	(mathematics)
10	carbon dioxide	(science)
11	crossroads	(general)
12	the Nazi–Soviet Pact	(history)

In My Mind's Eye

13	dog in the manger	(general)
14	pointillism	(art)
15	the French Revolution	(history)
16	meander	(geography)
17	negative numbers	(mathematics)
18	set-aside land	(geography)
19	forgive him	(general)
20	opposite poles attract	(science)
21	keep in perspective	(art)
22	the Ten Commandments	(religious education/the Bible)
23	going backwards	(general)
24	*Hard Times*	(literature – Charles Dickens)
25	going off at a tangent	(mathematics)
26	*Lord of the Rings*	(literature – J.R. Tolkein)
27	paying over the odds	(mathematics)
28	half-life	(science)
29	*Measure for Measure*	(literature – William Shakespeare)
30	chemical change	(science)
31	scatter graph	(mathematics)
32	showing one's true colours	(general)
33	the Civil War	(history)
34	streamlined	(general) (has scientific connections)
35	filtering	(science)
36	composition	(art)
37	computer error	(general)
38	antibiotics	(science)
39	square roots	(mathematics)
40	food chain	(science)
41	Sermon on the Mount	(religious education/the Bible)
42	primary, secondary and tertiary occupations	(geography)
43	random sampling	(mathematics)
44	isobar	(geography)
45	imperial units	(mathematics)

The Crustacean of Fashion

Everywhere around us are signs. Most of them are clear and straightforward. However, for those with a particular sense of humour, some signs conjure up wonderfully entertaining pictures. Such a person is Carly Cartoon, who has converted some signs into amusing, pictorial interpretations.

See if you can get inside Carly Cartoon's mind!

Your Tasks

1 Look at the 11 pictures drawn by Carly Cartoon.
2 For each one: a) write down what the sign would actually say
                   b) describe what is misleading about Carly's interpretation
                   c) explain what the sign really means.
3 Decide which of these pictures is linked to the title of this piece.

THE PICTURES

Extension Tasks

1 Look about you, at the shops, on the roads, in your school and anywhere else. Discover other signs that can be misinterpreted.
2 Draw the pictures to illustrate the signs.
3 Write down, for each one, what the sign says, how the picture is misleading and what the sign really means.

Problem-solving and Thinking Skills Resources for Able and Talented Children
© Barry Teare (Network Continuum Education, 2006)

The Crustacean of Fashion

Teaching Notes

This is a light, fun piece for able pupils to enjoy. So many able children have a particular sense of humour that delights in word humour and second meanings.

Key Elements
- wordplay
- word humour
- visual interpretation
- lateral thinking
- imagination and creativity (especially in the extension tasks)
- drawing of a particular type (in the extension task).

Contexts
'The Crustacean of Fashion' can be used in the following ways:
- as extension work in lessons concerning wordplay
- as a particular exercise in art lessons
- as an enrichment activity for those who have completed other tasks
- as differentiated homework
- as an activity during an enrichment day, weekend or summer school
- as an open-access competition, where the extension tasks would act as discriminators
- as an activity for the English Club or Society, or the Art Club

The Solution
1. a) Clocks 25% off.
   b) You lose a quarter of the clock.
   c) Clocks are being sold at a discount.
2. a) Horse trials.
   b) The animals are in court on charges.
   c) The horses are involved in competitions, demonstrating their skills.
3. a) Lamb going cheap.
   b) Sheep have changed their cries from 'baa' to 'cheep'.
   c) There is a reduction in the price of lamb.
4. a) Heavy plant crossing.
   b) A large plant has left the garden and is crossing the road.
   c) Large machines and vehicles may be encountered as they cross the road ahead.
5. a) Traffic calming.
   b) Vehicles are being soothed.
   c) There are features such as bumps in the road to deliberately slow traffic down.
6. a) Dressed crab.
   b) The crab likes to wear clothes.
   c) The crab is prepared for sale by the fishmonger.
7. a) All-day breakfast.
   b) The breakfast is so large that it will take you all day to eat it.
   c) Breakfast is available at any time of the day.
8. a) Closed for bank holiday.
   b) The bank has gone on its holiday.
   c) Most businesses, including banks, are closed for days at Christmas, Easter, and in August and May.
9. a) Police slow.
   b) Police personnel or vehicles are moving at a very leisurely pace, or have been ordered to do so.
   c) The police are telling motorists to go slow because of some hazard.
10. a) Cured meat.
    b) The animals have been made healthy again.
    c) Meat has been cooked and processed in a particular way to preserve it (salting, smoking or pickling).
11. a) Bridle path.
    b) A route for a woman on her wedding day.
    c) A track suitable for riding or leading horses.

It is, of course, **'Dressed Crab'** that is linked to the title **'The Crustacean of Fashion'**.

Problem-solving and Thinking Skills Resources for Able and Talented Children

1/2

N O W O R D S N E E D E D

Many companies, charities, schools and organizations use a logo – an emblem that catches the eye and conveys a visual message as to their core purpose or activity. A logo provides a quick and dramatic method of conveying information. Interpretation and creation of logos involves careful analysis of the intended visual message.

An American publishing company, Corwin Press, uses as its logo a raven striding across an open book. The explanation given is that the logo 'represents the happy union of courage and learning' and these qualities are at the heart of the company's publications.

Now, how well do you operate when no words are needed?

TASK ONE

The author carries out a number of activities linked to able and talented children – training teachers, running enrichment courses and writing suitable materials. The logo to the right was designed for his business. What do you think are the messages conveyed and why has it been chosen for the author's business?

TASK TWO

Below and opposite there are ten logos. Study each of them in turn and then write down what they convey to you and which group of people is likely to use such a logo. Do not stop at one answer. Write down a number of explanations where you believe that there are alternative interpretations.

NOTE: These logos are made up. Any similarity to existing logos, actually used by groups of people, is coincidental and should not influence interpretation.

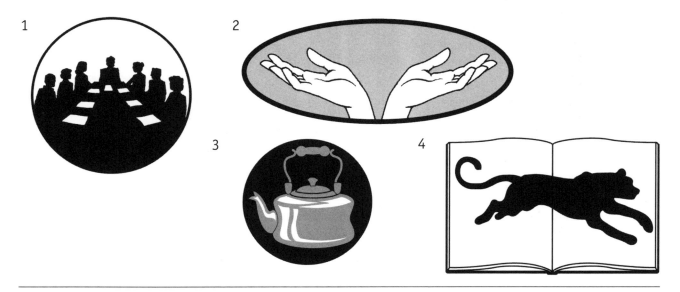

1

2

3

4

Problem-solving and Thinking Skills Resources for Able and Talented Children

5

6

7

8

9

10

TASK THREE

For each of the groups, companies, charities and businesses below, design a suitable logo.

1. An association of architects.
2. A publisher specializing in garden books.
3. An angling club in Scotland.
4. A charity looking after stray cats and dogs.
5. A sports and leisure centre.
6. A chain of theatres.
7. An association of organic farmers.
8. A charity working for people with sight problems.
9. A company promoting meditation and relaxation.
10. An amateur art society.

NO WORDS NEEDED

Teaching Notes

'No Words Needed' looks at the fascinating world of logos. It will be appreciated particularly by pupils who have a strong visual intelligence, although strength in interpretation may not be matched in creation of logos and vice-versa.

Key Elements

- ❖ visual interpretation
- ❖ symbolic thinking
- ❖ lateral thinking
- ❖ alternative answers
- ❖ creativity and imagination
- ❖ succinct visual presentation
- ❖ design.

Contexts

'No Words Needed' can be used in a number of ways:

- ❖ as classwork in English, art or media studies, where differentiation by outcome will operate
- ❖ as enrichment work for those who have completed other tasks
- ❖ as differentiated homework
- ❖ as an activity during an enrichment session, cluster day or summer school
- ❖ as an open-access competition.

Answers

There cannot be any set answers. Many different responses could be equally valid. Certain success criteria are likely to be important:

TASKS ONE AND TWO

- ❖ the quality of the analysis of the pictorial material
- ❖ the level of fluency – the number of appropriate alternative answers
- ❖ the degree to which the interpretation is conveyed within the written responses.

TASK THREE

- ❖ the creativity and originality displayed
- ❖ the suitability for the group to be represented
- ❖ the clarity of the message conveyed in what has to be a simple format.

Section 5

Prediction

Predicting the future fascinates many people. Being as accurate as possible can bring many benefits beyond the fanciful wish to know the National Lottery winning numbers in advance! Seeing patterns enhances the chances of predicting correctly the consequences of decisions; all of our actions and decisions have consequences. Predicting is an essential element in problem solving. If a particular route is taken, will it achieve the desired outcome? Is it the best route? What side effects might there be of the decision? This can never be exact, as predicting the consequences of actions and decisions must be based upon the strength of probabilities rather than upon certainties.

Prediction should be based upon existing evidence. What is it that is already known? Are there lessons to be learned from other examples? Has the scenario got similarities with other situations? All three of the higher-order thinking skills are involved. Predicting and hypothesizing are part of synthesis, a thinking skill that is also involved because sense needs to be made of data from different sources. Thinking about a changed situation requires analysis of existing information to be able to predict the outcome. The third higher-order thinking skill then comes into play, as evaluation occurs – making a judgement or forming an opinion based upon existing information.

Predicting plays an important role in a number of curriculum areas, including the subjects linked to the following quotations from the National Curriculum 1999:

 … use their knowledge of sequence and story language when they are retelling stories and predicting events.
(English)

 … considering alternatives and anticipating consequences. 99
(English)

 … decide whether the conclusions agree with any prediction made and/or whether they enable further predictions to be made. 99
(science)

 … that it is important to test explanations by using them to make predictions and by seeing if evidence matches to predictions. 99
(science)

 … recognize simple spatial patterns and relationships and make predictions about them.
(mathematics)

 … to use simulations and explore models in order to answer What if …? questions. 99
(information and communication technology)

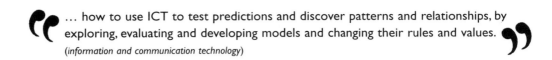

... how to use ICT to test predictions and discover patterns and relationships, by exploring, evaluating and developing models and changing their rules and values.
(*information and communication technology*)

Certainly, linked to the final two quotes are models trying to predict the future in situations such as climate change.

- **'Crystal Ball'** places ten major areas of public interest in front of children, asks them to research one or more of them, based upon existing evidence and consideration of trends and patterns, and make predictions as to what is going to happen one year from now, five years from now and 100 years from now.

- 'What if?' and 'What if not?' questions have been promoted to stimulate high-quality thinking by able children in a variety of subjects. This is very much the basis of **'Let Us Suppose...'**. The situations chosen cover many areas – citizenship, mathematics, science, politics, art and the environment.

- **'Final Curtain'** is a very substantial piece of work. The theatre murder context makes the tasks extremely enjoyable. Synthesis of various sources is an important ingredient. Various methods can be used, including an active team format involving crime squads. After analysis of the data and evaluation of the evidence, pupils are asked to predict a sensational development later in the investigation and also the verdict at the trial.

There are many examples of people trying to predict the future. A French physician and astrologer called Nostradamus became famous for his controversial prophecies. Another well-known example was the oracle at Delphi, in ancient Greece. Both made ambiguous predictions that could be interpreted in different ways.

Fêtes and fairs often include a fortune teller among the attractions. For a small fee people can have their fortunes predicted via the use of a crystal ball or the reading of the palms of the hands. Tea leaves in cups are also used. These methods are mainly for fun and should not be taken too seriously.

However there are more substantial attempts to predict the future. Journalists discuss likely developments in their particular area. Scientists model the future on computers to try to look at the consequences of global warming. Politicians try to assess how the electors would react to proposed policies. In these cases the predictions are based upon existing knowledge and past experience.

Here is your chance to predict the future. Rather than rely upon the mystical and mythical 'crystal ball', use what you already know in prophesizing what will happen.

Your Tasks

1 Choose one or more of the ten areas listed below.
2 Research the areas through books and the internet.
3 Make predictions as to what is going to happen:
   a) one year from now; **b)** five years from now; **c)** 100 years from now.
4 Give explanations as to the reasons for your predictions.

The Ten Areas

1 Food and drink
2 Technology
3 Clothes
4 The planet
5 The British Royal Family

6 Popular entertainment
7 Transport
8 Medicine
9 The political situation in Britain
10 Sport

Crystal Ball

Teaching Notes

'Crystal Ball' is very much concerned with the higher-order thinking skills of hypothesizing and prediction. Children should be encouraged to base their views upon existing knowledge and likely developments, rather than fanciful methods that have no validity.

Key Elements

- change and continuity
- hypothesizing
- prediction
- synthesis
- analysis
- use of existing data
- research
- creativity and imagination but based upon clear thinking.

Contexts

'Crystal Ball' can be used in the following ways:

- as part of a thinking skills course
- as part of general thinking within history courses
- as an enrichment activity for those who have completed other tasks
- as differentiated homework
- as part of normal lessons where an individual item is selected
- as an activity on an enrichment day, weekend or summer school
- as an open-access competition.

Practical Notes

1   The students' sheet suggests that a choice of one or more from the ten is made. This is an arbitrary suggestion. Teachers can alter that instruction to suit their purposes.

2   Areas have been left as large general themes deliberately to allow students to tackle the topic in their own individual way. That, in itself, is instructive.

Success Criteria

It is difficult to lay down a tight assessment scheme for such a piece of work. The following success criteria are, however, likely to be important:

- the extent to which existing situations have been analysed
- the creativity and imagination displayed within a realistic framework
- the quality of the research undertaken
- the appreciation of the pace of change and, therefore, the likely differences between one year, five years and 100 years
- the recognition that some things will change but others are constant
- the understanding shown of the complexity of some issues, and the possibility of various directions of future developments in a given area.

Let Us Suppose ...

Speculating or hypothesizing involves many skills when given serious consideration. Thinking about a changed situation requires analysis of existing information to be able to predict the outcome. People often speculate on what might have happened to them personally if they had taken a different decision or option.

Your Task

For each of the following situations, get into the mindset of predicting what might happen if a key factor changed. Let your imagination run but remember to give proper consideration to existing information.

Let us suppose ...

1 that a law was passed forbidding cars being driven without at least one passenger in addition to the driver.
2 that there was no zero in our number system.
3 that locusts became carnivorous.
4 that Britain moved to a system of proportional representation.
5 that there was a cheap and effective method of extracting salt from sea water.
6 that the dates of birth and the birthplaces of Lowry and Picasso were reversed.
7 that footballers were not allowed to earn more than teachers, nurses, fire fighters and police officers.
8 that each person could make only five journeys by aeroplane during his or her lifetime, to reduce pollution.
9 that the countries of western Europe left the present European Union and formed a new economic community.
10 that vast new gold reserves were discovered.
11 that there was a binding referendum on the reintroduction of capital punishment.
12 that the age for retirement was increased to 70.
13 that the maximum rate of income tax was restricted to 25 per cent.
14 that smoking was limited to one's own home.
15 that only women could inherit property.
16 that a programme of planting doubled the number of hedgerows.
17 that there was a 9p.m. curfew for those under the age of 18.
18 that political leaders undertook television interviews under lie detector conditions.
19 that no new roads were constructed.
20 that Parliament and all government departments moved from London to Newcastle upon Tyne.
21 that all computers crashed irreversibly.

Extension Task

Create some 'Let Us Suppose...' examples of your own.

Let Us Suppose...

Teaching Notes

Many 'what if?' or 'just imagine' exercises include situations that involve evaluation. 'What if you were able to resurrect one person from history to run your country?' would be an example. 'Let Us Suppose...' concentrates upon prediction. Good answers necessarily involve consideration of much existing information.

Key Elements

- ❖ prediction
- ❖ hypothesizing
- ❖ research
- ❖ analysis of existing information
- ❖ synthesis
- ❖ logical thinking
- ❖ lateral thinking.

Contexts

'Let Us Suppose ...' can be used in a variety of ways:

- ❖ individually as extension work to particular subject-based topics
- ❖ as discussion material in normal lessons
- ❖ as enrichment material for those who have completed other work
- ❖ as differentiated homework
- ❖ as topics for the Debating Society
- ❖ as an activity during an enrichment day, weekend or summer school
- ❖ as an open-access competition.

Answers

There can be no set, prescribed answers although, for each situation, there will be a number of factors that a good response would include. Relevant research is required.

Example: 'Let Us Suppose' that the maximum rate of income tax was restricted to 25 per cent.

Research is needed on the various rates in present use, the total taken by all taxes and the different elements of source. Two routes are then possible. Either the additional revenue is abandoned and there are serious consequences for the provision of services and public expenditure, or, more likely, the Treasury would want to retain a similar level of revenue. In this case the shortfall has to be made good by an increase in other existing taxes or by the introduction of new taxes.

Some of the suggestions are highly controversial and should spark lively debate. A 9p.m. curfew for the under-18s is likely to stir up the emotions. How will boys react to the notion of female-only inheritance? It should be an interesting discussion!

Final Curtain

At the end of the rehearsal period for a play or musical, a dress rehearsal is held before the production is put in front of a paying audience. For director Colin Brown the dress rehearsal for 'What's Your Poison?' turned out to be his 'final curtain'. The fictional whodunnit turned out to be a real whodunnit for, during dress rehearsal at the Theatre Royal in York Street, Colin Brown was murdered.

Enquiries are at a reasonably early stage but, already, there is substantial evidence to study. As a consequence, the crime squad has arrested Bryony Green for the murder of Colin Brown. Can you predict what the verdict of the court will be?

Your Tasks

1 Study all the evidence that has been gathered from a variety of sources.
   (a) The Cast List for 'What's Your Poison?'
   (b) The Costume List for 'What's Your Poison?'
   (c) Summary of the script for 'What's Your Poison?'
   (d) The plan of the Theatre Royal.
   (e) Norset County Constabulary Report Form from PC Wilkins.
   (f) Norset County Constabulary Pathology Report Form from Dr J. Peterson.
   (g) Description of the forensic evidence.
   (h) Transcript of a taped interview between theatre critic Ashley Harrison and PC Dent.
   (i) Written information from Margaret Dancy of Many Parts Theatrical Agency.

2 Consider the significance of that evidence and how it all adds to the total picture.

3 Put together two written statements drawing upon the detailed evidence. One is to show what you predict the main arguments at Bryony Green's trial will be from the Defence Counsel, trying to prove her innocence. The second is to outline the main points against Bryony Green as likely to be used by the Prosecution Counsel.

4 In constructing the two statements, you will find it helpful to consider the following points:
   (a) MOTIVE – which people had reason to kill Colin Brown?
   (b) OPPORTUNITY – who could have killed Colin Brown, bearing in mind the critical period during which the murder occurred and the location of the suspects?
   (c) PRIME SUSPECTS – does the evidence point to Bryony Green being the main suspect? Is anybody else an equally strong suspect?
   (d) STRENGTH OF EVIDENCE – does the evidence fit together? Are there gaps? Are there conflicts? Is some evidence of no consequence?

5 There was a sensational development later in the investigation. From the evidence, predict what that was.

6 Predict the verdict at the trial of Bryony Green. Was she found 'Guilty' or 'Not guilty'? Explain, in detail, why you have reached that conclusion. Remember that the defendant has to be proved guilty beyond reasonable doubt.

Success Criteria

You accounts and the predictions will have regard to:

★ the clarity of the written statements
★ the care taken in examining the evidence to get full meaning from it
★ the degree to which deductions from different pieces of evidence have been brought together
★ the quality of the conclusions reached
★ the degree to which gaps and doubts have been identified.

Problem-solving and Thinking Skills Resources for Able and Talented Children
© Barry Teare (Network Continuum Education, 2006)

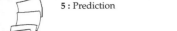
 Final Curtain

Theatre Royal

What's Your Poison?

CAST LIST

JASON COLLINS, a successful businessman   ROBERT MORRISON

JUDITH COLLINS, wife of Jason   DONNA HARGREAVES

FRANK COLLINS, Jason's younger brother   MICHAEL MERCHANT

GRACE SEABROOK, Personal Assistant to Jason   BRYONY GREEN

STEWART DANCE, a friend of the Collins family   GEORGE HOBBS

OLIVER BRAND, a rival businessman   DAVID HERBERT

HARRY BETWOOD, a financial consultant   SIMON TRAIN

PRODUCTION TEAM

DIRECTOR   COLIN BROWN

DESIGNER   SUSAN DAVIES

COSTUMES   ANGELA BLUNT

SOUND   HILARY MOON

LIGHTING   BERNARD GRIFFIN

Problem-solving and Thinking Skills Resources for Able and Talented Children
© Barry Teare (Network Continuum Education, 2006)

Costume list for the production of 'What's Your Poison?'

Robert Morrison playing JASON COLLINS
Act One Scene One — Dark navy suit, white shirt, red tie, black shoes
Act One Scene Two — Ditto
Act Two Scene One — Ditto
Act One Scene Three — Blue short-sleeved shirt, grey trousers, no tie, black casual shoes
Act Two Scene Two — Red silk shirt, navy trousers, smart black shoes

Donna Hargreaves playing JUDITH COLLINS
Act One Scene One — Light blue blouse, navy blue trousers, white casual shoes
Act Two Scene One — Ditto
Act One Scene Three — Green dress with white collar and cuffs, a white belt, smart white evening shoes
Act Two Scene Two — Dark blue trouser suit, navy blue high-heeled shoes

Michael Merchant playing FRANK COLLINS
Act One Scene One — Blue casual shirt, yellow golf jumper, blue trousers, black and grey shoes, a blue golf cap
Act One Scene Three — White shirt, dark green trousers, brown shoes
Act Two Scene One — as Act One, Scene One but no cap
Act Two Scene Two — Beige shirt, light brown trousers, brown shoes

Bryony Green playing GRACE SEABROOK
Act One Scene Two — Black ladies suit, white blouse, black high-heeled shoes
Act Two Scene One — Ditto
Act Two Scene Two — Green evening dress, green high-heeled shoes
Act Two Scene Three — Dark blue top and rough trousers – 'prison garb'

George Hobbs playing STEWART DANCE
Act One Scene Three — A blue-and-white striped shirt, red tie, dark-grey trousers, black shoes
Act Two Scene One — Charcoal-grey business suit, white shirt, blue tie, black shoes
Act Two Scene Two — White shirt, black trousers, black shoes

David Herbert playing OLIVER BRAND
Act One Scene Two — Dark-blue pin-striped suit, white shirt, blue tie, black shoes
Act Two Scene One — Ditto
Act Two Scene Two — Yellow shirt, brown cravat, brown checked trousers, brown shoes

Simon Train playing HARRY BETWOOD
Act One Scene Two — Medium-blue suit, blue shirt, red tie, black shoes
Act Two Scene One — Ditto
Act Two Scene Two — White shirt, blue tie, black trousers, black shoes

Final Curtain

Summary of the script for 'What's Your Poison?'

ACT ONE

Scene One

The lounge of the Collins' home. It is smartly and expensively furnished. It is mid-morning on a warm, fine day in May. The sunny weather is not matched by the atmosphere in the room.

Jason Collins is preparing to go to his office. He has had a loud argument with his wife Judith who accuses him of ignoring his family and of being totally engrossed in work. During the row, Frank Collins enters the room. He is dressed to play golf, wearing a golf cap and carrying a golf glove. Frank takes offence at the tone of Jason's comments to Judith, a woman he much admires. Jason vents his anger upon his younger brother, accusing him of being idle and useless. The older man is keeping Frank financially and wants to see him secure decent employment.

The ringing of the telephone interrupts the heated exchanges. Grace Seabrook has called to ask if Jason will be long as he has important visitors in his office. Jason is extremely unpleasant with Grace, even though she is only doing her job.

Scene Two

The city office of Jason Collins and the administrative centre of his profitable quarrying company. There is evidence everywhere of the latest technology.

Grace Seabrook is entertaining Oliver Brand and financial consultant Harry Betwood. She is not in the best of moods having just been insulted by her boss. Oliver tries to cheer her up by commenting upon her reputation within the industry for efficient, hard work and good organization. These sentiments are supported by Harry Betwood who has a high regard for Grace's work. She is pleased by their remarks but still complains about the way she is treated, almost like a slave.

Jason Collins then arrives. He is gruff and rather unwelcoming to the two men. Before they get down to business, Jason gives Grace a tremendously long list of tasks with rather unrealistic deadlines. She raises her eyes to the ceiling and grimaces at Oliver Brand as she leaves the room.

The meeting concerns a possible joint enterprise between Jason Collins and Oliver Brand. This had occurred as a result of some preliminary investigation by Oliver. Harry Betwood had been brought in to carry out a more detailed survey. All this becomes clear at the start of the meeting.

Jason shocks Oliver and Harry by explaining that he has now arranged to undertake the work through his own company alone. Oliver complains that Jason has stolen the business opportunity. Equally, Harry is very upset because he has undertaken a great deal of research, for which he is not now going to be paid. Jason just laughs at them, saying that each man must look after himself. Oliver and Harry leave in an angry state.

 ## Scene Three

Back in the lounge of the Collins' home. The time has moved on two days. It is early evening. Jason, Judith and Frank have just finished dinner with a guest, Stewart Dance, a family friend.

The atmosphere starts off as a social one although there is tension between the members of the Collins family. Stewart then explains that he has a wonderful business opportunity in which he can invest. He explains the possibilities but adds that he has not got sufficient funds available. He asks Jason for help. Both Judith and Frank are enthusiastic about the opportunity but Jason dismisses it with contempt, calling it amateurish and unlikely to succeed.

The evening ends unpleasantly. Judith and Frank are both exasperated and embarrassed. Stewart leaves stating that 'one day somebody will do for Jason'.

ACT TWO

 ## Scene One

This scene is set on Platform Four of the local railway station. Time has moved on three days. By huge coincidence, several of the characters are waiting for the same train, although they do not form a single group. Attention switches back and forward, and parts of the conversations are heard.

Judith is saying goodbye to Jason, having brought him to the station. She complains that he seems to be going out of his way to upset people. Jason takes the criticism better than usual. He is going to sign an important contract and is in good spirits. He promises to try to 'mend a few fences' on his return.

Grace Seabrook is seen talking to Oliver Brand and Harry Betwood. They are off to seek legal advice about Jason's manoeuvrings. She wishes them luck. The three talk about the problems Jason has caused. Grace leaves the two men to join her boss.

Further along the platform, Frank Collins and Stewart Dance hold a conversation. Stewart is going to London to try to secure investment for his business opportunity – the one that Jason turned down. Frank is embarrassed about his brother's behaviour and wishes Stewart well.

The scene ends as the train is heard close to the station and an announcement heralds its arrival.

Final Curtain

Scene Two

Another week has passed. A drinks party is underway at the Collins' home. The set is of the lounge but clearly guests are positioned in other rooms. All the main characters are at the party which is to celebrate Jason's latest deal. The invitations to Oliver Brand, Harry Betwood and Stewart Dance seem tactless given what has happened previously.

Jason is seen asking everybody what they want to drink. Indeed, he actually asks 'What's your poison?' thus providing the title for the play. Oliver Brand accepts a whisky, somewhat reluctantly, leaves the room and is not seen again. Judith is very concerned and goes off in search of him. She does not return to the lounge. At this point, Stewart Dance excuses himself and goes out into the garden. Frank Collins spends a small time at the start of the scene in the lounge but he does not talk to anybody else. He soon departs towards the kitchen to get something to eat. That is the last we see of him.

Harry Betwood has decided to cut his losses. He holds a long conversation with Jason about how he can help in the new venture. Shortly after the start of that conversation Grace Seabrook joins the two men. She was not in the lounge up to this point as she was dealing with some business papers in another room. She spends some time then supporting Harry's suggestions. Jason is clearly interested.

After a considerable time, Jason leaves the room, taking his drink with him, and sets off to search out his other guests. Harry and Grace remain in the lounge discussing the chance of Harry being taken into the new business arrangement. After some three or four minutes of conversation, a strangled cry is heard from the garden. 'What's that cry?' asks Harry and the lights fade as the scene ends.

Scene Three

In a dramatic last scene, Grace Seabrook sits alone in a prison cell. Considerable time has passed. Taped conversations of the police investigation, the replies of the guests and Grace's own answers are heard. The truth emerges that Grace has poisoned Jason's drink. She has been romantically attached to Oliver Brand and took Jason's treatment of him very badly. At the end of the play she says 'What's your poison, Jason?'.

Problem-solving and Thinking Skills Resources for Able and Talented Children
© Barry Teare (Network Continuum Education, 2006)

Ground plan of the Theatre Royal

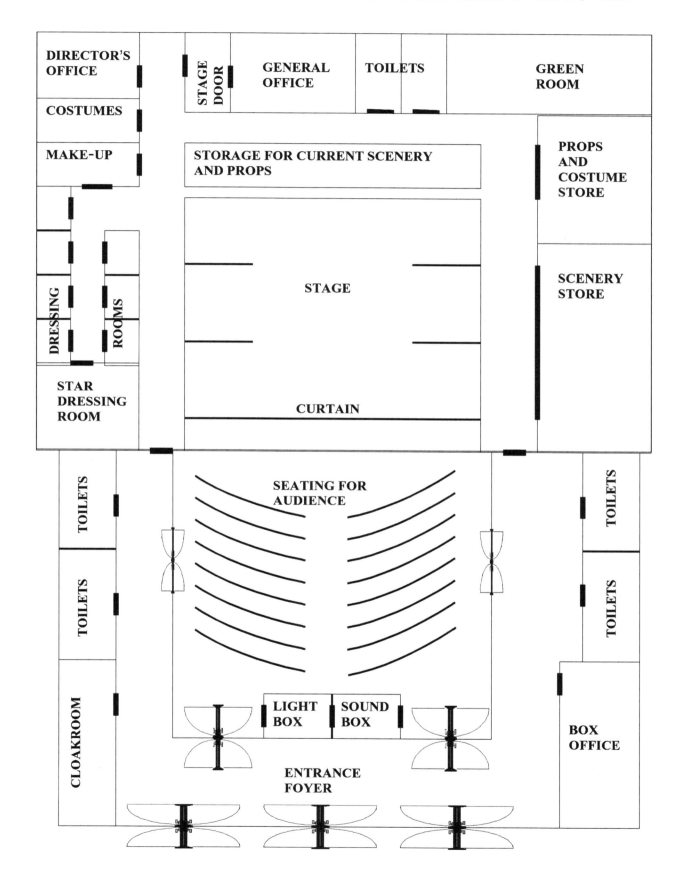

Final Curtain

Norset County Constabulary

REPORT FORM

CASE REFERENCE NUMBER:	SUSD/1429/C

REPORTING OFFICER:	PC Wilkins

I was summoned on my mobile to go to the theatre on York Street. When I arrived I was met by the lighting engineer, Bernard Griffin. He was in quite a state. Mr Griffin met me at the front foyer entrance. He explained that up to my arrival that door and every other outside door had been locked. The company had been doing a dress rehearsal for their performance of 'What's Your Poison?'. It was the normal practice to lock all outside doors so that they would not be interrupted.

The Director, Colin Brown, is Bernard Griffin's brother-in-law. Colin's body had been found by the costume designer, Angela Blunt, in the Director's Office.

It became clear that Colin Brown had been seated in the front row of the stalls watching the rehearsal until he had called a short break, at the end of a particular scene, when he was dissatisfied. Apparently Colin had spoken to all the cast and production team at that point because, in the scene just ended, the stage layout for the railway platform was causing problems with the position of the actors and the delivery of the lines. He had shouted at the designer, Susan Davies, complaining that such problems should already have been sorted out and that it was ridiculous to have to stop a dress rehearsal in such a way.

Anyway, things were sorted out and everyone went back to their places – all, that is, except Colin Brown himself. He said that he was going to talk to a member of the staff about a small technical problem. He was not seen alive again.

That brings us to a very strange thing – an incredible coincidence in fact. The costume director, Angela Blunt, had spotted something which she felt could be improved on stage. She went to talk to Colin Brown and found him dead in his office. She screamed loud and long. Her scream coincided with a loud cry on tape which is heard from off-stage as part of the play. Indeed Harry Betwood has to ask 'What was that cry?' – on this occasion it went on and on!

The scene in the office was one of chaos. Furniture had been overturned – clearly a struggle had taken place. There was no sign of the murder weapon.

Some actors were on stage when the dreadful scream was heard; others were backstage, sometimes alone. Hilary Moon and Bernard Griffin had been back in their sound and lighting boxes respectively since the discussion after Colin Brown's interruption of the rehearsal. They confirmed that they could see each other throughout that period.

Susan Davies, the designer, had been wandering about, worrying about the director's criticisms of the railway station scene.

Problem-solving and Thinking Skills Resources for Able and Talented Children

Norset County Constabulary

PATHOLOGY REPORT FORM

CASE REFERENCE NUMBER: SUSD/1429/C

REPORTING PATHOLOGIST: Dr J. Peterson

Death was clearly from a fatal lunge by a knife into the chest. The murder weapon had a thin, extremely sharp blade of some five to six inches (12.7 to 15.24cm) in length. The dead man had scratches and marks in a number of places, and there had obviously been a violent struggle immediately prior to his death. With such violence it is almost certain that the assailant will bear signs of the struggle on his or her person. The fatal injury, especially the approach and angle of entry, suggests that the attack was made by a left-handed person. It would not have needed any particularly great strength to have caused so much damage – the type of knife and the organs pierced would have been enough.

A much fuller report will be issued within the next 24 hours.

Forensic Evidence

SUSD/1429/C
EXHIBIT A

British Airways

Name: ....
Address: ....
....
Flight Number: .... Date: ....

Luggage label found in corridor near the stage door.

SUSD/1429/C
EXHIBIT B

Grand Hotel

Digital hotel key recovered from corner of Costume/Props Store.

SUSD/1429/C
EXHIBIT C

Colin,
When you have a moment during the dress
rehearsal, can I have a word please - it is about
the administering of the poison
B.G.

Note in the dead man's pocket – was folded.

SUSD/1429/C
EXHIBIT D

Golf tee found on the floor of the Director's Office

SUSD/1429/C
EXHIBIT E

To D.H.
Good luck in our
enterprise. It is long
overdue.
Slave no more!
From D. H.

Greetings card found behind the lockers in the Green Room.

SUSD/1429/C
EXHIBIT F

Small piece of torn, brown check material found on the floor of the
Director's Office, among the overturned furniture.

SUSD/1429/C
EXHIBIT G

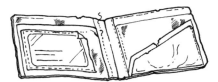

Empty credit cards plastic wallet (rather battered condition) found
in the Director's Office.

Final Curtain

Norset County Constabulary

REPORT FORM

CASE REFERENCE NUMBER: SUSD/1429/C

REPORTING OFFICER: PC Dent

THIS REPORT IS A TYPED TRANSCRIPT OF A TAPED INTERVIEW WITH THEATRE CRITIC ASHLEY HARRISON.

PC Dent:	I am sorry to bother you Mr Harrison. Colin Brown's death must have come as an awful shock.
A.H.:	Well … yes … I suppose so. The sudden death of anyone you know is a shock. On the other hand I am not that surprised.
PC Dent:	Why do you say that?
A.H.:	Colin Brown was not the most popular man in the world. He pushed people very hard. Sometimes it seemed as though nothing was good enough for him. Also … he was very arrogant. He was a good director but, my word, he knew that. That's alright, I suppose, but he didn't recognize the contributions of other people – not saying 'thank you' and 'well done'.
PC Dent:	That might be the case but it hardly seems strong enough for somebody to murder him!
A.H.:	Perhaps not … but there were other points of conflict. Take Simon Train as an example. Colin and Simon have worked together before and there is always tension.
PC Dent:	Strong enough to provoke murder?
A.H.:	Simon believes that there have been times when Colin Brown has bad-mouthed him to others – not uncommon in our business where people live and work on top of one another – but this was a bit more serious. Simon claims that he actually lost one or two plum parts because of the damage that Colin did.
PC Dent:	Are there other problems you know about that might be relevant to the case?
A.H.:	Colin normally finds fault with other members of the production team. He doesn't like the sound effects or the lighting. The set is not atmospheric

Final Curtain

enough for the impression he is trying to create. That sort of thing. Last year, for instance, he told Angela Blunt that some of her costumes looked as though they had come from a junk shop. Strange, really, because he normally gets on quite well with Angela – in fact they play tennis together for relaxation.

PC Dent: Is there anything else you can tell me about the relationships between Colin Brown and others involved in this particular production?

A.H.: Colin wasn't very pleasant to George Hobbs, taunting him and making fun. You see George used to be quite a leading actor but now the best he can do is what you would call 'bit parts' – that is if he is working at all. George's problem is that he is rather too fond of a drink and there have been one or two unfortunate incidents on stage when George has had too much for his own good. Colin keeps reminding George of what he has been and what he is reduced to now.

PC Dent: How did George Hobbs feel about this teasing?

A.H.: He was none too happy as you can imagine. George has made that very clear. His friend, David Herbert, tried to calm him down – take him out of the way, play a round of golf with him when there was time – that sort of thing. In fact when George had forgotten his clubs once David lent him his set as they were both left-handed players. Of course Colin would then have a dig about that. 'How did George see the ball on the tee?' 'Did he ever hit it?' Colin didn't rate golf as a game anyway.

PC Dent: Is there anything else you can add?

A.H.: Not much really. Colin was not a popular man although most people recognized his ability in the theatre. I did hear rumours of money problems – something to do with a venture that he and Susan Davies were partners in but I don't know the details. That's about all I can tell you.

PC Dent: Well thank you Mr Harrison for your time. It has been most helpful. If anything else comes to mind please contact me at the station.

Many Parts Theatrical Agency

32a Dock Road, BANTON, Norset BN5 7EL 01639 456789

Margaret Dancy, one of the partners of the agency, has pieced together the following information from Many Parts' knowledge of the people.

DAVID HERBERT

He has made good progress in his career moving to more important roles. David is regarded as a very ambitious man. He has been trying to break into production where he believes his future lies. Colin Brown recognized how good an actor David is, although never telling him that, but he has poured scorn on David's ambition to direct. This has led to a certain amount of friction between the two. Indeed, it was surprising that they joined forces for the current production.

ROBERT MORRISON

Born into a wealthy family, Robert is now short of money. He has had a very successful career and is much in demand. The problem is his gambling. Robert went through a small fortune on the horses, the dogs, the roulette wheel, cards – wherever he could make a wager. He says that he has now kicked the habit but he always seems to be short of cash. During one production, two or three years ago, Colin Brown lent him some money so that he could pay off his most pressing debts. Robert claims that he was charged excessive interest on that loan and that Colin made a fortune out of him.

DONNA HARGREAVES

Colin Brown helped her to get her first big part. They were seeing each other at the time and others saw it as favouritism and rather unfair. They split up some while back – it was not a very amicable parting by all accounts, with recriminations on both sides.

BRYONY GREEN

Bryony used to be a dancer but then changed to acting. She has been reasonably successful in recent years although she struggled at first. Indeed, when she was first on our books she used her real name, Dora Harley. It's funny but when she changed to her current stage name her fortunes changed as well. Colin Brown once sacked her from a production in the days when she was struggling. The really strange thing is that she was very keen to work with him again.

GEORGE HOBBS

George used to be in great demand and there was always work for him. However, the bottle took over and his drinking has cost him dearly. Nowadays he is lucky to get small parts and only then sometimes at reduced rates of pay. He has become very bitter and is jealous of those who are doing well.

HILARY MOON

Hilary now works as a sound engineer and designer but at one time she was an actress – not a very good one and her performances left much to be desired. Then she took up sound work and is now much respected. Colin Brown asked for her to work with him as much as possible.

The agency has not had professional dealings with the others and there is little that I can tell you. Bernard Griffin is Colin Brown's brother-in-law. Michael Merchant went to school with Colin Brown although they were not in the same year.

Final Curtain

Teaching Notes

Predicting is carried out effectively when there is substantial evidence to draw upon. The scenario used here is one that fascinates many people, including a good proportion of able children, namely a whodunnit. The three higher-order thinking skills of synthesis, analysis and evaluation are central to a successful outcome. The techniques employed are very important in problem solving in a number of curriculum areas and, especially, in the humanities subjects.

Key Elements

- ❖ predicting and hypothesizing
- ❖ synthesis
- ❖ deduction and inference
- ❖ analysis
- ❖ evaluation
- ❖ close engagement with text
- ❖ seeing connections
- ❖ logical thinking
- ❖ lateral thinking
- ❖ putting together a reasoned report
- ❖ prioritization of the importance of data.

Contexts

'Final Curtain' can be used in the following ways:

- ❖ as part of a thinking skills course
- ❖ as extension work to the use of evidence in subjects such as history, geography and science
- ❖ as enrichment material for those who have completed other work
- ❖ as differentiated homework
- ❖ as a team activity
- ❖ as an open-access competition
- ❖ as an activity during an enrichment day, weekend or summer school
- ❖ as an activity for the Problem-solvers' Club.

An Alternative Form of Delivery

'Final Curtain' can be tackled individually by able students or in teams, so that discussion of the evidence with others becomes a major feature. A team basis can also be employed in a much more active format that increases the excitement and enjoyment.

The evidence is placed at a number of distinct locations. Teams visit the locations for perhaps 15 to 20 minutes each on a rotation basis. If necessary, they can request a shorter return to a maximum of two locations.

THEATRE ROYAL, YORK STREET

Here is the plan of the theatre. Transferring it onto a large piece of card is more effective, especially if a toy theatre is placed in the central area. The costume list is also located here.

Final Curtain

THEATRE SHOP, DOWNS ROAD
The summary of the script for 'What's Your Poison?' is placed here, a copy for each team. The pupils take one copy with them. As a consequence this is not a location to be revisited, if such a scheme is operated.

NEWSPAPER OFFICE OF THE *DAILY TIMES*
Here is to be found the transcript of the conversation between PC Dent and theatre critic Ashley Harrison. This works even better if two people record the conversation and the pupils play the tape at the location.

MANY PARTS THEATRICAL AGENCY, DOCK ROAD
Teams read the written information from Margaret Dancy.

FORENSIC LABORATORY, VALLEY WAY
On view here are the pathologist's initial report and the forensic evidence. This can be just a list but it is much more satisfying and engaging if physical evidence is put into plastic bags. Each bag has a label on it with SUSD/1429/C and then EXHIBIT A/B and so on, and a note as to where it was found.

Some need to be exactly as described on the Forensic Evidence Sheet – Exhibits C, D, E and F. The others are not necessarily connected with the case – they just happened to be there. Therefore, alternatives can be bagged for Exhibits A, B and G.

At the start, the pupils are briefed. They are given the title sheet explaining the tasks, the Cast List and PC Wilkins' Report Form. Everything else they examine en route. Evidence is left for the next team at the location, with the exception of the script summary at the theatre shop on Downs Road. Sufficient copies are provided there so that each team takes a copy with them.

The method above is the one used extremely successfully by the author on enrichment courses. Pupils have been very enthusiastic. They have employed crucial thinking skills without believing that they are working hard. Levels of concentration have been very impressive, including children from 'challenging' geographical areas.

'Solution'
Clearly there has to be considerable latitude in assessing pupil responses. Credit should be given for good logical thinking that is supported by evidence. There are, however, some key clues that should be spotted.

MOTIVE
This can be pieced together from the written account submitted by Margaret Dancy of the Many Parts Theatrical Agency and from the answers given by theatre critic Ashley Harrison in his taped interview with PC Dent.

General
Colin Brown was very unpopular. He pushed people very hard. He was never satisfied and failed to acknowledge other professionals' contributions. By nature, Colin Brown was arrogant.

Simon Train – Colin Brown criticized him to others and, as a result, Simon felt that he had lost parts.

Angela Blunt – Colin Brown had told her previously that her costumes looked as though they had come from a junk shop. She shared in the general criticisms of the production team. Against that, the two normally got on well and they played tennis together.

George Hobbs – Colin Brown taunted him about his drink problem, reminding him of his downfall. George Hobbs was jealous of successful people and Colin Brown was certainly one of them.

David Herbert was trying to break into production and Colin Brown poured scorn on his ambition. He may also have resented Colin's ridicule of George Hobbs, David's friend.

Final Curtain

Susan Davies – There was a suggestion about money problems when she and Colin Brown were partners. Susan suffered from the criticism directed at all the production team. Colin had shouted at her during the dress rehearsal about the design for the railway station scene (PC Wilkins' report).

Robert Morrison had gambled away his rich background. As a result he was always short of cash and Colin Brown had lent him money at excessive interest.

Donna Hargreaves and Colin Brown had been romantically attached and the split-up was acrimonious. Colin had, however, secured her first part for her.

Bryony Green had been sacked by Colin Brown in the past, when she was struggling.

OPPORTUNITY

From PC Wilkins' report it is clear that Colin Brown was alive at the end of Act Two Scene One. He complained at that point to Susan Davies about design problems for the railway station scene. Then Colin Brown went off saying that he was going to talk to a member of staff about a technical problem. He was dead by the end of Act Two Scene Two as the finder of the body, Angela Blunt, screamed at the discovery of the murder and her scream coincided with a cry in the play.

Who, then, had an opportunity during Act Two Scene Two to murder Colin Brown?

Hilary Moon and Bernard Griffin can be eliminated as they were in full view in their sound and lighting boxes respectively. This is clear from PC Wilkins' report. Simon Train (Harry Betwood) is on stage for the full scene and could not have been the killer.

Robert Morrison (Jason Collins) was involved for nearly all the scene. He can almost be ruled out. Bryony Green (Grace Seabrook) is off-stage for the first part of the scene but, for most of the time, she is involved on stage. She had some time but not a lot.

Donna Hargreaves (Judith Collins), George Hobbs (Stewart Dance) and Michael Merchant (Frank Collins) were only involved at the very start of a long scene. During most of the critical period they were not on stage. This is even more true of David Herbert (Oliver Brand) who left the stage almost immediately after Act Two Scene Two started.

Two members of the production team also had very good opportunity. Susan Davies, the designer, was wandering about and the person responsible for costumes, Angela Blunt, actually found the body. Was Colin Brown already dead or did she commit the murder?

THE DEFENCE CASE

- ❖ An outsider cannot be blamed because the doors were locked for the dress rehearsal, but there are others who have an equally strong motive for wanting to kill Colin Brown.

- ❖ The murder has to be carried out during a fairly narrow 'window' during the rehearsal. Bryony Green is off-stage for only a limited part of that time. Many others are off-stage or unaccounted for during much or the whole of that critical period.

- ❖ There is little forensic evidence to link Bryony Green with the murder. The note from her in the Director's pocket is hardly conclusive.

- ❖ The attacker was left-handed and this was not true of the accused woman (this is supposition as nothing is said definitely).

- ❖ Exhibit G is an empty credit card wallet. If the motive involved theft then there are others with more financial problems, especially Robert Morrison and George Hobbs.

Final Curtain

THE PROSECUTION CASE

❖ Bryony Green had a strong motive.

❖ She had opportunity at the start of Act Two Scene Two before coming onto the stage as Grace Seabrook.

❖ The pathologist's report stated that no great force was necessary and that, therefore, a woman could have done the killing.

❖ Colin Brown had gone off to see a member of staff about a technical problem. In his pocket was a note saying 'When you have a moment during the dress rehearsal, can I have a word please? It is about the administering of the poison.' It was signed B.G., the initials of either Bryony Green or Bernard Griffin. However, Bernard Griffin was always to be seen in the lighting box. What is more, it was Bryony Green, as Grace Seabrook, who administered the poison in the play. This is made clear in Act Two Scene Three of the script summary.

❖ The handwriting on the note found in Colin Brown's pocket was the same as on Exhibit E, the greetings card discovered behind the lockers in the Green Room. That said 'To D.H. Good luck in our enterprise. It is long overdue. Slave no more! From D.H.' This could be difficult to unravel. Is Donna Hargreaves implicated? The keen-eyed will have spotted that Bryony Green's real name is Dora Harley and she changed her name to bring about a change of fortune. 'Slave' is a reference to her role as Personal Assistant to Jason Collins in 'What's Your Poison?', and to how many people felt when working for Colin Brown. So this card is from Bryony Green. But who is the other person? Is it Donna Hargreaves? She had a motive and there was opportunity.

❖ This is where the forensic evidence kicks in. David Herbert must be considered carefully. He had a strong motive and very good opportunity during Act Two Scene Two. He is left-handed and this fits the murderer. A golf tee was found on the floor of the Director's Office (exhibit D) and David Herbert plays golf. Most convincingly of all, a piece of torn cloth found on the floor of the Director's Office matches his suit from the costume list. The damage was probably done during the struggle before the stabbing.

❖ This then is the sensational development – that two people were involved: Bryony Green and David Herbert. The probable scenario is that Bryony Green fixed up a meeting with Colin Brown to discuss the administering of the poison in the play. She had time to go to the Director's Office at the start of Act Two Scene Two before appearing on stage again. Having got Colin Brown out of public view, David Herbert was able to take over and it was he who carried out the murder.

THE VERDICT

If students untangle all the evidence their predicted verdict should be guilty, not just for Bryony Green but also for David Herbert. The note to D.H. from D.H. might lead them astray. The verdict is then much less certain as Bryony Green had a limited time opportunity.

NOTES

1 Some forensic evidence may have nothing to do with the case. At the scene-of-the-crime there are always items that are there coincidentally. Pupils should not feel that every exhibit has to be worked into their explanation.

2 All the names used in this piece are fictional and any links with real people are purely coincidental.

Section 6

Evaluation

Evaluation is one of the three higher-order thinking skills in Bloom's Taxonomy. Nobody should be surprised by the importance given to evaluation as it concerns judgement, giving an opinion and prioritization.

Many areas of the National Curriculum 1999 feature the skill:

    … analyse and evaluate evidence and draw and justify conclusions.
(geography)

    … when investigating and evaluating products.
(design and technology)

    … thinking skills, through helping pupils to engage in social issues that require the use of reasoning, understanding and action through enquiry and evaluation.
(citizenship)

    … evaluating critically what they hear, read and view, with attention to explicit and implied meaning, bias and objectivity, and fact and opinion.
(English)

    … discuss and evaluate their own and others' writing.
(English)

    evaluate critically performances of dramas that they have watched or in which they have taken part.
(drama)

    … thinking skills, through analysis and evaluation of music … .
(music)

    … analyse and evaluate their own and others' work, express opinions and make reasoned judgements.
(art and design)

    … adapt and refine their work and plan and develop this further, in the light of their own and others' evaluations.
(art and design)

    … critically evaluate aspects of performance.
(physical education)

    They evaluate their work, in particular the strength of the evidence they and others have collected.
(science)

> ... considering and evaluating the benefits and drawbacks of scientific and technological developments, including those relating to the environment, personal health and quality of life, and those raising ethical issues.
> (*science*)

> ... reflect critically on their own and others' use of ICT to help them develop and improve their ideas and quality of their work.
> (*information and communication technology*)

> ... evaluating and suggesting improvements to existing systems.
> (*information and communication technology*)

> ... to evaluate interpretations.
> (*history*)

> ... evaluate the sources used, select and record information relevant to the enquiry and reach conclusions.
> (*history*)

- **'Myself'** deals with, perhaps, the most difficult task of all: self-evaluation. There is a wide-ranging questionnaire for pupils to complete. Knowing yourself is important in overcoming obstacles and making progress. It fits many of the quotes above from the National Curriculum 1999. This piece of work also fits the area labelled by Howard Gardner as intrapersonal intelligence.

- Able children need to be placed in positions where they see various points of view. This, in turn, requires weighing up all the evidence. **'Those in Favour? ... Those Against?'** presents eight discussion points from areas of public concern.

- **'The Going Rate'** is one of the pieces in the book that asks able pupils to evaluate the society in which they live. It has obvious links with citizenship and personal and social education. Children are asked to place 15 occupations in a league table in terms of how well they are paid and to analyse the consequences of that situation. They then use their own judgement to rewrite the league table as they think it should be.

- **'Decisions by the Decade'** gives an unusual opportunity to consider the twentieth century as an overview while exercising evaluation skills. This major piece of work puts emphasis upon selecting key elements from a huge amount of data.

- In **'Looking for Clues'**, pupils are asked to draw up a list of success criteria by which to judge the quality of a detective story. This is a genre that promotes hypothesizing, speculation, analysis and synthesis. It is a popular area of reading for many able children.

- Evaluation of particular and substantial information is at the centre of **'Devon Loch'**. A presentation is involved as pupils take on the role of television programme makers. A number of other key thinking skills result from an examination of the evidence surrounding one of the greatest sporting mysteries ever to take place.

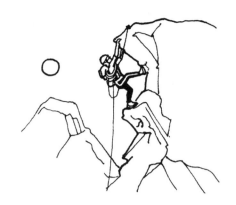

Myself

We are asked to evaluate many situations and people. We pass judgement over events in history, over decisions and policies in politics, over decisions affecting the environment, over the morality and social consequences of scientific developments. The most difficult task of all, though, is to evaluate ourselves – to carry out self-evaluation or self-analysis.

Your Task

'Run the rule' over yourself by answering the questionnaire below. To help you do that, read, and act upon, the suggested sources of information.

Suggested Sources of Information

★ Think back to how you reacted to particular events and opportunities.
★ Look at comments in your exercise books.
★ Recall conversations with teachers.
★ Take note of school reports.
★ Seek the opinions of friends, parents, adults you know and other children at school.
★ **Most important of all – look deep into yourself, being as honest as possible.**

The Questionnaire

What do you really enjoy doing?

Which activities do not interest you?

What sort of a person are you?

What are your strengths?

What are your weaknesses?

Problem-solving and Thinking Skills Resources for Able and Talented Children

How do you solve problems best?

How do you make decisions?

Which working methods work best for you?

Are there areas you feel you could improve?

Do you always make a determined effort?

How do you fare working in a group or a team?

In which activities do you most want to succeed?

Can you identify any barriers to personal success?

What do you want to achieve over the next two years?

Do other people make comments that confirm your own opinion about yourself?

Have you learned anything from other people's comments that surprise you?

If there are several things to do, which do you do first?

What makes you happy?

What makes you sad?

What makes you angry?

Do you model yourself on anybody else?

If you make New Year resolutions, what are they?

What is the best piece of work that you have done recently and why is it good?

What was the worst piece of work that you have done recently and why was it poor?

Myself

Teaching Notes

This is a very different piece of work if, indeed, it should be classed as a piece of work at all. Intrapersonal intelligence is one of the seven original intelligences identified by Howard Gardner. 'Knowing yourself' is important in overcoming obstacles and making progress. OfSTED, often identifies 'not enough pupil participation in their own learning' as a weakness during the inspection of schools.

Key Elements

- ❖ analysis
- ❖ synthesis
- ❖ self-evaluation
- ❖ intrapersonal intelligence.

Contexts

'Myself' can be used in the following ways:

- ❖ as part of a personal and social education course
- ❖ as an activity during a form period
- ❖ as part of a thinking skills course
- ❖ as a specialized homework
- ❖ as part of the identification process of able and talented pupils
- ❖ as part of the information transferred during transition from one school to another.

NOTE: The information generated from this exercise could be put to valuable use in the pastoral system of the school. To get the best from able pupils, we need to look after the whole child.

Those in Favour?...Those Against?

Before making up one's mind about something, it is helpful to weigh up all the evidence. This is particularly true when considering important issues. Seeing the other person's point of view helps reduce prejudice and conflict.

Your Tasks

1 Choose one of the statements or discussion points below.
2 Research your chosen issue by using the internet, reference books and newspapers.
3 Get a feel of contrasting viewpoints by talking to a variety of people about their opinions on the subject.
4 Write two short accounts – one in favour of the statement and the other against. Comment upon which you feel is the stronger argument, explaining why.

THE DISCUSSION POINTS

1 Mobile phones have become a public nuisance.
2 As aircraft do serious damage to the ozone layer, people should fly as little as possible.
3 Health and safety concerns have reduced the quality of life for children.
4 Organized religions are a positive force for peace.
5 'Binge drinkers', who require medical assistance, should be charged for the help given.
6 Solicitors should be prevented from offering 'no win, no fee' services in personal accident injury cases.
7 Viewing figures show that television programmers have lost sight of what the viewing public want.
8 Defendants found not guilty should be retried if important new evidence comes to light at a later time.

Extension Task

Make suggestions of your own as to other discussion points that would produce interesting 'for' and 'against' arguments.

'Those in Favour? ... Those Against?'

Teaching Notes

Seeing both sides of an argument is a vital ingredient in the successful discussion of issues within many subject areas, including English, science, history, geography, religious education, politics, law, philosophy and economics. Hopefully able children will influence sensible policy formulation, decision making and legislation in the future.

Key Elements

* research
* weighing up evidence
* evaluation
* appreciation of both sides of a case.

Contexts

'Those in Favour? ... Those Against?' could be used in the following ways:

* as a piece of classwork within study skills, thinking skills or specific subject lessons
* as a differentiated homework
* as an open-access competition
* as an activity during an enrichment day, weekend or summer school.

The Going Rate

The 'going rate' is the normal price paid for a product or service. It can also be regarded as the current wage paid for a particular job. When you compare the going rate for different occupations, the information provides much food for thought.

Your Tasks

1 Study the list of occupations below. This list has no particular order.
2 Use your understanding of how society in Britain operates to place the occupations in a league table, with the highest paid at the top and the lowest paid at the bottom.
3 Write down what you think the implications are of this league table.
4 Now rewrite the league table in the order that you, personally, believe should operate.
5 Write an explanation of your own league table to show the thinking behind the positions.

THE OCCUPATIONS

Nurse
Prime Minister
Star footballer at a top Premiership club
Doctor
Television newsreader
Police Constable
Teacher
Machine operator
Pilot
Dentist
Social Services Care and Support Assistant
Farm worker
Member of Parliament
Benefits Claims Officer
High Court Judge

NOTES

1 This is to be considered within Britain rather than abroad.

2 Assume that comparison should be made for equivalent age and experience, when appropriate.

The Going Rate

Teaching Notes

'The Going Rate' is one of the pieces in the book that asks able students to evaluate the society in which they live.

Key Elements

- ❖ evaluation
- ❖ analysis
- ❖ synthesis
- ❖ justifying one's views
- ❖ weighing evidence
- ❖ personal values.

Contexts

'The Going Rate' can be used in the following ways:

- ❖ as written work within subjects such as personal and social education and citizenship
- ❖ as a topic for debate
- ❖ as a differentiated homework
- ❖ as an enrichment activity during an enrichment day, weekend or summer school.

Answers

The league table in real life would be:

1 **Star footballer at a top Premiership club**: players vary considerably but a few are now earning £100,000 a week or over £5 million a year. The average Premiership player earns £1 million a year.

2 **Television newsreader**: there was a major row in June 2005 when it became clear that some were earning over £400,000 a year.

3 **Prime Minister**: salary, at the time of writing, is just under £184,000 a year.

4 **High Court Judge**: just over £155,000 was quoted for 2005–2006.

5 **Dentist**: over £60,000 is the average given.

6 **Member of Parliament**: the actual salary for 2005–2006 was just under £60,000 but there are a number of allowances as well.

{ 7 **Pilot**: over £50,000 is the average given.
  8 **Doctor**: circa £50,000 on average.

{ 9 **Teacher**: basic entry in September 2005 was just over £19,000 but the top for a classroom teacher was just under £33,000. Those in management earn more.

10 **Police Constable**: after ten years' service the figure stood at just over £32,000 in September 2005. Overtime can push that figure up considerably and there are plans for substantial improvements.

11 **Nurse**: in 2005 the basic was just under £11,000 but the top of the scale was just under £23,000.

{ 12 **Machine operator**: circa £15,000.
  13 **Social Services Care and Support Assistant**: circa £15,000.

{ 14 **Benefits Claims Officer**: circa £13,000.
  15 **Farm worker**: £12,000 was the going rate at the time of writing.

Special Note
Considerable research has been done to acquire the figures for the league table. However, averages are sometimes the only figures that are available. Overtime payments can make quite a difference as, for instance, with Police Constables; similarly, allowances can alter incomes. Time moves on and salaries will increase. The data used here are from 2005. Those positions that are bracketed together are more-or-less the same.

Some of the Implications
Some really important occupations get poor remuneration. The danger is that recruitment and retention will be harmed. Those concerned with popular entertainment look to have grossly inflated salaries. It is difficult to justify a television newsreader earning more than double the Prime Minister when the relative responsibilities are taken into account.

Tasks 4 and 5
Outcomes will vary considerably. The students' own league tables and reasoning will say a good deal about them as people.

DECISIONS by THE DECADE

19?? 19?? 19??

When you watch television programmes with a setting in the past, you may sometimes wonder what it would have been like to live in another time and whether you would have preferred that to being alive in the present. If you have elderly relatives or acquaintances, they will have lived through a period of enormous change. Some of their stories will sound very far removed from your own experiences.

'Decisions by the Decade' gives you the opportunity to choose what you would most like to have experienced from the twentieth century, a period of very rapid change.

Your Tasks

1. Research the twentieth century from the point of an overview rather than very detailed knowledge. Get a feel for what each decade in that century was like – the lifestyle and the major events.
2. Choose three of the ten decades available. Assume that a newly invented time machine allows you to sample those decades simultaneously.
3. Explain why you have chosen the three particular decades and write down the features that appeal to you. These may concern transport, dress, leisure activities, technology, science, quality of life, major events or, indeed, anything else.
4. Make brief comments as to why you rejected the other seven decades when making your choices.
5. Comment on any clashes or difficulties produced by choosing the three separate decades.

THE DECISIONS ARE YOURS!
THE DECISIONS BY THE DECADE
19?? 19?? 19??

Problem-solving and Thinking Skills Resources for Able and Talented Children

Decisions by the Decade

Teaching Notes

'Decisions' by the Decade' gives an unusual opportunity to consider the twentieth century as an overview while exercising evaluation skills.

Key Elements

- ❖ twentieth-century history
- ❖ research
- ❖ prioritization
- ❖ selecting key elements from a huge amount of data
- ❖ evaluation
- ❖ judgement and opinion
- ❖ empathy
- ❖ analysis
- ❖ self-awareness
- ❖ synthesis.

Contexts

'Decisions by the Decade' can be used in the following ways:

- ❖ as extension work to normal syllabus coverage of the twentieth century
- ❖ as enrichment work for those who have completed other tasks
- ❖ as a differentiated homework project
- ❖ as an activity for an enrichment day, weekend or summer school
- ❖ as an activity for the History Club or Society
- ❖ as a debate, if the format is changed
- ❖ as an open-access competition.

NOTE: whatever the circumstances, clearly this is a major piece of work; sufficient time needs to be allowed to enable considered and substantial responses.

Success Criteria

Responses may vary considerably in terms of approach. The quality of answers is likely to include consideration of the following criteria:

- ❖ the quality displayed in the selection of key points
- ❖ the degree to which research allowed the pupil to make reasoned decisions
- ❖ the level of appreciation shown of the particular 'feel' of the three decades chosen
- ❖ the judgement shown in both the positive choice of three decades and the rejection of the other seven
- ❖ the quality of thinking in terms of cause and effect shown by the justification for the three decades chosen
- ❖ the level of realization that choices across the three decades may be for distinct or even contradictory reasons
- ❖ an appreciation of the influence of their personality or stage of development.

NOTE: These success criteria should be shared with the pupils before they commence work.

Looking for Clues

Evaluation of objects, situations and proposals, looking for strengths and weaknesses, is a very important skill. You need to have 'success criteria' in mind by which to make your judgement. It could be said that you are 'Looking for Clues'. This would be particularly true if you were evaluating a detective story, either in book form or on television. What, in your view, makes a good detective story?

There has been unfavourable comment about how some detective stories on television have 'cheated' by not laying clues in front of the viewer fairly. One such criticism has concerned the late appearance in a story of an identical twin so that the solution was never possible for those watching.

Your Tasks

1   Draw up a list of 'success criteria' by which you can judge the quality of a detective story.
2   Choose a suitable detective story for your age. (Your teacher will assist you with this.)
3   As you read or watch it, make brief notes about motive, opportunity and evidence.
4   When you come to the denouement (the explanation of the crime or mystery), evaluate the story against the success criteria that you have drawn up. What are the strengths and weaknesses of the story? Were the success criteria met?

All the time you will be 'Looking for Clues'.

Extension Task

Write a synopsis for a detective story of your own. Show clearly how you intend to meet the success criteria.

Looking for Clues

Teaching Notes

Evaluation is one of the three higher-order thinking skills. It has widespread application. Here the skill is used in a particular context: that of the detective story. This is a genre with particular opportunities for thinking skills; the reader is engaged in hypothesizing and speculation, analysis and synthesis, as he or she tries to solve the case ahead of the denouement. It also appeals to many able children.

Key Elements

- ❖ evaluation
- ❖ close engagement with text
- ❖ deduction
- ❖ inference

- ❖ analysis
- ❖ synthesis
- ❖ using success criteria
- ❖ writing a synopsis (in the extension task).

NOTES

1   It would be helpful for the teacher to assist in the selection of detective fiction. The age of the child will be a determining factor, not so much because of reading age but, rather, the context of the story and how adult the background material is. Many able children have started reading in this genre with Agatha Christie. The writing may not be particularly wonderful but the plots are excellent, the solutions are ingenious and the supporting material does not contain themes that some would consider unsuitable for children.

2   The alternative to a book is a programme on television. This can change the timescale dramatically.

Contexts

'Looking for Clues' can be used in a number of ways, although the decision to use a book or a television programme will have a considerable impact because of the difference in time involved:

- ❖ as differentiated homework(s)
- ❖ as an enrichment activity for those well ahead on other tasks
- ❖ as extension material to work on detective fiction
- ❖ as part of a problem-solving/thinking skills course
- ❖ as an activity during an enrichment day, weekend or summer school
- ❖ as an open-access competition
- ❖ as an activity for the English Club or Society, or Detective Club.

Success Criteria

Children may suggest a number of success criteria. They can be seen as two types. Some will apply to all stories:

- ✓ a good plot
- ✓ strong characters
- ✓ logical development

- ✓ imaginative vocabulary
- ✓ interesting images.

However, in this particular genre, others may be important:

- ✓ an intriguing mystery
- ✓ a number of viable suspects
- ✓ the cleverness of the solution
- ✓ a good balance between being fair with the clues and not making the solution too easy
- ✓ good use of 'red herrings'.

Devon Loch

If you had been listening to the radio commentary on the Grand National in 1956 you would have heard something like this on the final stages of the race, after the leaders had jumped the last fence:

'Devon Loch is holding off ESB. He's drawing 1½ lengths clear. Devon Loch is stretching away. The hats are coming off. He is three lengths clear with 100 yards to go. Devon Loch has gone down .... He's gone down and has been passed by ESB!'

THE FULL RESULT OF THE RACE

1 ESB (D.V. Dick)
2 Gentle Moya (G. Milburn)
3 Royal Tan (P. Taaffe)
4 Eagle Lodge (A. Oughton)

ALSO RAN

Carey's Cottage	Key Royal	Clearing	Wild Wisdom
Early Mist (fell)	Mariner's Log (fell)	Sundew (fell)	High Guard (fell)
Dunboy II (fell)	Much Obliged (fell)	Armorial (fell)	Must (fell)
M'as-tu-vu (fell)	Reverend Prince (fell)	Witty (fell)	Domata (fell)
Athenian (fell)	No Response (fell)	Ontray (fell)	Devon Loch (fell on the flat)
Pippykin (refused)	Martinique (refused)	Border Luck (refused)	Polonius (refused)
Merry Windsor (baulked)			

Your Work

You and your colleagues make television programmes for your living. The speciality of your company is the investigatory documentary with a mystery element. A television channel is looking for a team to produce a programme on Devon Loch, as part of a series on unsolved mysteries. One of the aims of the series is to allow the viewer to evaluate the evidence and to make a personal judgement. Another major aim is to entertain the viewing public. Your company is anxious to win the contract. You, and other rival units, have been invited to make a presentation to the channel's programmers.

Tasks

1 Study the data gathered previously. This consists of the radio commentary and the 'Full Result of the Race' (above), 'The Basic Facts' and 'Opinions' (on separate sheets).

2 Explain what was so unusual in the Devon Loch incident.

3 Evaluate the evidence. How strong is it? Are there problems with the evidence?

Problem-solving and Thinking Skills Resources for Able and Talented Children
© Barry Teare (Network Continuum Education, 2006)

4 Make a plan of further research that you intend to carry out. What limitations are there on your work?

5 Give an outline of the way in which you intend to present the case, trying to make it compulsive viewing but honest journalism.

6 Within your team, come to a conclusion on what caused Devon Loch to collapse and how you intend to support this verdict. Use known evidence involving the race, the conditions and the opinions of leading figures involved in the incident.

7 Complete the planning sheets for your presentation.

8 Make your presentation.

Success Criteria

The contract will be awarded to the company on the basis of the following success criteria:

- the existing evidence has been used well

- the strengths and weaknesses of the evidence have been identified

- the degree to which the suggested further research would assist making an informed judgement

- how well the team has worked together

- the balance maintained between entertaining the television viewers and presenting the evidence fairly

- the quality of the presentation itself.

THE BASIC FACTS

THE RACE

The Grand National is perhaps the most famous race in the world. It is run in the spring of each year at Aintree in Liverpool. The course is long and difficult. The distance is approximately 4½ miles and the horses jump 30 formidable fences (by doing almost two circuits of the track). Among them are very famous obstacles, such as Valentines, The Chair, The Canal Turn and Becher's Brook. The 'National' is an extremely important race to win, not only for the high prize money but also for the prestige that goes with it.

THE HORSE

Devon Loch began his racing career in 1951. He showed great promise and was soon winning races. His main target was the Grand National. Devon Loch had great stamina – an important quality for a horse hoping to win that race.

THE OWNER

The Royal Family has a long history of interest in horse racing. Elizabeth, the Queen Mother, favoured steeplechasing rather than 'the flat'. As owner of Devon Loch, she looked forward to the Grand National of 1956. The Queen Mother had become a very popular supporter of the sport and the great majority of racegoers loved to see a royal victory.

Devon Loch

THE JOCKEY

Dick Francis started riding as an amateur but later turned professional and made a highly successful living. He was regarded as one of the best jump jockeys of the time and it was no surprise when he became Champion Jockey. He has since written very successful 'thrillers'.

THE INCIDENT

Devon Loch ran brilliantly and, on the second circuit, he began to overtake other horses. He took the lead three fences from 'home'. After jumping the last fence he started to pull away from the second horse, ESB. It seemed certain that Devon Loch would win but less than 100 yards from the finishing post he made a sort of jump and collapsed. ESB went on to win, followed by Gentle Moya and Royal Tan.

Map of the end of the race

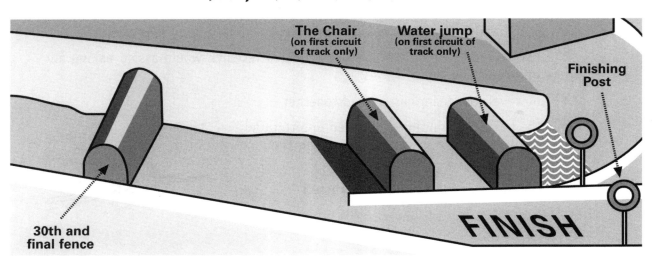

OPINIONS

THE JOCKEY - DICK FRANCIS

In his autobiography, Dick Francis gave his views on the main theories as to why his horse fell. One suggestion was a heart attack but the horse was not blowing (breathing hard) badly at the end of the race. A heart attack would mean that Devon Loch was at the end of his strength, and yet he did not feel like a tired horse. Dick Francis had ridden many tired horses over a number of years. Before his collapse the horse was running easily and, if he had finished, he would have broken the time record. Devon Loch recovered within minutes and this is unlikely after an attack severe enough to stop him so suddenly.

The second theory was a very popular one. Many newspapers tried to show that Devon Loch had attempted to jump the water-jump fence which he saw to his left. They suggested that the horse pricked his ears in the manner typical before a jump. Dick Francis was adamant that the 'ghost jump' theory was incorrect. He believed that the jumping action would occur in any case when a horse stopped suddenly after galloping at 30 miles an hour. Devon Loch had too much experience to try to jump the water from outside the wings. He had just passed The Chair without any reaction and he was well used to galloping alongside fences without attempting to jump them. Dick Francis made the point very strongly that as a jockey, and a very experienced one at that, he would know whether the horse had been going to jump. There is an unmistakable feeling of the horse gathering himself to jump, and this did not occur.

The third theory is that Devon Loch suffered a sudden and severe attack of cramp. As this occurred at great speed the horse was thrown down. Tiredness would produce such a condition. With horses, cramp is known as 'setfast' and it lasts for six hours or so. Devon Loch was walking normally again within a few minutes. The condition is quite rare but Dick Francis had spoken to a huntsman who had once owned a horse that had suffered three separate cramp attacks. Francis felt that cramp was a reasonable suggestion but it did not explain why Devon Loch pricked his ears.

The jockey himself supported a fourth possibility. He felt that the incident could be explained by the fact that the owner was the Queen Mother. She was a tremendously popular figure in racing. When the crowd saw Devon Loch in the lead, so close to the finish, they cheered very loudly. This tremendous noise was funnelled down the course from the stands and it was carried by the light breeze. On hearing this, Devon Loch pricked his ears and he was hit by the wave of noise. The effect was to stop him in his stride and bring him down.

THE TRAINER OF ESB - FRED RIMMELL

Fred Rimmell talked about the enormous crowd which was delighted at seeing Devon Loch pulling away from ESB after the last fence. He had resigned himself to seeing his own horse finish second. He described the incident as he saw it – Devon Loch appeared to jump something that was not there, slithering along the ground and coming to a complete halt with his forelegs stretched in front of him. He then mentioned the newspapers' support of the 'ghost jump' and Dick Francis' own ideas.

Fred Rimmell's view was clear. 'I believe that Devon Loch suffered a spasm or heart attack.' He supported this by likening Devon Loch to a long-distance runner who suddenly does not know where he is, and by the fact that he saw the horse swerve across the course at the finish of a race at Sandown the following year.

JOURNALIST - TIM FITZGEORGE-PARKER

He also quoted the race at Sandown in support of his belief that Devon Loch had a temporary heart problem at Aintree brought about by extreme pressure. Although rare, the condition could have been caused by the tremendous speed of Devon Loch during the very gruelling race.

DEVON LOCH PLANNING SHEETS

YOUR COMPANY'S NAME:

MEMBERS OF YOUR TEAM:

WHAT WAS SO UNUSUAL IN THE DEVON LOCH INCIDENT?

EVALUATION OF THE EXISTING EVIDENCE

FURTHER RESEARCH

Problem-solving and Thinking Skills Resources for Able and Talented Children
© Barry Teare (Network Continuum Education, 2006)

PROGRAMME PLANNING/OUTLINE

THE VERDICT YOU INTEND TO PRESENT, WITH SUPPORTING EVIDENCE

CONCLUSION: WHY YOUR COMPANY SHOULD BE GIVEN THE CONTRACT

PLEASE CONTINUE ON ANOTHER SHEET IF NECESSARY

Devon Loch

Teaching Notes

'Devon Loch' relates to one of the greatest sporting mysteries ever to take place. It provides an intriguing vehicle to demonstrate a number of key thinking skills.

Key Elements

- ❖ evaluation
- ❖ analysis
- ❖ synthesis
- ❖ careful interpretation of data
- ❖ research
- ❖ working as a team
- ❖ presentational skills
- ❖ organizational skills.

Contexts

'Devon Loch' can be used in a number of ways, as it currently is presented:

- ❖ as a team activity
- ❖ as an activity during an enrichment day, weekend or summer school
- ❖ as part of a problem-solving/thinking skills course.

Teachers can, however, change the suggested format so that it does not involve working as a television company or making an actual presentation at the end of the work. The final product can be a written report, either individually or as a team, giving a balanced verdict on the reason for Devon Loch's amazing 'fall'.

Other uses can be:

- ❖ as a differentiated homework
- ❖ as an activity during normal lessons but with a written outcome
- ❖ as an enrichment activity for those ahead on other work
- ❖ as an open-access competition
- ❖ as an activity for the Problem-solvers' Club.

Success Criteria

These are listed on the pupil sheets. They will need to be amended when a presentation is not to be the outcome. In all versions one would look for pupils to consider the various options before deciding upon their preferred explanation. Strong answers would refer to the weaknesses, gaps and problems in the existing evidence – the incident took place a long time ago, many witnesses have died, the absence of a vet's report, the fact that you cannot then, or now, get evidence from Devon Loch, and so on.

Section 7

Classification

Classification involves the ability to recognize similarities and differences. This, in turn, leads to looking for patterns. Which objects or events fit together and where, therefore, are the anomalies?

In curriculum terms, science is the subject most closely associated with classification. The following four quotes from the science section of the National Curriculum 1999 are just a sample of many examples:

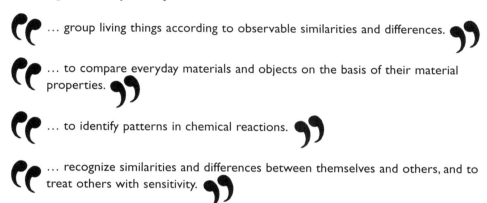

> … group living things according to observable similarities and differences.

> … to compare everyday materials and objects on the basis of their material properties.

> … to identify patterns in chemical reactions.

> … recognize similarities and differences between themselves and others, and to treat others with sensitivity.

Humanities' subjects, too, involve seeing what fits together and what is different. Patterns of settlement, for instance, are part of the geography syllabus. The history section of the National Curriculum 1999 has a number of comments such as:

> … identify differences between ways of life at different times.

These skills are key in mathematics. One factor in solving problems is to see the connections with other situations.

- **'In a Class of their Own'** asks children to sort out 150 items into 30 groups or classes of five and then to explain what links them. Elements of geography, science, English, mathematics, sport, music, religious education, geology and general knowledge are included, thus not only making the exercise truly cross-curricular but also increasing the challenge significantly. The difficulty has also been increased by including items that could fit more than one category until a full solution is achieved that results in 30 groups of five. Strategy and organization are placed at a premium.

- The second piece in the section, **'Spoof Proof Reader'**, is heavily based in English. Pupils take the role of proof reader to identify 30 errors in a passage and then organize those errors into six groups of five. A number of key areas of the English curriculum are involved – punctuation, forming plurals, grammar and the correct use of capital letters. Here, therefore, strong content is coupled with a classification exercise.

● Dictionary work is often unimaginative. '**Pawn in the Game**' requires use of a dictionary, reference books and/or the internet. Sixty words and phrases have to be classified according to the nature of their origin. Wordplay is, therefore, a strong feature. The material is taken from a wide range of curriculum areas – science, English, religious education, French, mythology, history, ancient languages, computing, popular music and games.

● The fourth, and final, piece is light-hearted but it involves wordplay and classification. '**The Following Parties**' is based upon a real-life garden centre known to the author. Lunch in the restaurant is booked on arrival but, due to the popularity of the garden centre, there is often a wait. Families are told when their tables are ready by a tannoy announcement. In this exercise the 60 families have to be placed into 20 appropriate groups of three with an explanation of the classifications employed. Many able children have a particular sense of humour and they will enjoy the images created by the tannoy announcements. Various methods can be used, including the use of slips of paper, thus pleasing those who prefer a tactile or kinesthetic style.

In a Class of their Own

Sorting things out can be very satisfying. Some items go together as groups or classes. Indeed the process is called classification. Are you a class act when it comes to grouping similar items?

Your Tasks

1 Sort out the list of 150 items detailed below into 30 groups or classes of five.

2 For each group or class explain what it is that links them.

NOTES

★ Some of the groups are more obvious than others.

★ Try to develop a strategy to get into this piece of work that will make your task easier.

★ You may need to research some of the entries.

★ Some items could go into more than one list initially. Be prepared to make changes when necessary.

The List

1	Wagner	19	topaz	37	question mark
2	kappa	20	camomile	38	Exodus
3	measles	21	Jurassic	39	wren
4	leek	22	boat	40	fritillary
5	n	23	2	41	Bakewell tart
6	Seine	24	baritone	42	beret
7	comma	25	a	43	i
8	Monopoly	26	faraday	44	Clearface
9	amethyst	27	Helvetica	45	29
10	deerstalker	28	black widow	46	volley
11	limerick	29	delta	47	Earl Grey
12	lob	30	Beethoven	48	Cambrian
13	Genesis	31	greenfinch	49	full stop
14	triple jump	32	Swiss roll	50	bowler
15	Elgar	33	Dublin	51	Cluedo
16	tibia	34	Amazon	52	trapdoor
17	red admiral	35	high jump	53	mumps
18	gully	36	beta	54	fibula

In a Class of their Own

55	carrot	87	serve	119	Gothic
56	s	88	herbal	120	tarantula
57	bye	89	Devonian	121	exclamation mark
58	ampere	90	11	122	65
59	broccoli	91	Nile	123	bus
60	free verse	92	alpha	124	tenor
61	soprano	93	femur	125	Folio
62	Madrid	94	Dundee	126	5
63	Mozart	95	bouncer	127	o
64	pole vault	96	bobble hat	128	bass
65	starling	97	d	129	tram
66	speckled wood	98	Vienna	130	Thames
67	Madeira	99	Congo	131	Rome
68	garnet	100	omega	132	mezzo-soprano
69	volt	101	chickenpox	133	haiku
70	Times New Roman	102	opal	134	turnip
71	train	103	trilby	135	half volley
72	25	104	Silurian	136	China
73	javelin	105	jawbone	137	Palaeozoic
74	hyphen	106	Job	138	whooping cough
75	Proverbs	107	discus	139	money
76	chess	108	German measles	140	Indian
77	e	109	17	141	aeroplane
78	Eccles	110	Paris	142	u
79	crease	111	75	143	blank verse
80	smash	112	Deuteronomy	144	marrow
81	Scrabble	113	sparrow	145	backgammon
82	robin	114	55	146	coulomb
83	funnel-web	115	metatarsal	147	t
84	Tchaikovsky	116	cabbage white	148	sonnet
85	peacock	117	googly	149	joule
86	diamond	118	15	150	v

Extension Tasks

1 Analyse the factors that make this piece of work difficult to handle.

2 Explain sensible strategies and working methods to help the solution.

3 Create a similar piece of your own using groups other than those here (perhaps not as many as 30). Mix up the order of the items. Get somebody else to try to sort out the items into appropriate groups with an explanation for each group.

Problem-solving and Thinking Skills Resources for Able and Talented Children

In a Class of their Own

Teaching Notes

Classification is an important thinking skill. Here the difficulty has been increased dramatically by the large number of items together with the variety of the groups. Organizational skills are therefore put at a premium. Working in teams would allow pooling of ideas. Some items, for example bowler, will fit more than one group but the need to find 30 groups of five points to a particular solution.

Key Elements

- ❖ classification
- ❖ research
- ❖ elements of geography, science, English, mathematics, sport, music, religious education, geology and general knowledge
- ❖ strategy
- ❖ organizational skills
- ❖ mental agility
- ❖ dictionary use
- ❖ deduction and inference.

Contexts

'In a Class of their Own' can be used in the following ways:

- ❖ as part of a thinking skills course
- ❖ as an enrichment activity for those who have completed other tasks
- ❖ as an activity for an enrichment day, weekend or summer school
- ❖ as differentiated homework
- ❖ as an activity for the Thinking Skills Club
- ❖ as a team activity.

Teaching Points

Children should be encouraged to develop strategies and organizational methods. They need to look for clues to identify groups. They should be encouraged to find a strategy to handle items that could appear in more than one group. Children should be encouraged to use any effective method that suits them. A kinesthetic method of slips of paper would work well.

A Solution

A possible solution is given below. Credit should be given for alternative answers so long as 30 viable groups of five are created.

GROUP 1	COMPOSERS			
1 Wagner	15 Elgar	30 Beethoven	63 Mozart	84 Tchaikovsky
GROUP 2	GREEK ALPHABET			
2 kappa	29 delta	36 beta	92 alpha	100 omega
GROUP 3	CHILDHOOD ILLNESSES			
3 measles	53 mumps	101 chickenpox	108 German measles	138 whooping cough
GROUP 4	VEGETABLES			
4 leek	55 carrot	59 broccoli	134 turnip	144 marrow
GROUP 5	CONSONANTS			
5 n	56 s	97 d	147 t	150 v

In a Class of their Own

GROUP 6	**RIVERS**			
6 Seine	34 Amazon	91 Nile	99 Congo	130 Thames
GROUP 7	**PUNCTUATION MARKS**			
7 comma	37 question mark	49 full stop	74 hyphen	121 exclamation mark
GROUP 8	**GAMES**			
8 Monopoly	51 Cluedo	76 chess	81 Scrabble	145 backgammon
GROUP 9	**GEM STONES**			
9 amethyst	19 topaz	68 garnet	86 diamond	102 opal
GROUP 10	**HATS**			
10 deerstalker	42 beret	50 bowler	96 bobble hat	103 trilby
GROUP 11	**POETIC FORMS**			
11 limerick	60 free verse	133 haiku	143 blank verse	148 sonnet
GROUP 12	**TENNIS STROKES**			
12 lob	46 volley	80 smash	87 serve	135 half volley
GROUP 13	**BOOKS OF THE OLD TESTAMENT**			
13 Genesis	38 Exodus	75 Proverbs	106 Job	112 Deuteronomy
GROUP 14	**FIELD EVENTS IN ATHLETICS**			
14 triple jump	35 high jump	64 pole vault	73 javelin	107 discus
GROUP 15	**BONES**			
16 tibia	54 fibula	93 femur	105 jawbone	115 metatarsal
GROUP 16	**BUTTERFLIES**			
17 red admiral	40 fritillary	66 speckled wood	85 peacock	116 cabbage white
GROUP 17	**CRICKET TERMS**			
18 gully	57 bye	79 crease	95 bouncer	117 googly
GROUP 18	**TYPES OF TEA**			
20 camomile	47 Earl Grey	88 herbal	136 China	140 Indian
GROUP 19	**GEOLOGICAL AGES**			
21 Jurassic	48 Cambrian	89 Devonian	104 Silurian	137 Palaeozoic
GROUP 20	**TYPES OF TRANSPORT**			
22 boat	71 train	123 bus	129 tram	141 aeroplane
GROUP 21	**PRIME NUMBERS**			
23 2	45 29	90 11	109 17	126 5
GROUP 22	**TYPES OF SINGING VOICE**			
24 baritone	61 soprano	124 tenor	128 bass	132 mezzo-soprano
GROUP 23	**VOWELS**			
25 a	43 i	77 e	127 o	142 u
GROUP 24	**SCIENTIFIC UNITS**			
26 faraday	58 ampere	69 volt	146 coulomb	149 joule
GROUP 25	**TYPEFACES**			
27 Helvetica	44 Clearface	70 Times New Roman	119 Gothic	125 Folio
GROUP 26	**SPIDERS**			
28 black widow	52 trapdoor	83 funnel-web	120 tarantula	139 money
GROUP 27	**GARDEN BIRDS**			
31 greenfinch	39 wren	65 starling	82 robin	113 sparrow
GROUP 28	**CAKES**			
32 Swiss roll	41 Bakewell tart	67 Madeira	78 Eccles	94 Dundee
GROUP 29	**EUROPEAN CAPITAL CITIES**			
33 Dublin	62 Madrid	98 Vienna	110 Paris	131 Rome
GROUP 30	**MULTIPLES OF FIVE**			
72 25	111 75	114 55	118 15	122 65

SPOOF PROOF READER

Publishers use proof readers to check texts for mistakes before books are printed and sold. Moira Scrutiny is such a proof reader and she is very good at her job, as befits somebody with her name! Normally she finds just a few mistakes but, on one day, she was horrified to identify no fewer than 30 errors in one relatively short passage for a book to be published in England. Authors may have particular weaknesses regarding spelling, punctuation or other features but this passage displayed a variety of types of error. Out of interest, Moira listed the mistakes into groups or categories. In the method that she used, Moira found that the 30 mistakes were placed into six groups with five errors in each group. The high level of error was afterwards explained by the fact that the passage was a 'spoof' sent as a joke by a colleague.

Here is a chance for you to pit your skills against Moira Scrutiny!

Your Tasks

1. Read the passage below.
2. Identify the 30 mistakes in the passage.
3. Organize the 30 errors into six groups of five depending upon the nature of the error.

THE PASSAGE

The man walked down the street purposefully. He went past the theater and crossed to the other side. quickly he moved to the next road junction. There was a short delay until the green pedastrian light came on. Jack daley, for that was the mans name, glanced into the windows as he passed the bank the bakery and the garage In the center of the next block of shops was a newsagent. Jack entered and looked around him. On the shelfs there were boxs of birthday cards. The proprieter was stood near the counter looking at a catalog of magazines.

'Where are the sheets of wrapping paper!' Jack asked the owner. The shopkeeper indicated an area with a nod of his head. There was quite a colection of sheets. Some were designed in pastel shades, others were much stronger in color. There were amusing examples among them, showing a sense of humor. A number of sheets feetured animals. Groups of deers adorned one particular sheet. Elephants, snakes, monkeys and lions dominated another sheet. A gaggle of gooses produced a striking image on yet another. Jack chose a sheet showing a mass of wild flowers and took it back to the counter.

'Its hot today' commented the shopkeeper. Jack bought a copy of *The times* as that was the newspaper what he liked best. 'You and me know what suits us' said Jack and the shopkeeper smiled in agreemont. They chatted for a minute or two. Jack glanced down at his newspaper and saw a photograph of the prime Minister.

'Where are the local advertisement cards?' asked Jack. 'We have moved them' replied the owner. He leaded his customer to a board at one side of the shop. There Jack read some of the cards. One of them was advertising a meeting on the local environment and it was headed 'To who this may concern'. A second was appealing for more ladys to join the bowling club just north of stockport.

SPOOF PROOF READER

Teaching Notes

'Spoof Proof Reader' is a classification exercise that is heavily based in English.

Key Elements

- ❖ classification
- ❖ use of a dictionary
- ❖ close engagement with text
- ❖ spelling
- ❖ grammar
- ❖ plurals
- ❖ punctuation
- ❖ use of capital letters
- ❖ deduction and inference.

Contexts

'Spoof Proof Reader' can be used in a variety of ways:

- ❖ as extension work in English
- ❖ as part of a thinking skills course
- ❖ as enrichment work for those who have completed other tasks
- ❖ as differentiated homework
- ❖ as an activity during an enrichment day, weekend or summer school
- ❖ as an activity for the English Club or Society.

The Solution

NOTE: Opinions do differ on areas like grammar. The errors included here are very definite ones and they should be acknowledged by everybody.

THE PASSAGE

The man walked down the street purposefully. He went past the **theater** and crossed to the other side. **quickly** he moved to the next road junction. There was a short delay until the green **pedastrian** light came on. Jack **daley**, for that was the **mans** name, glanced into the windows as he passed the **bank** the bakery and the **garage** In the **center** of the next block of shops was a newsagent. Jack entered and looked around him. On the **shelfs** there were **boxs** of birthday cards. The **proprieter** was **stood** near the counter looking at a **catalog** of magazines.

'Where are the sheets of wrapping paper**!**' Jack asked the owner. The shopkeeper indicated an area with a nod of his head. There was quite a **colection** of sheets. Some were designed in pastel shades, others were much stronger in **color**. There were amusing examples among them, showing a sense of **humor**. A number of sheets **feetured** animals. Groups of **deers** adorned one particular sheet. Elephants, snakes, monkeys and lions dominated another sheet. A gaggle of **gooses** produced a striking image on yet another. Jack chose a sheet showing a mass of wild flowers and took it back to the counter.

'**Its** hot today' commented the shopkeeper. Jack bought a copy of ***The times*** as that was the newspaper **what** he liked best. 'You and **me** know what suits us' said Jack and the shopkeeper smiled in **agreemont**. They chatted for a minute or two. Jack glanced down at his newspaper and saw a photograph of the **prime** Minister.

SPOOF PROOF READER

'Where are the local advertisement cards?' asked Jack. 'We have moved them' replied the owner. He **leaded** his customer to a board at one side of the shop. There Jack read some of the cards. One of them was advertising a meeting on the local environment and it was headed 'To **who** this may concern'. A second was appealing for more **ladys** to join the bowling club just north of **stockport**.

Punctuation Errors

1   apostrophe missing in 'the man's name'

2   comma missing after 'the bank'

3   full stop missing after 'the garage'

4   exclamation mark used incorrectly instead of a question mark after 'wrapping paper'

5   apostrophe missing from 'It's hot today'.

Capital Letters

1   Quickly

2   Jack Daley

3   *The Times*

4   Prime Minister

5   Stockport.

American Spelling

1   theater should be theatre

2   center should be centre

3   catalog should be catalogue

4   color should be colour

5   humor should be humour.

Incorrect Plurals

1   shelfs should be shelves

2   boxs should be boxes

3   deers should be deer

4   gooses should be geese

5   ladys should be ladies.

Spelling Errors

1   pedastrian should be pedestrian

2   proprieter should be proprietor

3   colection should be collection

4   feetured should be featured

5   agreemont should be agreement.

Grammatical Errors

1   The proprietor was standing (not 'stood')

2   newspaper that he liked (not 'what')

3   You and I (not 'You and me')

4   led his customer (not 'leaded')

5   To whom this may concern (not 'who').

PAWN IN THE GAME

The derivation or source of words is a fascinating subject. Words and phrases come into our language via many routes. Some date back a long time, although others are very modern because the English language is constantly changing.

Your Tasks

1 Look at the list of 60 words and phrases below.
2 Use a dictionary, reference books or the internet for those with which you are not familiar.
3 You will find that a number of themes or groups can be identified. Classify the words and phrases into categories or groups depending upon the nature of their origin. You should be able to find at least three words and phrases to fit a particular group.
4 Write down the groups of words and phrases, giving a definition for each. Explain what is the basis of your classification – what links the group together.

THE LIST OF WORDS AND PHRASES

1 quixotic
2 laser
3 DVD
4 home page
5 alabaster
6 emperor
7 pasteurization
8 anorak
9 volt
10 Judas
11 Achilles' heel
12 hip-hop
13 pawn in the game
14 ammoniac
15 wellingtons
16 democracy

17 pound of flesh
18 fait accompli
19 bad hair day
20 CBI
21 download
22 the Midas touch
23 doubting Thomas
24 cruncher
25 trump card
26 boycott
27 bête noire
28 BSE
29 meet your Waterloo
30 agoraphobia
31 bull's eye
32 glass ceiling

33 Galahad
34 bowler hat
35 enfant terrible
36 nihilism
37 David and Goliath (situation)
38 malapropism
39 AIDS
40 panacea
41 stalemate
42 morse
43 Jekyll and Hyde
44 garage
45 spartan
46 radar
47 sandwich

48 nemesis
49 laissez-faire
50 reboot
51 badminton
52 Herculean
53 ampere
54 Job's comforter
55 Balaclava helmet
56 alibi
57 house
58 Scrooge
59 CFC
60 level playing field

Extension Task

Find, and write down, further examples of the categories not included in the original list.

Problem-solving and Thinking Skills Resources for Able and Talented Children
© Barry Teare (Network Continuum Education, 2006)

PAWN IN THE GAME

Teaching Notes

'Pawn in the Game' has been included in the classification section as that is a very important element of the activity. However, the piece could also have been placed in the wordplay section. There is a wide coverage in terms of subject material.

Key Elements

- ❖ material from science, English, religious education, French, mythology, history, ancient languages, computing, popular music and games
- ❖ classification
- ❖ derivation of words
- ❖ use of the dictionary
- ❖ wordplay
- ❖ application (in the extension task)
- ❖ appreciation that the language changes.

Contexts

'Pawn in the Game' can be used in a number of ways:

- ❖ as extension work to vocabulary or dictionary based exercises
- ❖ as an enrichment activity for those who have completed other tasks
- ❖ as differentiated homework
- ❖ as part of a thinking skills course
- ❖ as an activity during an enrichment day, weekend or summer school
- ❖ as an open-access competition
- ❖ as an activity for the English Club or Society.

A Possible Solution

Below there is one solution to the exercise. The classification used is strong and logical. However, pupils may devise equally good groups that are different. If so, credit should be given for those alternative solutions providing that the instruction of at least three words or phrases in a group has been followed.

CLASSIFICATION	NO.	WORD	MEANING
Based upon literature	1	quixotic	Impractically idealistic: from the character of the hero of Cervantes' book *Don Quixote de la Mancha*.
	17	pound of flesh	Something that you are entitled to but is unreasonable: from Shakespeare's play *The Merchant of Venice* when Antonio promised a pound of flesh if he could not repay a loan.
	33	Galahad	A person known for nobility and good character: from Arthurian legend – the stories of the Round Table.
	38	malapropism	The use of a wrong word, similar in sound to the correct word: from the character Mrs Malaprop in Sheridan's *The Rivals*.
	43	Jekyll and Hyde	A split personality showing both good and evil: from Robert Louis Stevenson's book *The Strange Case of Dr Jekyll and Mr Hyde*.
	58	Scrooge	A miser or mean person: from the character of Scrooge in Charles Dickens' book *A Christmas Carol*.

PAWN IN THE GAME

Acronyms (words formed from the initial letters or syllables of other words)	2	**laser**	A device for converting light into an intense narrow beam: an acronym of light amplification by stimulated emission of radiation.
	39	**AIDS**	A medical condition that destroys a person's immune system: an acronym of Acquired Immune Deficiency Syndrome.
	46	**radar**	The technique of using reflections of radio waves for locating objects: an acronym of radio detecting and ranging.
Abbreviations	3	**DVD**	A digital recording medium with large capacity: stands for Digital Versatile Disc.
	20	**CBI**	An organization of companies: stands for Confederation of British Industry.
	28	**BSE**	An incurable brain condition in cattle: stands for Bovine Spongiform Encephalopathy.
	59	**CFC**	Compounds known to be harmful to the ozone layer: stands for ChloroFluoroCarbon. **NOTE**: students should recognize the difference between acronyms and abbreviations.
Computer terms	4	**home page**	The first page to access on an internet site.
	21	**download**	Transferring the contents of an electronic data file from one computer to another.
	24	**cruncher**	A computer or computer application that undertakes extensive calculation or processing of data.
	50	**reboot**	Restart a computer.
Based upon places	5	**alabaster**	Semi-transparent gypsum: said to be derived from Alabastron, a town in Egypt.
	14	**ammoniac**	Gum resin: traditionally obtained in Libya, near the temple of Ammon.
	29	**meet your Waterloo**	Face a major defeat: Napoleon was defeated at the Battle of Waterloo in 1815.
	45	**spartan**	Very strict or austere: from the ancient Greek city of Sparta which was famous for its discipline and for its harsh and austere way of life.
	51	**badminton**	A game played with a shuttlecock and racquets: from the home of the Duke of Beaufort where the game was first played. **NOTE**: this should not really be placed in the games category as it is not a term from a game but, rather, a place.
	55	**Balaclava helmet**	A woollen hood that covers the ears and neck: from a seaport in the Crimea where British soldiers fought in the nineteenth century.
Latin base	6	**emperor**	The person ruling an empire: from the Latin *imperator* which means 'a commander'.
	36	**nihilism**	A political doctrine that works against all established authority: from the Latin *nihil* meaning 'nothing'.
	56	**alibi**	A plea that somebody was in another place when a crime was committed: from the Latin *alibi* meaning 'elsewhere'.

PAWN IN THE GAME

Real people	7	**pasteurization**	The process of heating substances to destroy micro-organisms: from the work of the chemist, Louis Pasteur.
	9	**volt**	Unit of electrical potential: named after the Italian physicist, Count Volta.
	15	**wellingtons**	Rubber boots: named after the Duke of Wellington.
	26	**boycott**	To isolate and ignore a person or an organization: from Captain Boycott, treated this way in Ireland in the nineteenth century.
	34	**bowler hat**	A stiff hat with a rounded crown: named after the manufacturer, Bowler.
	42	**morse**	A system for transmitting messages: named after the inventor, Samuel Morse.
	47	**sandwich**	A type of food: named after the fourth Earl of Sandwich, who ate such a snack so as not to have to leave the gaming-table.
	53	**ampere**	The unit by which an electrical current is measured: named after the French physicist Ampère.
Metaphorical or symbolic	8	**anorak**	A person who pursues an interest with obsessive dedication: from wearing an anorak, considered to be unfashionable and boring.
	19	**bad hair day**	A day on which everything goes wrong.
	32	**glass ceiling**	An unofficial or unacknowledged barrier to personal advancement, especially at work.
	60	**level playing field**	Fair conditions for everybody.
The Bible	10	**Judas**	A person who betrays a friend: named after Judas Iscariot who betrayed Jesus for 30 pieces of silver.
	23	**doubting Thomas**	A person who needs proof before believing: from Thomas who would not accept the resurrection of Christ without seeing for himself.
	37	**David and Goliath** (situation)	A struggle between somebody small and a much more powerful person: from the story in the Old Testament.
	54	**Job's comforter**	Somebody who makes worse the distress of the person who has come for help and comfort: from the story in the Old Testament.
Mythology	11	**Achilles' heel**	A small but important weak point: from the Greek myth where Achilles was dipped into the river to make him invincible but he was held by the heel which remained vulnerable.
	22	**the Midas touch**	The ability to succeed, especially where money is concerned: from the story of King Midas who turned everything he touched into gold.
	48	**nemesis**	Retributive justice: from Nemesis, the Greek goddess of retribution.
	52	**Herculean**	A difficult task requiring great strength: from Hercules, a hero in Greek mythology who had superhuman physical strength.

Pawn in the Game

Popular music	12	**hip-hop**	A culture involving rap music, graffiti art and break dancing.
	44	**garage**	A variety of music from New York that incorporates elements of soul music.
	57	**house**	Popular music typically featuring the use of drum machines, sequencers, sampled sound effects and prominent synthesized bass lines.
Games terms	13	**pawn in the game**	Somebody who is manipulated and not given much consideration: in the game of chess, the pawn is the piece of least value.
	25	**trump card**	A particularly advantageous tactic or action: in card games, such as bridge, trumps have more weight than other cards in winning tricks.
	31	**bull's eye**	Something that 'hits the target' exactly: in the game of darts the bull's eye is the small central area that scores highly.
	41	**stalemate**	A deadlock situation: in the game of chess no further moves are possible and the game is drawn
Greek base	16	**democracy**	A political system in which everybody has influence: from the Greek *demos* which means 'people' and *kratos* meaning 'strength'.
	30	**agoraphobia**	Fear of open spaces: from the Greek *agora* meaning 'marketplace' and *phobos* meaning 'fear'.
	40	**panacea**	A universal remedy, originally relating to illness but used also more generally: from the Greek *pan* meaning 'all' and *akos* meaning 'cure'.
French words, phrases used directly	18	**fait accompli**	Something already done or finished.
	27	**bête noire**	A person or thing that one especially dislikes or fears.
	35	**enfant terrible**	A person, especially young, whose behaviour is embarrassing or unconventional.
	49	**laissez-faire**	A policy of non-intervention: the French literally means 'let do'.

The Following Parties

It was a week before Christmas and the restaurant at the Villa Garden Centre was extremely busy. Sixty different family groups were booked in for lunch. At very regular intervals a voice on the tannoy system said 'Would the following parties please proceed to the restaurant where their tables are ready'. There then followed, on each occasion, three family names.

Your Task

Study the list of 60 family names placed in alphabetical order. Now, divide the 60 into 20 appropriate groups of three names so that each trio makes a famous saying or a combination of similar items, such as trees, musicians or writers. Some names will go into more than one combination but a particular placement will allow all 60 names to be positioned in appropriate groups. Explain the reason for each grouping.

Practical Suggestion

You can use any method that suits you, but you may find it helpful to write the 60 names on slips of paper that you can move about physically.

The family groups in alphabetical order

1 Able	16 Drake	31 Lamb	46 Scott
2 Ash	17 Drink	32 Lance	47 Sinker
3 Barrel	18 Eat	33 Line	48 Snow
4 Birch	19 Faith	34 Lion	49 Spear
5 Blyton	20 Fine	35 Livingstone	50 Starling
6 Carpenter	21 Frost	36 Lock	51 Stock
7 Charity	22 Greenwood	37 Love	52 Storm
8 Charles	23 Henry	38 Merry	53 Swallow
9 Churchill	24 Holly	39 Morse	54 Sword
10 Cook	25 Holmes	40 Oak	55 Thatcher
11 Cooper	26 Hook	41 Pike	56 Wardrobe
12 Cross	27 Hope	42 Poirot	57 Willing
13 Cub	28 Ivy	43 Ready	58 Wilson
14 Darling	29 James	44 Roach	59 Witch
15 Dear	30 Kitten	45 Rudd	60 Wren

Extension Task

Create your own list of names from other categories. Place them in alphabetical order. Get somebody else to try and group them in appropriate trios.

The Following Parties

Teaching Notes

'The Following Parties' is a light-hearted piece of work but it involves wordplay and the critical thinking skill of classification. Many able pupils have a particular sense of humour and they are likely to enjoy the wonderful images created by the announcements of the three family groups to go to the restaurant.

Contexts

'The Following Parties' would make a very suitable open-access competition with the extension task being used as a discriminator if needed. It could also be used:

❖ as differentiated homework
❖ as an activity in a thinking skills course
❖ as extension material to vocabulary extension work
❖ as an activity during an enrichment session, cluster day or summer school.

Possible Solution

19 Faith	+	27 Hope	+	7 Charity (saying)
24 Holly	+	28 Ivy	+	22 Greenwood (from the carol)
4 Birch	+	40 Oak	+	2 Ash (trees)
43 Ready	+	57 Willing	+	1 Able (saying)
8 Charles	+	23 Henry	+	29 James (male names, Kings of England)
36 Lock	+	51 Stock	+	3 Barrel (saying)
34 Lion	+	59 Witch	+	56 Wardrobe (book title)
55 Thatcher	+	9 Churchill	+	58 Wilson (British Prime Ministers)
31 Lamb	+	30 Kitten	+	13 Cub (young of animals)
15 Dear	+	37 Love	+	14 Darling (terms of affection)
48 Snow	+	21 Frost	+	52 Storm (weather)
39 Morse	+	42 Poirot	+	25 Holmes (fictional detectives)
18 Eat	+	17 Drink	+	38 Merry (saying)
53 Swallow	+	50 Starling	+	60 Wren (birds)
54 Sword	+	32 Lance	+	49 Spear (weapons)
41 Pike	+	44 Roach	+	45 Rudd (fish)
20 Fine	+	12 Cross	+	5 Blyton (children's writers)
16 Drake	+	46 Scott	+	35 Livingstone (explorers)
11 Cooper	+	6 Carpenter	+	10 Cook (jobs, occupations)
26 Hook	+	33 Line	+	47 Sinker (saying)

NOTES

● This combination uses all 60 names appropriately. Are there other solutions which allow total placement? Certainly, individual names can be placed in another group – for example, Cook with the explorers or Pike with the weapons. However, this is extremely likely to leave other names unplaced.

● Pupils may use a variety of working methods, including writing the names on 60 separate slips. Let them use the method that suits them best individually.

Section 8

Sequencing

Knowing the correct order is an essential factor for the successful completion of many activities. Problem solving is greatly assisted by a step-by-step approach. Understanding sequences assists predicting what is likely to follow. It also helps the appreciation of patterns and trends. Flow charts are based upon the logical sequencing of events. Stories have an essential chronological order although, ironically, it is the sophisticated writer, with a strong understanding of sequencing, who challenges the reader by mixing up time and using flashbacks. Many physical activities also depend upon appropriate sequencing. Edward de Bono in *Teaching Thinking* (Pelican, 1978) says:

> Pattern is the basis not only of how the mind works but of how the world itself works
>
> (*page 84*)

The same author, in his book *Po: Beyond Yes and No* (Pelican, 1973), gives an amusing example of how important the sequence of events is:

> In your own personal life things happen one after another. You acquire experience piece by piece. And the particular sequence in which experience is acquired makes a huge difference to the ideas and attitudes you hold. If you were rich and then lost all your money in the Great Depression, your attitude would be quite different from what it would have been if you went through the Depression and then became rich shortly afterwards.
>
> (*page 57*)

The breadth of the application of this thinking skill becomes clear when one looks at the following selection of quotes from the National Curriculum 1999:

> … suggest appropriate sequences of investigation.
> (*geography*)

> … plan what they have to do, suggesting a sequence of action and alternatives, if needed.
> (*design and technology*)

> … use their knowledge of sequence and story language when they are retelling stories and predicting events.
> (*English*)

> … use advanced compositional concepts and principles when composing their sequences.
> (*physical education – gymnastics*)

> … find the first terms of a sequence given a rule arising naturally from a context.
> (*mathematics*)

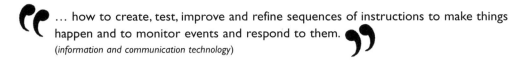

… how to create, test, improve and refine sequences of instructions to make things happen and to monitor events and respond to them.
(information and communication technology)

… place events and objects in chronological order.
(history)

- Many children have worked on number sequences, deciding what the next number should be. 'Next in Line' has 26 sequences where able pupils are asked to give the next two terms. Mental agility is put at a premium, as the examples are mixed up and contain elements of mathematics, science, history, geography and general knowledge.

- 'Tries So' is an anagram of 'stories', and rightly so, as the task is to rewrite, first of all, the sentences from a mixed-up order, then the nine sections of a confused story, and, finally, the ten sections of two overlapping mixed-up stories. As well as sequencing and engagement with text, deduction and inference play an important role.

- Anagrams are words out of order or sequence. 'Letters Rearrange' follows the travels of Anna Gram in the country of Muddle. She (and therefore the students) has to make sense of anagrams, written simply or within situations, which come from the widely different areas of history, science, English, mathematics, art and general knowledge. The challenging range and amusing contexts should appeal to many able children.

- The final piece, 'In Good Order', places sequencing very much in the real world. Many tasks need to be carried out in a particular order. If not, earlier work is spoiled or the sequence does not make practical sense. Pupils are asked to place the stages in correct logical order for, first, a case heard by a jury in court and, second, the decorating of a room. They then choose an area of their own to 'chunk down'. In all cases, the reasoning behind the suggested sequencing is requested.

Next in Line

In mathematics you may well have worked on number sequences.
You are given four or five terms and then have to say what the next one or two would be. You may have come across sequences involving letters or initials.
This piece of work looks at sequences from a wide variety of sources.

You will need to keep your wits about you.
So, what is 'Next in Line'?

Your Tasks

1 For each of the 26 examples below, look carefully at the terms that are given.
2 Work out what the next two terms should be. What, in other words, replaces the two question marks?
3 Explain your thinking by writing down the 'rule' that you are following to get to the next two terms.

Please Note

1 There is considerable variation in terms of difficulty.
2 In some examples the start of the sequence is given, while in others there are terms before those appearing.
3 The majority of the examples use only one rule but do watch out for an occasional example involving more than one sequence.

The Sequences

1	1	4	9	16	?	?
2	● —	— ● ● ●	— ● — ●	— ● ●	?	?
3	1	6	11	16	?	?
4	Red	Orange	Yellow	Green	?	?
5	○	◐	◔	◕	?	?

Next in Line

6	21		28		36		45		?	?
7	C	Ca		Cd		Ce		Cf	?	?
8	223		227		229		233		?	?
9	Calm	Light air	Light breeze	Gentle breeze	Moderate breeze		Fresh breeze		?	?
10	1		8		27		64		?	?
11	A	M		J		J		A	?	?
12	6561		2187		729		243		?	?
13	Rat	Ox		Tiger		Hare		Dragon	?	?
14	74		68		62		56		?	?
15	LII		LV		LVIII		LXI		?	?
16	M	T		W		T		F	?	?
17	1	5		12		22		35	?	?
18	Henry VII		Henry VIII		Edward VI		Mary		?	?
19	55	66		77	88		99	101	?	?
20	Aries		Taurus		Gemini		Cancer		?	?
21	9	26	13	29	17	32	21	35	?	?
22	pentagon		hexagon		septagon		octagon		?	?
23	1	2		6		24		120	?	?

24

25 90 75 88 70 86 65 84 ? ?

26   ? ?

Extension Task

★ Create some sequences of your own. These can involve numbers, letters, symbols or anything suitable.

★ Put question marks for the next two terms.

★ Ask somebody else to try to replace the question marks with the 'Next in Line'.

Problem-solving and Thinking Skills Resources for Able and Talented Children

Next in Line

Teaching Notes

Many children are familiar with number sequences and there is a selection included here. They will not be as familiar with some of the other examples. As the 26 sequences are really mixed up, the difficulty is increased.

Key Elements

- ❖ sequencing
- ❖ research
- ❖ mental agility
- ❖ explaining 'rules'
- ❖ application (in the extension task)
- ❖ elements of mathematics, science, history, geography and general knowledge.

Contexts

'Next in Line' can be used in a number of ways:

- ❖ within a thinking skills course
- ❖ a selection of examples during mathematics lessons
- ❖ as extension work to an exercise on sequences
- ❖ as enrichment work for those who have completed other tasks
- ❖ as differentiated homework
- ❖ as an activity during an enrichment day, weekend or summer school
- ❖ as an activity for the Investigators' Club
- ❖ as an open-access competition, where the extension task acts as a discriminator where necessary.

Some Answers

The following are the intended answers. If pupils produce a different response with a valid explanation, credit should be given.

1	25	36	(ascending square numbers)
2	●	● ● — ●	(E and F in Morse Code)
3	21	26	(add 5 to the previous number)
4	Blue	Indigo	(colours of the rainbow)
5			(cloud cover measured in oktas or eighths)
6	55	66	(triangular numbers; alternatively, adding one more than the last number added)
7	Cl	Cm	(chlorine and curium – in chemistry, part of the alphabetic order of symbols used for the elements)
8	239	241	(prime numbers in ascending order)
9	strong breeze	near gale	(the Beaufort Scale)
10	125	216	(cube numbers)

Problem-solving and Thinking Skills Resources for Able and Talented Children

Next in Line

11	S	O	(September and October – initials of the months of the year)
12	81	27	(divide by 3)
13	Snake	Horse	(animals, year by year, in the Chinese calendar)
14	50	44	(subtract 6 from the previous number)
15	LXIV	LXVII	(add 3 but in Roman numerals)
16	S	S	(Saturday and Sunday – days of the week)
17	51	70	(pentagonal numbers – a combination of square numbers and triangular numbers)
18	Elizabeth I	James I	(chronological reigns of kings and queens of England)
19	111	121	(ascending palindromic numbers)
20	Leo	Virgo	(signs of the zodiac)
21	25	38	(alternating sequences of adding 4 and adding 3)
22	nonagon	decagon	(polygons in ascending order of sides)
23	720	5040	($6!$ and $7!$ – factorials)
24			(E and F in Braille)
25	60	82	(alternating sequences of subtracting 2 and subtracting 5)
26			(10^4 and 10^5 – Egyptian numeral system)

Tries So

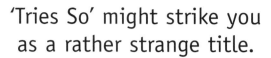

'Tries So' might strike you
as a rather strange title.

What's it all about? Well – 'Tries So' is an anagram of 'stories' or, in other words, this piece is about mixed-up stories. Most books tell a story in chronological order, starting with the first event and finishing with the last. How would you cope if the order had been mixed up? Here is your opportunity to find out.

Work hard on this exercise and the teacher's comment might well be 'Tries So'!

Your Tasks
Part A

This first section involves single sentences. The six examples here have been written out in a mixed-up order. Rewrite the sentences in their correct order.

1   January a strong often of are feature winds weather.
2   For essential boots ramblers walking good are.
3   Beginning global to on an warming species have is animal impact.
4   Be to tend children at puzzles able solving good.
5   Early sufficient in to Madeleine got always school time for up be.
6   Moods vehicle the the best a had puncture of driver was bus in not his as.

Part B

The nine sections of a story have been mixed up. Sort out the order to make the story be chronologically correct.

NOTE: use a method that suits you best. You might find it helpful in Parts B and C to write the sections on slips of paper to move around.

Section 1   On the bus Nadia thought back about the questions. She thought that she had done well.

Section 2   Then she had a stroke of luck. The bus was a couple of minutes late which meant that she caught it.

Section 3   She looked at the alarm clock. It had not gone off at the correct time.

Section 4   There were five other candidates for the post. Tea, coffee and biscuits were available as they waited for the interviews to start.

Section 5   Nadia heard the post drop through the letter box. She hastily tore open the envelope. A big smile crossed her face. She had been appointed to the job.

Section 6   On the bus Nadia met one of her old school friends. Nadia explained that she was on her way for an interview at a company called Crossley Computers.

Tries So

Section 7   Nadia got washed and dressed as quickly as she could. She decided that she would have to go without breakfast.

Section 8   Nadia was the last to be interviewed. She felt confident about her answers. She walked to the bus station.

Section 9   Nadia was woken up by the sounds of blackbirds squabbling in the garden.

Part C

Now let us take the process a stage further. Below there are ten sections, but not only are they mixed up in terms of order, they also form two separate stories of five sections each. Sort out the order to make two different stories that are chronologically correct.

Section 1   Jane returned from her meal, her hunger satisfied.

Section 2   He began to think about her name. Was this the Jane that he had met at a friend's birthday party in Bromley? Frank rather thought that it was.

Section 3   'My name is Frank Howard,' the man said. He explained who he was. 'You had better co-operate with your husband's lawyer now that I have seen the letters in your briefcase.' Jane's face fell. The game was up.

Section 4   Frank had eaten a large meal before his journey. He did not accompany other passengers, including Jane, who had gone to the restaurant car. While she was away, Frank continued his thoughts about that birthday party.

Section 5   The pilot boat left the great liner and returned to port. On board, Frank Howard, the detective, began to trail his suspect, Jane Dark. Firm evidence was needed.

Section 6   'Excuse me, but I think that we have met before', said Frank. Jane looked at him and smiled. 'Indeed we have' she said. 'I wondered if you would remember.'

Section 7   Frank took the opportunity to search her luggage. It was illegal, of course, to use skeleton keys but this was in a good cause. Inside the briefcase were the papers he was looking for. Now he had a real lead.

Section 8   Frank Vernon settled down into his seat. His luggage was safely stored in the rack above his head. The train left the station and picked up speed. The only other passenger in that particular group of seats was taking some papers out of her briefcase. Frank saw the name tag on the case – Jane Perkin.

Section 9   Jane made her way to the restaurant. She was hungry and looked forward to the meal. 'What was being prepared in the galley?' she thought.

Section 10   Jane returned from her meal, her hunger satisfied. She stood on deck watching the sights in the distance. She heard footsteps and turned to see a man watching her intently.

Extension Task

Write your own 'double story' with mixed-up sections as you were asked to sort out in Part C. You need to make sure that the two stories can be separated and put into chronological order while, at the same time, not making it too easy to do so. The material has to be similar enough but contain sufficient clues to allow a solution.

Tries So

Teaching Notes

First and foremost 'Tries So' is a piece of work about sequencing. However, many other skills are required, especially for Part C.

Key Elements

- ❖ sequencing
- ❖ analysis
- ❖ engagement with text
- ❖ deduction
- ❖ inference
- ❖ a very particular piece of writing in the extension task.

Contexts

'Tries So' can be used in a variety of ways:

- ❖ as a challenging piece of work in a thinking skills course
- ❖ as an enrichment activity for those who have completed other tasks
- ❖ as a differentiated homework
- ❖ as an activity during an enrichment day, weekend or summer school
- ❖ as an open-access competition where the extension task would be the discriminator.

Some Answers

Possible solutions are given but credit should be given for alternative answers that fit equally well. They cannot, however, ignore key clues such as the different locations used in the stories in Part C.

PART A (this is very much a warm-up exercise)

1 Strong winds are often a feature of January weather.

2 Good walking boots are essential for ramblers.

3 Global warming is beginning to have an impact on animal species.

4 Able children tend to be good at solving puzzles.

5 Madeleine always got up in sufficient time to be early for school.

6 The bus driver was not in the best of moods as his vehicle had a puncture.

PART B

Section 9	Nadia was woken up by the sounds of blackbirds squabbling in the garden.
Section 3	She looked at the alarm clock. It had not gone off at the correct time.
Section 7	Nadia got washed and dressed as quickly as she could. She decided that she would have to go without breakfast.
Section 2	Then she had a stroke of luck. The bus was a couple of minutes late which meant that she caught it.
Section 6	On the bus Nadia met one of her old school friends. Nadia explained that she was on her way for an interview at a company called Crossley Computers.
Section 4	There were five other candidates for the post. Tea, coffee and biscuits were available as they waited for the interviews to start.
Section 8	Nadia was the last to be interviewed. She felt confident about her answers. She walked to the bus station.
Section 1	On the bus Nadia thought back about the questions. She thought that she had done well.
Section 5	Nadia heard the post drop through the letter box. She hastily tore open the envelope. A big smile crossed her face. She had been appointed to the job.

Tries So

PART C
Story One

Section 5	The pilot boat left the great liner and returned to port. On board, Frank Howard, the detective, began to trail his suspect, Jane Dark. Firm evidence was needed.
Section 9	Jane made her way to the restaurant. She was hungry and looked forward to the meal. 'What was being prepared in the galley?' she thought.
Section 7	Frank took the opportunity to search her luggage. It was illegal, of course, to use skeleton keys but this was in a good cause. Inside the briefcase were the papers he was looking for. Now he had a real lead.
Section 10	Jane returned from her meal, her hunger satisfied. She stood on deck watching the sights in the distance. She heard footsteps and turned to see a man watching her intently.
Section 3	'My name is Frank Howard,' the man said. He explained who he was. 'You had better co-operate with your husband's lawyer now that I have seen the letters in your briefcase.' Jane's face fell. The game was up.

Story Two

Section 8	Frank Vernon settled down into his seat. His luggage was safely stored in the rack above his head. The train left the station and picked up speed. The only other passenger in that particular group of seats was taking some papers out of her briefcase. Frank saw the name tag on the case – Jane Perkin.
Section 2	He began to think about her name. Was this the Jane that he had met at a friend's birthday party in Bromley? Frank rather thought that it was.
Section 4	Frank had eaten a large meal before his journey. He did not accompany other passengers, including Jane, who had gone to the restaurant car. While she was away, Frank continued his thoughts about that birthday party.
Section 1	Jane returned from her meal, her hunger satisfied.
Section 6	'Excuse me, but I think that we have met before', said Frank. Jane looked at him and smiled. 'Indeed we have' she said. 'I wondered if you would remember.'

Extension Task

The success criteria for the extension task would include:

- the effectiveness of the two stories created
- the skill in selecting similarities within the two stories
- how well the clues are included to enable the separation of the two stories
- how well the clues have been mixed up.

Problem-solving and Thinking Skills Resources for Able and Talented Children

Letters Rearrange!

Anna Gram has lost her way on her travels and she has found herself in the country of Muddle. Wherever she goes she cannot understand the language as the words do not make sense to her. Switching channels on the television in her hotel room she comes across various programmes.

Your Task

Can you help Anna Gram to sort out what she is seeing and hearing on the television?

CLUeS

Anna Gram's name should help you to work out the words, and the fact that she is in the country of Muddle should tell you how to solve the problem.

PROGRAMMeS

Science equipment, substances and operations

Part 1	ben bus runner	(6, 6)
Part 2	u bet sett	(4, 4)
Part 3	laid oil tints	(12)
Part 4	close upper path	(6, 8)
Part 5	limp pasture	(6, 5)

famous scientists

Have you heard the story about the French scientist (9), the English scientist (7) and the Russian scientist (6)? It goes like this:

Sir love viola davy pa afar

Bird survey

One birdspotter reported his findings to the Royal Society for the Protection of Birds:

1	fen chin reg	(10)
2	red grape show	(5, 7)
3	little din goat	(4-6, 3)
4	a plaited wig	(4, 7)
5	my lame howler	(12)

Going round in a circle: a mathematical exploration of the circle

There is a definite relationship between the TEAM RIDE (8) and the RECCE FUR MINCE (13). To touch the circle a GANNETT (7) can be drawn. When there is more than one circle, they might be TECCNIC RON (10). One common calculation involves the DADS RISQUE RUA (6, 7).

Laughing with literacy

You will meet a number of terms where there might be similar sounds, general meanings, repeated sounds and bees going backwards!

1	tear lion tail	(12)
2	ample sir don	(11)
3	I moo on oat pea	(12)
4	my nosh mo	(8)
5	brev rops	(8)

A mixed-up gallery

These famous artists have got themselves into a tangle. One is French (7), one Dutch (9), one Spanish (7) and the last is English (9). The visitors to the gallery could see:

bald man comes across its best painter

British Prime Ministers of the last hundred years and their mixed vegetables

Four British Prime Ministers [(5), (8), (9) and (6)] met in a time capsule for a meal. They were:

at lunch with charles brill choir

They each ordered their favourite vegetables [(6), (9), (6) and (8)] – one yellow, one green, one orange and one deep red (but not necessarily in the order of the letters given above). The four Prime Ministers shouted out their orders at the same time so that their choices became mixed vegetables:

T stew crop rare rust once robot toe

Extension Task

Choose another television programme Anna Gram might have seen and create words that fit the country of Muddle in which she finds herself. Try to make interesting visual and verbal images with these words. Then say to somebody in your class: 'Letters Rearrange!'

Letters Rearrange!

Teaching Notes

'Letters Rearrange' deals with the popular format of anagrams. However, the level of difficulty has been increased by ranging over a number of curriculum areas and, on some occasions, by mixing anagrams together. An attempt has also been made to place the problems into interesting and amusing contexts.

NOTE: pupils should choose methods that suit them personally to solve the anagrams. Possible methods include writing the letters mixed up on paper and crossing off letters as they are used, or writing individual letters on pieces of paper and rearranging them to make words.

Key Elements

- ❖ sequencing
- ❖ wordplay
- ❖ mental agility
- ❖ strategic thinking
- ❖ elements of history, science, English, mathematics, art and general knowledge.

Contexts

'Letters Rearrange' can be used in the following ways:

- ❖ in sections within specific curriculum lessons
- ❖ as part of a thinking skills course
- ❖ as a team activity
- ❖ as an enrichment activity for those who have finished other tasks
- ❖ as a differentiated homework
- ❖ as an activity during an enrichment day, weekend or summer school
- ❖ as an open-access competition.

The Solution

Science equipment, substances and operations
1   Bunsen burner
2   test tube
3   distillation
4   copper sulphate
5   litmus paper.

Famous scientists
Lavoisier, Faraday and Pavlov.

The bird survey
1   greenfinch
2   hedge sparrow
3   long-tailed tit
4   pied wagtail
5   yellowhammer

Going round in a circle
1   diameter
2   circumference
3   tangent
4   concentric
5   radius squared.

Laughing with literacy
1   alliteration
2   palindromes
3   onomatopoeia
4   homonyms
5   proverbs.

A mixed-up gallery
Matisse, Rembrandt, Picasso and Constable.

British Prime Ministers and mixed vegetables
Blair, Thatcher, Churchill and Wilson.
Carrot, sweetcorn, sprout and beetroot.

Problem-solving and Thinking Skills Resources for Able and Talented Children   **211**

IN GOOD ORDER

On some occasions there are a number of jobs to be done but they are independent of each other – washing the car, doing the shopping, mending some clothes. It doesn't matter what order is followed. However, at other times, there are large tasks or events that take place in stages. Then the order is vital because earlier work can be spoiled or the sequence does not make logical sense. Then one can say that the steps need to be 'In Good Order'.

SECTION ONE

Your Tasks

1 Examine the mixed-up lists.
2 Place them in their correct chronological order.
3 Explain why this order is necessary.

ORDER IN COURT

THE MIXED-UP LIST OF EVENTS DURING THE HEARING OF A CASE BY A JURY

- 👉 Closing speech for the defence.
- 👉 The judge's summing up.
- 👉 The swearing-in of the jury.
- 👉 The jury retires to consider its verdict.
- 👉 The case for the defence.
- 👉 Sentence is passed by the judge.
- 👉 The defendant pleads guilty or not guilty.
- 👉 The case for the prosecution.
- 👉 Objections are made by the defence to members of the jury.
- 👉 Closing speech for the prosecution.

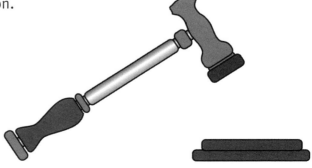

Problem-solving and Thinking Skills Resources for Able and Talented Children

ROOM FOR IMPROVEMENT

THE MIXED-UP LIST OF STAGES
DURING THE DECORATION OF A ROOM IN A HOUSE

- ☛ Hang the wallpaper.
- ☛ Undercoat the woodwork.
- ☛ Sand down all areas of woodwork.
- ☛ Clean all surfaces to get the grease off.
- ☛ Do a final clean-up, removing protective tape, covers and newspapers.
- ☛ Do the second coat of emulsion paint on the ceiling.
- ☛ Move and/or protect the furniture and curtains.
- ☛ Strip off the old wallpaper.
- ☛ Protect the carpet.
- ☛ Gloss paint the woodwork.
- ☛ Do the first coat of emulsion paint on the ceiling.
- ☛ Put the room back to normal use.
- ☛ 'Make good' any cracks and defects.
- ☛ Wipe dust off all areas of woodwork.

SECTION TWO

DON'T PUT THE CART BEFORE THE HORSE

Your Tasks

1 Choose one or more of the jobs that follow.
2 Carry out the necessary research.
3 Break the job down into its various stages.
4 Explain why the chronological order has to be as you have suggested.

THE JOBS

- ★ Making a Christmas cake.
- ★ Building a house.
- ★ Going on holiday.
- ★ Constructing a garden for a new house where there has not been a garden previously.
- ★ Setting up coarse fishing tackle.

OR Select any other similar situation that interests you and will fit the thinking behind 'In Good Order'.

IN GOOD ORDER

Teaching Notes

'In Good Order' takes the theory of sequencing into a number of very practical situations. In so doing, the piece of work involves a number of thinking skills.

Key Elements

- ❖ sequencing
- ❖ chronological order
- ❖ analysis
- ❖ evaluation
- ❖ logical thinking
- ❖ problem solving.

Contexts

'In Good Order' can be used in the following ways:

- ❖ as part of a thinking skills course
- ❖ as differentiated homework
- ❖ as an enrichment activity for those who have completed other tasks
- ❖ as an activity during an enrichment day, weekend or summer school
- ❖ as an open-access competition, where Section Two could act as a discriminator if required.

Some Answers

The court scenario has a particular solution. Decorating the room has a strong logical order but small switches are possible to save time. There may be some latitude in the second section. Great emphasis should be placed upon the reasoning shown.

SECTION ONE
ORDER IN COURT

1   The defendant pleads guilty or not guilty. (A guilty plea means that no jury is required.)

2   The swearing-in of the jury.

3   Objections are made by the defence to members of the jury. (Stages 2 and 3 take place in an overlapping manner; as each juror is sworn in, the defence has the opportunity to object.)

4   The case for the prosecution.

5   The case for the defence. (In English law there is an onus on the prosecution to prove the case against the defendant 'beyond reasonable doubt'. The defendant is innocent until proved otherwise. Speaking last is seen as an advantage.)

6   Closing speech for the prosecution.

7   Closing speech for the defence

8   The judge's summing up. (The defence, again, goes last. The judge sums up when all the evidence has been presented and the speeches have been made. He needs to draw important areas to the jury's attention and to make points of law clear.)

9 The jury retires to consider its verdict.

10 Sentence is passed by the judge. (If the verdict is guilty, the judge passes sentence. If the verdict is not guilty, stage 10 will not take place.)

ROOM FOR IMPROVEMENT

1 Move and/or protect the furniture and curtains.

2 Protect the carpet. (The top two must come first to prevent damage.)

3 Strip off the old wallpaper. (This is a messy job that would cause problems if done later.)

4 Clean all surfaces to get the grease off. (No other preparation works well if dirt remains on the surfaces.)

5 'Make good' any cracks and defects. (This needs to dry before painting or wallpapering takes place.)

6 Sand down all areas of woodwork (otherwise paint will not 'take').

7 Wipe dust off all areas of woodwork (necessary after stage 6 and before painting).

8 Put the first coat of emulsion paint on the ceiling.

9 Do the second coat of emulsionpaint on the ceiling. (The new decorations have now begun. It is best to do the ceiling first to avoid paint 'running' onto lower surfaces.)

10 Undercoat the woodwork.

11 Gloss paint the woodwork.

12 'Hang' the wallpaper. (If the painting is done after the wallpapering, marks could be made.)

13 Do a final clean-up, removing protective tape, covers and newspapers.

14 Put the room back to normal use.

NOTE: while the first coat of emulsion paint on the ceiling is drying, some people might want to be getting on with undercoating the woodwork. Some variation is possible.

SECTION TWO

Answers here will depend upon what the students have chosen. The key point is that the suggested order is logical and that the reasoning behind the sequencing is sound.

Section 9

Codes

Codes or, often more accurately, ciphers hold great fascination for adults and children alike. They play a part in a number of detective stories and thrillers. Recently, Dan Brown's *The Da Vinci Code*, which is a thriller filled with codes, became an international bestseller.

History teems with codes. Julius Caesar used a system of a 'shift of steps'. Spartan officers used their staffs to encode and decode messages. It could be said that Mary, Queen of Scots was executed because her code was not strong enough to prevent Walsingham from linking her actively with Catholic conspirators. The most well-known story of all is 'Station X', the remarkable cracking of the Enigma machine by the secret code-breakers of Bletchley Park. This was essential to the Allies' success and most historians believe that it shortened the Second World War. Bletchley Park was also the birthplace of the world's first programmable computer.

There are many good reasons to use codes with able pupils. As something stands for something else, there is an abstract quality. Abstract thinking is an element that many able children excel at. 'Abstract' appears throughout the curriculum – it is the whole area of mathematics called algebra, proverbs in English, chemical notation, musical notation, parables in religious education, symbolism, allegories and second meanings in stories.

Codes encourage good working habits. They do involve trial-and-error on some occasions but in a systematic way. Close engagement with the text is required, a feature of huge importance right across the curriculum.

Exercises on codes vary in length but some require a considerable period of time. It is vital that able pupils maintain concentration for more than a few minutes. Television and the media tend to have a 'dumbing down' effect. Nothing of any significance can be solved with a 'sound bite' approach.

Codes also vary in difficulty. Some have a high level of challenge and that is important, too, for able children. Too often they lack such challenge. On an undemanding diet they can become intellectually idle and then be reluctant to tackle anything beyond the standard material.

- **'The School for Surreptitious Spies'** provides a demanding challenge because of its scope. Ten types of code or cipher are included. The setting is a fictional school where spies are trained. Spoof lecture notes are provided and then there are ten secret messages to crack without knowing which type each is. The piece also provides the pupils with some of the theory behind this intriguing subject.

- **'New Meanings for Mnemonics'** is a general code with a small reference to trigonometry. At its heart is one of the tools for memory work – mnemonics. Logical thinking and close interpretation of data are key features. Pupils are invited to pit their wits against a problem set by teacher Miss Meta Cognition for her 'Think Big' club at school.

● Some codes are more closely associated with a particular subject. In previous books the author has set problems in English, science, French, mathematics and history. In fact any area of the curriculum could be used. Sherlock Holmes was renowned for his ability to solve codes and a number were featured in Sir Arthur Conan Doyle's stories. Holmes was also a keen student of chemistry. 'The Case of the Confused Chemist' does, therefore, use a spoof Sherlock Holmes case to set a code that is based upon chemical equations. This particular problem is heavily based on curriculum content. Logical thinking, following instructions carefully and synthesis of three sets of data are all involved.

● 'Spellbinding' is another curriculum based code. This time the target subject is English. Cryptic clues have to be understood. The solution depends upon spelling mistakes and homophones. Pupils need to be very exact in their interpretation of the information.

The School for Surreptitious Spies

You won't have heard about the School for Surreptitious Spies. Of course not, it has to be kept secret and under cover. Agents and spies are trained there. The curriculum of their school is somewhat different from the one delivered in your school.

Some of the subjects, like English and mathematics, are the same but there are fascinating additions and changes. Among them is an essential course on code breaking, for agents and spies often have to send secret messages.

How would you have fared if, instead of going to your local school, you had attended the School for Surreptitious Spies, at a location that cannot be disclosed?

Your Tasks

1 Read the lecture notes, on separate sheets, from an early stage of the course on code breaking. These detail ten types of code or cipher. Many more would follow later in the course.

2 Use what you have learned to crack the secret messages which you will find on a separate sheet. There is one example of each of the ten types, but not in the same order as the lecture notes. Sort out which is which and write out the messages that have been concealed.

Extension Tasks

1 Choose one, or more, of the ten types of code.

2 Construct your own passages that contain secret messages.

3 Get somebody else to try to solve them.

4 Design codes of your own.

Problem-solving and Thinking Skills Resources for Able and Talented Children

Notes from Lecture One on Code Breaking

First, some introductory comments.

Codes and ciphers

We use the name 'code', and therefore the activity 'code breaking', inaccurately much of the time. Strictly speaking, a code is only the correct description when a word or phrase is replaced by a word, number or symbol. An army group may be told to retreat by the codeword 'Pluto'.

On the other hand, ciphers work with discrete letters. Ciphers provide the bulk of the methods that we call codes even though that is technically inaccurate. However, in this course, we will stick with the general public acceptance and use code breaking to cover ciphers.

Transposition and substitution

Transposition takes place when the letters of a message are rearranged. Many of us are familiar with a particular type, especially linked with crosswords, called anagrams. Substitution involves letters being replaced by something else. The range of possibilities is large. Numbers or other letters perhaps are the most common. However, shapes, symbols or punctuation marks can be used. Playing cards provide a splendid method as, without jokers, there are 52 in a pack, exactly twice the number of letters in the alphabet.

Now let us introduce ten types of codes. You will meet many more later in the course.

Type One

The message is hidden within a larger passage. Only certain letters are extracted. These could be every third, fourth, fifth or sixth letter, for instance.

Type Two

Similar to Type One, but here you extract complete words from a passage rather than individual letters. The rule again applies of taking, for example, every fourth word.

The School for Surreptitious Spies

Type Three

A passage can be used in which only the first letter and last letter of each sentence is picked out to provide the secret message. Normally all the first letters are used and then all the last letters.

The passage is:

> 'Some voyages can be rough. Even in the summer it is common to have a gale. Nobody should get involved who does not sail well. Dangerous conditions often blow up.'

This would give the message 'send help'.

Type Four

This might be called a shift of steps. The letters, in alphabetical order, can be moved on a certain number of places. Julius Caesar used such a system. He progressed all the letters by three. Thus A became D, the B an E and so on. The shift of letters may involve numbers other than three.

Type Five

A simple reverse transposition involves writing a message backwards. Often the letters are divided into groups of five. Thus, 'attack without further delay' becomes 'yaledrehtruftuohtiwkcatta'. Broken into five-letter groups we have 'yaled rehtr uftuo htiwk catta'.

Type Six

A variation of Type Five is to write each word backwards and separately. Now 'attack without further delay' becomes 'kcatta tuohtiw rehtruf yaled'.

Type Seven

Here the message reads forwards but the letters are divided into groups of five and then, within those groups of five, two letters are exchanged. Grouping in fives 'attack without further delay' becomes 'attac kwith outfu rther delay'. Now exchange the second and fourth in each group and you see 'aattc ktiwh oftuu rehtr daley'.

Other combinations can be employed, exchanging the first and third letters or second and fifth, and so on.

Problem-solving and Thinking Skills Resources for Able and Talented Children
© Barry Teare (Network Continuum Education, 2006)

The School for Surreptitious Spies

Type Eight

There are many types of 'rail fence'. The simplest is illustrated here. The message to be delivered is 'military reserves arrive tomorrow'.

This is then divided into two lines:

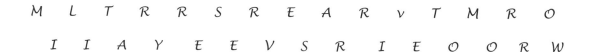

M   L   T   R   R   S   R   E   A   R   v   T   M   R   O

   I   I   A   Y   E   E   V   S   R   I   E   O   O   R   W

If five-letter groups are then used, the top line is written first, followed by the second line:

mltrr   srear   vtmro   iiaye   evsri   eoorw.

Type Nine

This is a rail fence with three lines in use instead of two. The message in Type Eight would be written as:

M   T   R   R   A   v   M   O

  I   I   A   Y   E   E   V   S   R   I   E   O   O   R   W

    L   R   S   E   R   T   R

This could be presented as the three lines:

mtrravmo   iiayeevsrieoorw   lrsertr.

The five-letter group version would be:

mtrra   vmoii   ayeev   srieo   orwlr   sertr.

Type Ten

There are many number codes. In some a two-digit number represents each letter. One method is to use a five-by-five square, and to put numbers from 1-5 across the bottom and up the side. This gives 25 spaces and there are 26 letters in the alphabet. Two letters, commonly I and J, are placed in the same square. When decoding, the rest of the word will tell you which it is. The letters are placed randomly into the square. Every letter can be coded as a two-digit number. In the

5/6

The School for Surreptitious Spies

grid below A is 23, B is 15, G is 55 and so on (the number along the bottom is the first in the two-digit number, followed by the number up the side).

	1	2	3	4	5
5	B	R	D	O	G
4	N	H	S	Z	C
3	U	A	I/J	Y	W
2	M	X	Q	E	K
1	P	F	T	L	V

The message 'come here as quickly as you can' would be coded as:

'54 – 45 – 12 – 42   24 – 42 – 25 – 42   23 – 34

32 – 13 – 33 – 54 – 52 – 41 – 43   23 – 34   43 – 45 – 13

54 – 23 – 14'.

As this is the first lecture, the words have been divided off for you, but that would change at a later stage.

Problem-solving and Thinking Skills Resources for Able and Talented Children

The School for Surreptitious Spies
Assignment One: The Secret Messages

Find the secret message hidden in each of the following examples. There is one each of the ten types covered in Lecture One, but not in the same order as in that lecture.

EXAMPLE A
The emergency services plan for a worst-case scenario. Hospitals make sure that they have sufficient room. Every administrator dreads being caught on the hop. Smooth planning helps to reduce the drama. Every detail is studied to restrict the level of danger. Checks are made for any defect. One mistake and the outlook could be grim. No errors can be made. Data are checked again and again. Confidence about dealing with a crisis is consequently built.

EXAMPLE B
xli   ribx   jypp   qssr   mw   e   kssh   xmqi

EXAMPLE C
alelg   ilehs   gatmv   bufaw   lbtei   nlooe

EXAMPLE D
noita   nracd   eragn   ireaw   namro   fkool

EXAMPLE E
My brother unfortunately has the habit of giving away secret information. He looks at papers and learns things that have been kept deliberately quiet, been, in fact, sealed and delivered to a safe place. To my dismay he turns his talents to dubious purposes. House rules should be kept.

EXAMPLE F

23 - 25 - 25   52 - 11 - 25   53 - 25 - 13 - 22 - 25 - 44   54 - 25 - 51 - 15 - 44 - 25

24 - 15 - 45   52 - 13 - 55 - 25   13 - 42 - 52 - 43 - 15 - 12

EXAMPLE G
eycrviet   nmfreaeoignhsuh   eosmnto

EXAMPLE H
ylrae   taerter   sekam   esnes

EXAMPLE I
You suppose bright work may be not all there is and more lasts in other slots of ideas, tracks by you.

EXAMPLE J
ehtna   lavtr   taeyh   bsaee   isngn   ndeow

The School for Surreptitious Spies

Teaching Notes

Many able children delight in code breaking with the accompanying background of mystery and secrecy. Here they can put themselves in the shoes of trainee spies, albeit in a tongue-in-cheek way. In this piece they are able to view some of the theory behind this intriguing subject. The intellectual demands are high, as ten types are involved in the one exercise.

Key Elements

- abstract – in a code, something stands for something else
- analysis
- synthesis
- deduction and inference

- close engagement with text
- good working methods
- following instructions
- logical thinking.

Contexts

'The School for Surreptitious Spies' can be used in a number of ways:

- as part of a thinking skills course
- as an enrichment activity for those who have completed other work
- as differentiated homework
- as an activity during an enrichment day, weekend or summer school
- as an open-access competition with the extension task as a discriminator
- as an activity for the Problem-solvers' Club
- as a competitive team activity.

NOTE: this is a substantial piece of work and a good block of time is required.

Solution

Able pupils can narrow down the types under consideration by looking at how the ten examples are presented. They may tackle them out of order and therefore make ground through a process of elimination.

EXAMPLE A
This is **Type Three**. Taking the first letter of each sentence and then the last letters, the message uncovered is: '**the second compartment**'.

EXAMPLE B
This is **Type Four**. The alphabet has been shifted four steps.

A	B	C	D	E	F	G	H	I	J	K	L	M	N	O	P	Q	R	S	T	U	V	W	X	Y	Z
E	F	G	H	I	J	K	L	M	N	O	P	Q	R	S	T	U	V	W	X	Y	Z	A	B	C	D

When the new positions are applied, the message says: '**the next full moon is a good time**'. A particular help is the one-letter word 'e' which gives a good starting point in discovering the number of steps.

EXAMPLE C
Here we have **Type Eight**. This is a two-line rail fence. The top line consists of the first three five-letter groups and the bottom line is formed from the remaining three five-letter groups.

```
A  L  E  L  G  I  L  E  H  S  G  A  T  M  V
   B  U  F  A  W  L  B  T  E  I  N  L  O  O  E
```

Taking letters one from the top and then one from the bottom, the message emerges: **'a blue flag will be the signal to move'.**

EXAMPLE D

Now we are dealing with **Type Five**. The message has been written backwards and then put into five-letter groups. When the order is reversed, the message reads: **'look for man wearing a red carnation'.**

EXAMPLE E

Type Two is in use here. A clue to the solver is the stilted appearance of the passage. It looks to be contrived. This is the consequence of having to place particular words at set intervals. Indeed, it is every fifth word that needs to be extracted: **'the secret papers have been delivered to his house'.**

EXAMPLE F

Clearly, as there is only one number code in the lecture, this is **Type Ten**. The five-by-five square that has been used is illustrated below.

	1	2	3	4	5
5	O	E	M	U	K
4	G	Y	P	R	B
3	A	S	Z	I/J	L
2	N	D	W	C	T
1	H	V	Q	X	F

There are no less than eight 25s. This is the 'e' and sets you well on the way. The message reads: **'see the leader before you take action'.**

EXAMPLE G

Here we have **Type Nine**, a rail fence with three lines. The setter has been kind. The letters have been set out in their three lines without being put into five-letter groups. This helps both recognition of the type and the actual solution.

This gives: **'enemy forces are moving in the south'.**

EXAMPLE H

Type Six is an easy one to spot. Each word has been written backwards. Reverse the order of each word to see the message: **'early retreat makes sense'.**

EXAMPLE I

Again, this is a very contrived passage and it results from having to place letters at set intervals while making some kind of sense. This is, then, **Type One**. In this example every sixth letter has to be extracted: **'problems today'.**

EXAMPLE J

The final example is **Type Seven**. An original message, written forwards, has been put into five-letter groups. Then in each group the first and third letters have been interchanged. Solving this message starts by experimenting with exchanges of letters. When an incorrect combination is tried the message is still nonsense. Interchanging the first and third letters gives: 'thena valtr eatyh asbee nsign ednow'. Look for breaks in words. The message then appears as: **'the naval treaty has been signed now'.**

new meaning for mnemonics

Miss Meta Cognition is a teacher who believes that thinking skills are vital for children to develop and to use. She organizes a 'Think Big' club after school. The members tackle a variety of puzzles, problems and study skills. They had recently been considering memory aids, including the use of mnemonics such as 'May I have a large container of coffee?' which reminds us that Π starts with 3.1415926, from the number of letters in each word. Many mnemonics consist of a saying that uses the initial letters of something that needs to be remembered. For instance, BODMAS stands for brackets, orders, division, multiplication, addition and subtraction and reminds us of the order in which to do a calculation.

One club evening, Miss Meta Cognition set a coded message for the members that was based upon mnemonics. Here is your chance to join the club and to 'think big'.

Your Tasks

1 Look at the poem below and work out what is the subject of it. Explain, in detail, the clues.

2 Think of the well-known mnemonic associated with the subject.

3 There is a less well-known mnemonic in mathematics that tells you whether all or some of sine, tangent and cosine are positive in the four quadrants of a circle. (HINT: look carefully here at the order of the sentence.) Don't worry too much about the trigonometry, you can work out the saying that is used from the nautical crossword clue.

4 Next, look at the advice on how to apply the two mnemonics, and how to deal with other letters and numbers.

5 Establish how the code works.

6 Decode the appropriate message.

the poem

Seven vibrant colours tied up in a bow,
Rain and shine are both required to make those colours show.
They are best remembered through a man from a certain place,
He who undertook a struggle that no success would grace.

Problem-solving and Thinking Skills Resources for Able and Talented Children
© *Barry Teare (Network Continuum Education, 2006)*

THE NAUTICAL CROSSWORD CLUE

'Without exception, seafaring men are advised to be cautious' (3, 7, 4, 4).

NOTE: don't forget the order referred to in Task 3.

ADVICE

The mnemonic for the subject of the poem takes the first seven places. Numbers 8–11 are linked with the mnemonic for the nautical crossword clue. Numbers 11–26 progress alphabetically with the letters not yet employed.

THE APPROPRIATE CODED MESSAGE

1 – 6 – 11 – 15 – 8 – 1 – 12   2 – 14

3 – 2 – 1 – 17   15 – 13 – 18 – 21 – 9

23 – 9   10 – 2

1 – 13 – 19 – 13 – 19 – 5 – 13 – 1

10 – 15 – 13   11 – 2 – 18 – 2 – 23 – 1 – 9

2 – 14   10 – 15 – 13

1 – 8 – 6 – 20 – 5 – 2 – 24

Extension Task

Discover other mnemonics and set clues to their identity.
Use them to create a similar code.
Write an appropriate message in that code.

Problem-solving and Thinking Skills Resources for Able and Talented Children

NEW MEANING FOR MNEMONICS

Teaching Notes

This is a code set around the fascinating subject of mnemonics. It plays to a number of skills.

Key Elements

- abstract
- number code
- synthesis
- close interpretation of data
- logical thinking
- mnemonics
- wordplay
- trigonometry.

Contexts

'New Meaning for Mnemonics' can be used in the following ways:

- as part of a thinking skills course
- as extension material on mnemonics in study skills
- as enrichment work for those ahead on other tasks
- as differentiated homework
- as an activity during an enrichment day, weekend, summer school or cluster day
- as an activity for the Puzzle Club.

Solution

1   The poem is clearly about a rainbow and the saying that goes with it to remember the order of the seven colours – 'Richard Of York Gave Battle In Vain' (Red, Orange, Yellow, Green, Blue, Indigo, Violet).

2   Combining the information in the tasks with the nautical crossword clue, gives us the saying 'All Sailors Take Care'. This gives All, Sine, Tangent and Cosine as being positive in the four quadrants working clockwise with 'the normal graph set-up' being the original quadrant. The order for the four words has been stressed in the additional hint within the task.

3   The letters from the first mnemonic are placed against numbers 1–7 in the code (in other word, ROYGBIV). Places 8–11 are matched with ASTC from the second mnemonic. Letters not already used are placed, in alphabetical order, against numbers 12–26.

The code is therefore:

1	2	3	4	5	6	7	8	9	10	11	12	13	14
R	O	Y	G	B	I	V	A	S	T	C	D	E	F

15	16	17	18	19	20	21	22	23	24	25	26
H	J	K	L	M	N	P	Q	U	W	X	Z

4   The message can now be broken:

1 – 6 – 11 – 15 – 8 – 1 – 12	2 – 14	3 – 2 – 1 – 17	15 – 13 – 18 – 21 – 9
R I C H A R D	O F	Y O R K	H E L P S

23 – 9	10 – 2	1 – 13 – 19 – 13 – 19 – 5 – 13 – 1	10 – 15 – 13
U S	T O	R E M E M B E R	T H E

11 – 2 – 18 – 2 – 23 – 1 – 9	2 – 14	10 – 15 – 13	1 – 8 – 6 – 20 – 5 – 2 – 24
C O L O U R S	O F	T H E	R A I N B O W

The Case of the CONFUSED CHEMIST

In a number of cases solved by Sherlock Holmes and chronicled by Dr Watson, codes play a part. 'The Dancing Men' with its strange hieroglyphics is, perhaps, the most famous. 'The Gloria Scott' and 'The Musgrave Ritual' are other adventures that contain coded information.

Even fans of the great detective may not have heard, however, of the code in 'The Case of the Confused Chemist' as the case was never recorded by Dr Watson. Can you take on the mantle of Sherlock Holmes and unlock its secret? Then you will be able to turn to your companion and say 'Elementary my dear Watson'!

YOUR TASKS

1 Read the summary of a part of the investigation of the case.
2 Study the sheet of chemical equations.
3 Make sense of Professor Gas's introductory note.
4 Work out the hidden message that was so important in the solution of the case.

COME ON. GET TO WORK. THE GAME IS AFOOT!

THE SUMMARY

Professor Gas had gone missing from his south London home. He was a well-known and highly respected chemist, as well as being a keen sailor. During a search of his laboratory a piece of paper was found with a note and a number of chemical equations written on it. The sheet gave Dr Watson no help but Sherlock Holmes, an enthusiastic student of chemistry, obtained vital information from it.

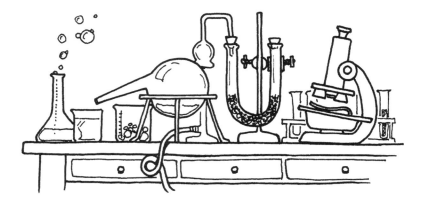

The Case of the CONFUSED CHEMIST

THE SHEET

A scribbled note in Professor Gas's handwriting stated:

> 1 *Numbers are very important.*
> 2 *Numbers have an effect upon the letter immediately preceding them.*
> 3 *Steps must be taken, forwards or backwards, to satisfy the letter of the law.*
> 4 *Only one number in each equation needs scrutiny.*
>
> ### *I AM UNBALANCED. PLEASE HELP.*

There followed a number of chemical equations:

1	$Mg_2 + H_2O$	→	$MgO + H_2$
2	$Li_2O + H_2O$	→	$2LiOH_2$
3	$C_2H_4 + H_2$	→	C_3H_6
4	$CH_5 + 2O_2$	→	$CO_2 + 2H_2O$
5	$CuO + 2HCl$	→	$CuCl_4 + H_2O$
6	$Ca(OH)_1 + 2HCl$	→	$CaCl_2 + 2H_2O$
7	$Ba_2 + 2H_2O$	→	$Ba(OH)_2 + H_2$
8	$2Na_5 + 2H_2O$	→	$2NaOH + H_2$
9	$2ZnS + 3O_2$	→	$2ZnO + 2SO_5$
10	$CuO + 2HNO_3$	→	$Cu(NO_3)_2 + H_2O_6$
11	$Mg_2 + H_2SO_4$	→	$MgSO_4 + H_2$
12	$Na_2S + 2HCl$	→	$2NaCl + H_2S_2$
13	$C_6H_{12}O_6$	→	$2C_2H_2OH + 2CO_2$
14	$H_2SO_4 + CuO$	→	$CuSO_3 + H_2O$

Extension Tasks

1 Write a short message in code using the same system as Professor Gas.

2 What problems do you face in creating such a message?

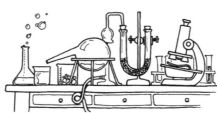

Problem-solving and Thinking Skills Resources for Able and Talented Children
© Barry Teare (Network Continuum Education, 2006)

The Case of the CONFUSED CHEMIST

Teaching Notes

This is a coded exercise within a spoof Sherlock Holmes situation. However, the scenario stands up to scrutiny. *A Study in Scarlet*, the book that brings Holmes and Watson together, contains a very early passage with the detective working upon an infallible test for blood stains. When the two men take up rooms in Baker Street, Holmes lists one of his shortcomings as 'I generally have chemicals about, and occasionally do experiments'. The code can only be solved by applying detailed knowledge of chemical equations.

Key Elements

- ❖ chemical equations
- ❖ code breaking
- ❖ abstract thinking
- ❖ following instructions
- ❖ synthesis
- ❖ logical thinking
- ❖ deduction and inference
- ❖ engagement with text
- ❖ application (in the extension task).

Contexts

'The Case of the Confused Chemist' can be used in the following ways:

- ❖ as extension work on chemical equations
- ❖ as an enrichment activity for those who have finished other work
- ❖ as a differentiated homework
- ❖ as an activity during an enrichment day, weekend or summer school
- ❖ as an open-access competition with the extension task acting as a discriminator, if needed
- ❖ as an activity for the Science Club.

NOTE: it is best for the pupils to solve the code with just the given data. It is possible, however, to add information by giving the word equations for some, or all, of the examples. This simplifies the task.

Solution

The note leads pupils to look carefully at the numbers in the equations for correctness. The pathetic plea from Professor Gas 'I am unbalanced' is because each equation has a mistake so that it does not balance, rather than being a comment upon his state of mind. Some chemical symbols consist of more than one letter and the professor's note makes it clear that pupils should concentrate on the last one. 'Forwards or backwards' refers to movement within the alphabet, the number of steps depending upon how much greater or less the number is than it should be. If O_2 is correct but it has been written O_5, we need to move three letters onwards from O in the alphabet, in other words, the letter R. If O_2 is correct but has been written O, we need to move one letter backwards from O in the alphabet, in other words, the letter N.

The Case of the CONFUSED CHEMIST

Each equation has one numerical error. The correct versions and the consequences of the mistakes on the professor's sheet are:

1 $Mg + H_2O$ $\rightarrow$ $MgO + H_2$ **One letter on from g is h**
   magnesium + water $\rightarrow$ magnesium oxide + hydrogen

2 $Li_2O + H_2O$ $\rightarrow$ $2LiOH$ **One letter on from h is i**
   lithium oxide + water $\rightarrow$ lithium hydroxide

3 $C_2H_4 + H_2$ $\rightarrow$ C_2H_6 **One letter on from c is d**
   ethene + hydrogen $\rightarrow$ ethane

4 $CH_4 + 2O_2$ $\rightarrow$ $CO_2 + 2H_2O$ **One letter on from h is i**
   methane + oxygen $\rightarrow$ carbon dioxide + water

5 $CuO + 2HCl$ $\rightarrow$ $CuCl_2 + H_2O$ **Two letters on from l is n**
   copper(II) oxide + hydrochloric acid $\rightarrow$ copper chloride + water

6 $Ca(OH)_2 + 2HCl$ $\rightarrow$ $CaCl_2 + 2H_2O$ **One letter back from h is g**
   Calcium hydroxide + hydrochloric acid $\rightarrow$ calcium chloride + water

7 $Ba + 2H_2O$ $\rightarrow$ $Ba(OH)_2 + H_2$ **One letter on from a is b**
   barium + water $\rightarrow$ barium hydroxide + hydrogen

8 $2Na + 2H_2O$ $\rightarrow$ $2NaOH + H_2$ **Four letters on from a is e**
   sodium + water $\rightarrow$ sodium hydroxide + hydrogen

9 $2ZnS + 3O_2$ $\rightarrow$ $2ZnO + 2SO_2$ **Three letters on from o is r**
   zinc sulphide + oxygen $\rightarrow$ zinc oxide + sulphur dioxide

10 $CuO + 2HNO_3$ $\rightarrow$ $Cu(NO_3)_2 + H_2O$ **Five letters on from o is t**
    copper(II) oxide + nitric acid $\rightarrow$ copper(II) nitrate + water

11 $Mg + H_2SO_4$ $\rightarrow$ $MgSO_4 + H_2$ **One letter on from g is h**
    magnesium + sulphuric acid $\rightarrow$ magnesium sulphate + hydrogen

12 $Na_2S + 2HCl$ $\rightarrow$ $2NaCl + H_2S$ **One letter on from s is t**
    sodium sulphide + hydrochloric acid $\rightarrow$ sodium chloride + hydrogen sulphide

13 $C_6H_{12}O_6$ $\rightarrow$ $2C_2H_5OH + 2CO_2$ **Three letters back from h is e**
    glucose $\rightarrow$ ethanol + carbon dioxide

14 $H_2SO_4 + CuO$ $\rightarrow$ $CuSO_4 + H_2O$ **One letter back from o is n**
    sulphuric acid + copper(II) oxide $\rightarrow$ copper(II) sulphate + water

The message therefore reads:

'hiding berth ten'

Clearly Sherlock Holmes can now investigate the sailing activities of Professor Gas and then locate the scientist himself and find out why he has gone into hiding.

Extension Task

Constructing a message is difficult because of the limited letters and numbers commonly in use. It is particularly awkward to create backward movement. How can you produce an 'a'?

SPELLBINDING

Mr Vowel and Miss Consonant run a problem-solving club at school. The members tackle a variety of exciting challenges including code breaking. The two teachers are now throwing out a challenge to you about one of the popular codes that they have used. They hope that you will find the exercise 'Spellbinding'!

Your Tasks

1. Solve the cryptic clues below.
2. Find a secret message hidden in the passage that follows. You should find the cryptic clues, and the title of this piece, very helpful in that process.
3. Explain how you worked out each letter in the secret message.

THE CRYPTIC CLUES

1. The number of different methods to spot is suggested by a stool or a triangle.
2. When looking at the sentence 'He used his too hands', we become interested in the twenty-third letter of the alphabet. It is always the first change to note.
3. When confused by troubled sleet, remember to concentrate upon the missing, second letter.
4. When a mistake is made that does not fit the other methods, you must stick to the letter of that error.

THE PASSAGE

Miss Terios looked about her furtively. After checking that no one was watching her, she crosed the road. It was a wonderful day and Miss Terios felt grate. The weather had improved and there was no danger of snow and slet. Miss Terios did not think that people would need there waterproof clothes. She had some time to wait. Diner time was still some way off. Miss Terios bought a newspaper to fill in some minutes. There was the usual scandal about a famous pog group. She also looked at the Art and Disign section. There was a pasing reference to a new range of garden sculptures. A variety of materials was involved – metal, wood, concrete and ruber.

In the greengrocer's window, a poster encouraged passers-by to sample as many vegetables as possible – carrots, turnips, peas, beans, sprouts and leaks. There was also an advertisement about a traveling circus that was about to visit town.

Miss Terios noticed a car in a short-term parking space. One window was half open to make sure that the dog inside did not get too hot and dye. Miss Terios, a dog-lover herself, complimented the owner. Then she realized that she was making herself conspicuous. She had bean foolish. She vanted to remain unnoticed. Thyme seemed to be dragging. Miss Terios went back to reading her newspaper. A baner headline trashed the latest government proposals on education. This was a sine of things to come as a general election loomed.

Extension Task

Using the rules in the cryptic clues, write a passage of your own that contains a hidden message. Ask someone else to try to solve the code.

SPELLBINDING

Teaching Notes

Abstract work, as in codes, is an important area for many able children but there are many skills at work.

Key Elements

- code breaking
- synthesis
- analysis

- deduction
- inference
- careful use of data

- spelling
- following instruction
- homophones.

Contexts

'Spellbinding' can be used in a number of ways:

- as extension work in literacy
- as an enrichment activity for those who have finished other work
- as differentiated homework
- as an activity during an enrichment day, weekend or summer school
- as an activity for the Problem-solvers' Club

The Solution

THE CRYPTIC CLUES

1. There are three different methods.

2. Method One – when a homophone is involved, take the first letter that would change when the correct word is used. 'Too' here should be 'two' and therefore the 'w' is extracted for the message.

3. Method Two – 'troubled sleet' is an anagram of 'double letters'. When a second one is missing, use that for the secret message.

4. Method Three – where there is a spelling mistake that does not result from a homophone or a double letter, use the letter that has been included incorrectly; for example, 'seperate' should be 'separate'. Therefore use the 'e' for the message.

THE SECRET MESSAGE

1	crosed	double letter error	should be crossed	S
2	grate	homophone	should be great	E
3	slet	double letter error	should be sleet	E
4	there	homophone	should be their	I
5	diner	double letter error	should be dinner	N
6	pog	other spelling error	should be pop	G
7	disign	other spelling error	should be design	I
8	pasing	double letter error	should be passing	S
9	ruber	double letter error	should be rubber	B
10	leaks	homophone	should be leeks	E
11	traveling	double letter error	should be travelling	L
12	dye	homophone	should be die	I
13	bean	homophone	should be been	E
14	vanted	other spelling error	should be wanted	V
15	thyme	homophone	should be time	I
16	baner	double letter error	should be banner	N
17	sine	homophone	should be sign	G

The message reads:

SEEING IS BELIEVING

Section 10

Thinking Like Crazy

This is only a short section but it is an important one. 'Thinking Like Crazy' may sound a strange title. However, much of the education for able children has become very dull and uninteresting, with many of them becoming bored and 'switched off'. They thrive on something different, an unusual approach, a spark, quirkiness and intriguing contexts.

Thinking 'outside the box' can be very productive. During brainstorming sessions, it is sometimes the initially rather strange ideas that turn out to be the best. Creative and innovative designers do not rehash what is already there; they think on new and different lines.

All the materials in this book, and in the six previous titles for Network Continuum Education, try to present serious and necessary content and processes in an unusual, and often amusing, way. Fun is a commodity in short supply in our present education system. One of my own sarcastic comments is that: 'Some people see education rather like medicine. Unless it tastes nasty, it doesn't do you any good!'

In this section the emphasis is very much upon a humorous and unusual approach. However, don't be fooled into thinking that the pieces are trivial for, collectively, they deliver some important skills.

- **'Hiss, Moo, Quack, Baa'** is about the wonderful world of nursery rhymes. Following a competition launched by a satellite children's channel, and supported by *The Times* newspaper, the author uses his four entries as a starting point for children to write modern nursery rhymes of their own. In a few, quirky lines, major thoughts can be delivered.

- **'The Pentire Point'** is based upon the premise that playing around with words is a delicious thing to do. Pupils are encouraged to create amusing phrases based upon common sayings, similes, proverbs and idioms, that each include a place from within the British Isles. Quoting from the children's sheet: 'The Pentire Point is that you have fun while, at the same time, learning.'

- **'Humanimals'** does just what it says on the tin. We often link animal behaviour and human behaviour. For 30 people, some real, others fictional, some alive, others dead, children are asked to suggest an appropriate animal with an explanation for their choice.

- **'You don't need to be Christopher Columbus'** completes the section. Examples explain that 'you don't need to be Christopher Columbus to come across Americans' nor that 'you don't need to be Goldilocks to show bare-faced cheek'. Children are encouraged to be witty and imaginative for 30 other 'you don't need to be …'.

HISS, MOO, QUACK, BAA

When you were little, were you told nursery rhymes? Did you hear the exploits of Jack and Jill, Little Miss Muffet, Humpty Dumpty, Little Bo-Peep and many others. The fascination with nursery rhymes never ends; so much so that a satellite children's channel, Nick Jr, recently launched a competition for composing modern nursery rhymes – rhymes for the here and now. The competition was promoted by *The Times* newspaper. It was called 'Time for a new rhyme'. How do you think you might have got on? Here is the chance to find out.

Your Tasks

1 Re-read a selection of traditional nursery rhymes.
2 Analyse how they work and what the essential ingredients are.
3 Take a look at the four rhymes below, written by the author.
4 Write one, or more, nursery rhymes that follow the traditional pattern but which are about modern life. They can be political or concern everyday life or anything else in the twenty-first century.

FOUR EXAMPLES

The author submitted four entries to the competition.

The first one concerns animal cloning and gives its name to the title of this piece.

Hiss, moo, quack, baa,
Cloning animals has gone too far.
Twenty black horses all alike in the race,
Crufts classes of dogs of identical face.
Hiss, moo, quack, baa,
Different animals, hurrah, hurrah!

The second followed from the news item of chef Jamie Oliver trying to improve the quality of school meals. The first line is reminiscent of 'Hot Cross Buns'.

One a euro, two a euro, burgers and chips,
Deep fried nuggets, chocolate and dips.
Jamie's in the kitchen, Jamie's in the school,
Five portions of fruit and veg will be the new rule.

Problem-solving and Thinking Skills Resources for Able and Talented Children

Entry three picked up the theme from the 2005 General Election of postal votes fraud. The rhythm is similar to 'Baa, Baa, Black Sheep'.

Ha-ha election, have you any postal votes?
Just to separate the sheep from the goats.
There's one for the dead man and another just the same,
And lots for anybody you'd care to name.

The fourth, and final, entry stemmed from the author's irritation at the current celebrity culture, where ridiculous sums are earned for dubious talent.

Celebrities, celebrities, how do you grow?
Through offal and waffle and nought else to show.
Celebrities, celebrities, what do you know?
Nonentities, nonentities, all in a row.

These four examples were political and social. Yours do not need to be the same.

LET YOUR MIND WANDER. ENJOY THE ABSURD.

TELL A NONSENSE STORY IN JUST A FEW LINES.

'HISS, MOO, QUACK, BAA' – NOW YOU ARE IN THE MOOD.

Problem-solving and Thinking Skills Resources for Able and Talented Children
© Barry Teare (Network Continuum Education, 2006)

HISS, MOO, QUACK, BAA

Teaching Notes

For any section entitled 'Thinking Like Crazy', what could be better than nursery rhymes? Many of them are 'off the wall'. It is a surreal world where the cow jumps over the moon, a pig is shaved and a garden grows with silver bells and cockle shells and pretty maids all in a row.

Key Elements

- ❖ imagination
- ❖ creativity
- ❖ analysis
- ❖ wordplay
- ❖ application
- ❖ word humour
- ❖ abstract thinking
- ❖ creative writing of a particular kind.

Contexts

'Hiss, Moo, Quack, Baa' can be used in a number of ways:

- ❖ as creative writing in the classroom
- ❖ as extension material to vocabulary work
- ❖ as an enrichment activity for those who have completed other work
- ❖ as differentiated homework
- ❖ as an activity during an enrichment day, weekend or summer school
- ❖ as an open-access competition
- ❖ as an activity for the English Club.

Answers

Pupils are likely to cover a wide range of subjects. Success criteria may well include:

- ❖ telling a story in a succinct way
- ❖ unusual choice of words
- ❖ strong rhythm
- ❖ an element of repetition
- ❖ rhyming
- ❖ a musical flow
- ❖ the use of allegory and/or symbolic, abstract or surreal imagery.

Playing around with words is a delicious thing to do. The names of many places lend themselves to wordplay. 'The entire point' is a phrase used in discussions and arguments. To the mischievous lover of words, this changes to 'the Pentire point', as Pentire is a place in north Cornwall.

Similar changes can be made to common phrases, similes, proverbs and idioms. Some examples follow.

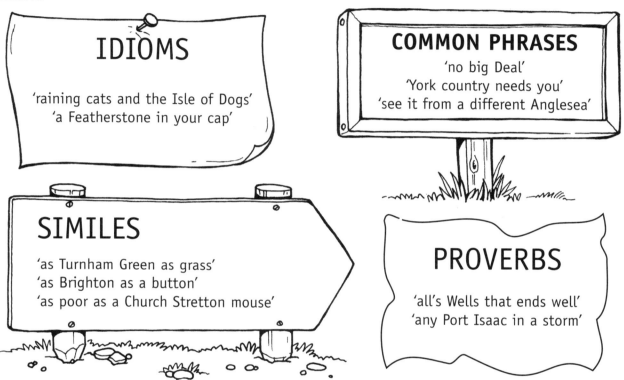

IDIOMS

'raining cats and the Isle of Dogs'
'a Featherstone in your cap'

COMMON PHRASES

'no big Deal'
'York country needs you'
'see it from a different Anglesea'

SIMILES

'as Turnham Green as grass'
'as Brighton as a button'
'as poor as a Church Stretton mouse'

PROVERBS

'all's Wells that ends well'
'any Port Isaac in a storm'

THE CHALLENGE

1 Look at a map of the British Isles and select some suitable places.
2 Research common phrases, idioms, similes and proverbs.
3 Create examples of your own like those given above.

BE CREATIVE; BE IMAGINATIVE; USE YOUR SENSE OF HUMOUR. 'THE PENTIRE POINT' IS THAT YOU HAVE FUN WHILE, AT THE SAME TIME, LEARNING.

THE SUPER CHALLENGE

Use the following places to change a common phrase, an idiom, a simile or a proverb:

1 Bolton	4 Ironbridge	7 Shottery	10 Motherwell
2 Newquay	5 Cooling	8 Mousehole	11 Oxford
3 Lately Common	6 Hay-on-Wye	9 Kettleshulme	12 Hawk Green

THE PENTIRE POINT

Teaching Notes

So many serious purposes can be achieved through fun methods and 'The Pentire Point' is a perfect example. Children are being encouraged to 'think like crazy' but there is great content, substance and understanding behind that thinking.

Key Elements

- wordplay
- word humour
- the British Isles
- vocabulary
- research

- creativity and imagination
- understanding of idioms, similes and proverbs
- delivery of sections of the literacy framework.

Contexts

'The Pentire Point' can be used in a number of ways:

- as extension work either to vocabulary extension or to the geography of the British Isles
- as an enrichment activity for those who have completed other tasks
- as differentiated homework
- as an activity during an enrichment day, weekend or summer school
- as an activity for the English Club or Society or the Geography Club
- as an open-access competition.

Some Answers

In 'The Challenge', the answers can be very varied indeed. The following are possible answers for 'The Super Challenge' but credit should be given for alternative, appropriate replies.

1   Like a Bolton from the blue
2   A Newquay broom sweeps clean
3   See you Lately Common
4   Strike while the Ironbridge is hot
5   As Cooling as a cucumber
6   Make Hay-on-Wye while the sun shines
7   A Shottery in the dark
8   To play cat and Mousehole
9   A pretty Kettleshulme of fish
10   We never miss the water until the Motherwell runs dry
11   As strong as an Oxford
12   Watch like a Hawk Green

Success Criteria

The quality of the answers in both 'The Challenge' and 'The Super Challenge' may be judged on a number of factors, including the following:

- the creativity and imagination displayed
- the selection of suitable places to use
- the degree to which idioms, similes and proverbs have all been used
- the skill and subtlety displayed
- the quality of research skills displayed.

Humanimals

Have you ever wondered what it is like to be a particular animal? Do you sometimes think of somebody you know as being like an animal because of shared characteristics? For instance, a man or woman with a sleek appearance might resemble a member of the cat family, especially a cheetah. It is claimed that some dog-owners resemble their pets. In the Harry Potter books, Professor McGonagall transforms herself into a tabby cat. Golf commentators talk of Tiger Wood 'stalking the green'. In other cases, the link between the person and an animal might not be due to physical appearance but rather a perceived shared characteristic such as strength or playfulness or meanness.

Your Tasks

1　For each of the people listed below, suggest an animal that you believe he or she could be linked with. Some of the people are real, some are fictional. Some of the real people are no longer alive.

2　Explain briefly the reasons for your suggestions.

3　For those people with whom you are not familiar, perhaps because they are no longer alive, carry out the necessary research.

THE PEOPLE

1 Robin Hood	11 Roger Federer	21 Ant and Dec
2 David Beckham	12 Florence Nightingale	22 The BFG
3 Roald Dahl	13 Germaine Greer	23 Sir Francis Drake
4 Albert Einstein	14 Ronan Keating	24 Kylie Monogue
5 Tony Blair	15 Terry Wogan	25 Jonny Wilkinson
6 J.K. Rowling	16 Queen Victoria	26 William Shakespeare
7 Hugh Grant	17 Sherlock Holmes	27 Richard Branson
8 Mother Theresa	18 Napoleon	28 Violet Baudelaire
9 Tracy Beaker	19 Shane Warne	29 Pablo Picasso
10 Abraham Lincoln	20 David Attenborough	30 Kelly Holmes

Extension Task

Make a representation of the humanimals: you can draw, paint, model or use computer graphics if you wish.

Humanimals

Teaching Notes

'Humanimals' is an unusual piece of work, trying to get able children to think rather differently. There is a real fun element within it. However, good answers require quality thinking. They also require knowledge of the animal kingdom.

Practical Notes

1 The pupils' sheet asks them to answer all 30 parts. Teachers may wish to alter that number or give a choice of a certain number out of the 30.

2 This piece can be used directly, or it can be used as exemplar material. It is perfectly reasonable to substitute names for those currently in the list to better suit the group of children.

Key Elements

❖ seeing connections
❖ identifying key characteristics
❖ living processes
❖ research
❖ creativity and imagination
❖ lateral thinking.

Contexts

'Humanimals' can be used for a number of purposes:

❖ as extension work to material on animals
❖ as an unusual piece of enrichment work for those who have finished other tasks
❖ as a differentiated homework
❖ as an activity during an enrichment day, weekend or summer school
❖ as an open-access competition
❖ as an activity for the Science Club or Society
❖ as an activity for the Art Club if the extension task is tackled.

You don't need to be Christopher Columbus

Have you got the sort of mind that sees unusual connections and conjures up interesting images? If so, this is the opportunity for you to exercise your imagination about people, real and fictional, alive today and from the past.

Your Task

For each of the people listed below, create a saying that starts with 'You don't need to be', then place the person's name, and, finally, put an amusing conclusion that is appropriate for the particular person.

Examples

★ You don't need to be Christopher Columbus to come across Americans.
★ You don't need to be Goldilocks to show bare-faced cheek.

Be witty, amusing, creative and imaginative. After all, you don't have to be William Shakespeare to write something that will entertain others!

THE PEOPLE

1 Jane Eyre	11 Charlie Dimmock	21 Terry Pratchett
2 Gordon Brown	12 James Bond	22 Catwoman
3 Luke Skywalker	13 Frankie Dettori	23 George Stephenson
4 Roman Abramovich	14 Queen Elizabeth II	24 Sir Walter Raleigh
5 Vincent van Gogh	15 Indiana Jones	25 George W. Bush
6 Bart Simpson	16 Little Red Riding Hood	26 Little Jack Horner
7 Steve Redgrave	17 Paula Radcliffe	27 Naomi Campbell
8 Alex Ryder	18 Isaac Newton	28 Inspector Morse
9 Thierry Henry	19 Natasha Bedingfield	29 A child in Africa
10 Johann Sebastian Bach	20 Jeremy Paxman	30 Ruby Wax

Extension Task

Suggest other people or characters not included in this list and write the appropriate line for them.

You don't need to be Christopher Columbus

Teaching Notes

This is a novel and unusual piece, very much in keeping with the notion of 'thinking like crazy'. It is the type of exercise that tells you a great deal about the pupils themselves. This is part of informal identification. Some children will write predictable answers but others will produce totally unexpected responses.

NOTE: teachers can suggest that pupils choose a certain number, rather than all 30. If so, it would be helpful if they kept a variety of people rather than concentrating only on certain areas. Teachers can also make changes to the list if they believe that such alterations would be more appropriate for particular students.

Key Elements

- ❖ seeing connections
- ❖ wordplay
- ❖ word humour
- ❖ differentiation by outcome
- ❖ creativity and imagination
- ❖ succinct creative writing of a very particular type
- ❖ cross-curricular material.

Extension Task

It will be interesting to see the additions made by the students themselves. Do the people come from just one or two areas of human activity? Is there a mixture of real people and fictional characters? Are all the people still alive? Can we detect the students' heroes and heroines? Again, this will add to our knowledge of the children.